Case Studies in Whole Language

Case Studies in Whole Language

Richard T. Vacca and Timothy V. Rasinski
Kent State University

Harcourt Brace Jovanovich College Publishers

Fort Worth   Philadelphia   San Diego   New York   Orlando   Austin   San Antonio
Toronto   Montreal   London   Sydney   Tokyo

Publisher: Ted Buchholz
Acquisitions Editor: Jo-Anne Weaver
Project Management: Publications Development Company of Texas
Production Manager: Erin Gregg
Cover Design: Nick Welch

ISBN: 0–03–0522544

Address Editorial Correspondence To: Harcourt Brace Jovanovich, Publishers
301 Commerce Street, Suite 3700
Fort Worth, Texas 76102

Address Orders To: Harcourt Brace Jovanovich, Publishers
6277 Sea Harbor Drive
Orlando, Florida 32887
1-800-782-4479, or 1-800-433-0001 (in Florida)

Library of Congress Cataloging-in-Publication Data
Vacca, Richard T.
    Case studies in whole language / Richard T. Vacca and Timothy
V. Rasinski.
        p.   cm.
    Includes bibliographical references and index.
    ISBN 0-03-052254-4
    1. Language experience approach in education—United States—Case
studies. I. Rasinski, Timothy V. II. Title.
    LB1576.V33   1992
    372.4'144—dc20   91-46857
                                                                  CIP

Printed in the United States of America.

3 4 5 016 9 8 7 6 5 4 3

Harcourt Brace Jovanovich Publishers
The Dryden Press
Saunders College Publishing

CONTENTS

PREFACE

Emblazoned on the cover of a recent edition of *Teacher Magazine* is the headline: "WHOLE LANGUAGE: Some teachers love it. Some teachers hate it. Many don't even know what it is. But it's changing America's schools." The headline, as eye-catching and provocative as it is, captures what happens when a good idea begins to rock the status quo.

Whole language is a good and powerful idea whose time has come. With its emphasis on the child as learner and on the authentic uses of language within meaningful contexts, some teachers—those who "love it"—are viewing whole language as one way to overcome the perceived malaise that afflicts American education. Others—those who "hate it"—are convinced that whole language threatens a generation of students who will not develop the skills needed to read, write, and learn effectively. The majority of teachers, we believe, presently are caught somewhere in between. Although the whole language movement is changing the face of language, literacy, and learning in today's schools, it still remains a nebulous, slippery concept for many teachers.

Whole language is reaching monolithic proportions in American education. Based on our experiences, many preservice and inservice teachers are intrigued with the possibilities of whole language, but have trouble envisioning, if you will, how to plan, manage, and sustain whole language instruction in classrooms. One major obstacle is defining and describing whole language theory and practice with clarity. What is whole language? And how does whole language teaching differ from what teachers presently do in classrooms?

This book is about how preschool and elementary teachers define themselves within a whole language framework. We explore whole language through their beliefs and actions in the classroom as well as the problems and issues they confront in their ever evolving transitions to whole language education.

What is whole language? First consider what it isn't. Whole language is not a prescriptive concept. A narrowly defined, single-minded whole language curriculum is neither possible nor desirable. The application of whole language principles will vary from instructional context to instructional context, based upon a host of interrelated, situational factors. As a result, whole language classrooms can look very different from one another depending upon the types of teachers, students, grade levels, and school and community contexts involved.

Yet the problem persists for teachers who want to move toward whole language teaching: How can they get a good grasp of how whole language is played out in real classrooms? Discussions of whole language are often "strategy-centered" and, consequently, mired in abstraction because the instructional strategies presented are not grounded in the context of real classrooms.

Although whole language rests upon the assumption that language learning shouldn't be fragmented, it has been our observation that whole language is often presented to teachers in a fragmented manner that runs counter to a holistic spirit. That is to say, an instructor (or textbook author) informing others about whole language identifies the major elements of a whole language curriculum and then, more often than not, presents these elements as separate parts to be analyzed and studied. Thus, an introductory textbook on whole language may include chapters on emergent literacy, shared book experiences, reading-writing connections, literature-based instruction, using language to learn, and thematic units. Within this analytical, part-to-whole approach, instructional strategies are also presented, such as procedures for reading aloud or journal writing. In addition, other "elements" of whole language instruction are presented and analyzed, for example, collaborative, cooperative learning. Do the parts add up to the whole?

Although an analytical approach to the study of teacher education is necessary, it is not sufficient. There is an inherent problem with this approach to learning about whole language. By analyzing its components, the very assumption upon which whole language rests is often violated. An analytical or segmented approach may lead preservice and inservice teachers who wish to move toward whole language to conceptualize it by its parts or elements and to implement it in their classrooms in ways that are similar to the status quo, as an alternative skills-based curriculum.

Lee Shulman, past president of the American Educational Research Association, has argued that simply learning the facts and principles of teaching is insufficient for becoming an effective teacher. He believes that the teachers need to learn how the facts and principles can be applied in real classroom contexts and events and how teachers deal with multiple and sometimes contradictory principles in the classrooms. He suggests that a case method approach may be the best way to help teachers, new to an educational idea, to develop these higher forms of understanding about teaching. We agree with Schulman, especially as his argument pertains to learning about whole language. Teachers need to get a feel for whole language in the context of its use before they can begin to consider its individual elements.

Case Studies in Whole Language tells the stories of six teachers in preschool through fifth grade classrooms who are in various stages of transition in their thinking about whole language and their enactment of curriculum that reflects their theories. You will study why and how these teachers gravitated toward whole language and where they are in their own transition as professionals. Through these multiple immersions into whole language classrooms, you will begin to understand what makes a classroom "whole language" and what roles teachers play in the development of whole language curriculum.

Whole language is more than a set of instructional principles and activities. It is a philosophy of education. It requires teachers to transform and to expand their knowledge of language, teaching, learning, and children in order to more completely take on the role of professional. The case studies we present go beyond how teachers teach in whole language classrooms. We provide insight into how these teachers think, what they are committed to, their fears and concerns, and how they interact with others. These cases will demonstrate to novice and veteran teachers alike that whole language has considerable depth and extends beyond the hours of the school day.

The teachers whose stories we tell are not new to us. We value our relationships with them as friends and colleagues. They have been our teachers, and we have been theirs. Each plies her craft in Ohio. Each is a veteran and has been teaching, on average, seventeen years. Two teach in relatively large urban areas; one teaches in a university-based child development center with a sizable number of international students; three teach in suburban schools.

Many books about whole language are written as first-person accounts by actual teachers. Certainly this approach lends itself to an authentic, subjective "insider's view" of whole language. We have chosen to write the case studies ourselves as relative outsiders to the classrooms we describe. Although we have collaborated with the teachers over the years, we approached our task as learners/researchers whose aim was to make sense of phenomena associated with whole language teachers and classrooms. Using the tools of inquiry—observation, interview, and document analysis—we maintained a healthy distance in order to create—to the extent that it is possible—objective depictions of whole language in action. Each teacher read preliminary drafts of their cases in order to insure that the stories we are telling mirror valid reflections of their classrooms. By developing the cases ourselves, we were able to present them in a way that allows you to make ready comparisons and draw distinctions among the teachers. Although each case is different, all are presented in a similar format.

This book is organized into four parts. Part I, *Understanding . . .* overviews the conceptual bases for whole language and distinguishes it from the status quo. Part II, *Emerging . . .* presents three case studies of teachers who work with beginners in preschool and primary classrooms. Part III, *Maturing . . .* , presents three case studies around problems and issues of whole language teaching in grades three, four, and five. Part IV, *Becoming . . .* explores how teachers can move toward whole language as they engage in a process of transition and change.

There is no one way to use this book. However, we do recommend you allow yourself considerable time and freedom to respond to each chapter. This book is meant to be read, reflected upon, and discussed. Write down your thoughts as you read the cases and use these comments as the basis for discussion. At the end of Parts II and III, there are a set of "thought questions" to help you think about each case and to make comparisons across cases.

We wish to thank Dona Bolton, Sylvia Jackson, Betsy Pryor, Gay Fawcett, Ann Burns, and Brenda Church—the teachers whose stories we tell and their students who served as powerful curriculum informants. We extend our appreciation to the editorial team at Harcourt Brace Jovanovich, especially to Jo-Anne Weaver, whose extraordinary patience and gentle hand shepherded this project home. Additionally, we thank the reviews whose commentaries guided the rethinking of initial drafts of the text: Dr. Ellen Jampole, SUNY Cortland; Dr. Sandra Wilde, University of Oregon; Dr. Mary Ann Manning, University of Alabama-Birmingham; Dr. Neil McLeod, North Adams State College; and Dr. Michael Ford,

University of Wisconsin-Oshkosh. Kudos to Drew Tiene, our colleague at Kent State University, for the photos that appear throughout the book.

Whole language empowers teachers as professionals. We hope that this book serves in some small way as a springboard to a lifetime of classroom exploration and professional growth.

RTV
TVR

Kent State University
Kent, Ohio

I
UNDERSTANDING...

Whole language is, first and foremost, about the theories and philosophies that teachers bring to literacy learning and education in general. The way teachers think about language, learning, and teaching involves a complex set of beliefs, values, and attitudes that is rooted in a strong knowledge base. Whole language teachers are active learners: the more they know about language, children, and teaching, the more they want to know. Understanding, inquiry, and self-reflection characterize the work of whole language teachers.

Part I creates a context in which to better understand the stories of the six teachers that we will profile in this book. What is the common ground that these teachers share? What principles of whole language are reflected in their classroom practices? How are their practices different from the status quo?

Chapter 1

WHOLE LANGUAGE TEACHERS, WHOLE LANGUAGE CLASSROOMS

"An idea as dynamic as whole language indeed creates its own 'muddy water.'" Teachers who gravitate toward whole language often do so with a certain sense of curiosity and ambiguity.

Beat the drums. Sound the trumpets. The movement is for real. Whole language is a grassroots phenomenon that has captured the fascination and the imagination of teachers, administrators, parents, and educational policymakers across the country. And in the process of doing so, it has become a *cause celebre* in the field of literacy education.

Open an educational journal on literacy today and you are likely to find an article, pro or con, on whole language. Attend a literacy-related conference and you are bound to hear participants engaged in lively dialogue in meeting rooms and hallways over the merits or shortcomings of THE MOVEMENT. With the debate likely to go on for some time, it may appear to many that confusion and controversy surround the concept of whole language.

Yet, for the teachers whose classrooms we profile in this book—and for thousands of others throughout the country and the world—there is no doubt, no confusion, no controversy over the meaning of whole language in their professional lives. They have developed *theories* about how language works, how children use language to learn and to communicate, how teachers go about the business of plying their craft, and how teachers—with children—negotiate, integrate, and enact curriculum. Their theories provide the *conceptual energy* that fuels how they define whole language in their classrooms.

What do we mean by theory? Simply this: A whole language teacher operates from a philosophical perspective—a theory—of teaching and learning that is rooted in an organized body of knowledge, beliefs, values, assumptions, and principles. This philosophical perspective or theory underlies a whole language teacher's intentions, instructional decisions, and practices. The way whole language teachers think about language, learning, and teaching is apparent in their day-to-day interactions and transactions with children, parents, and colleagues. No wonder Altwerger, Edelsky, and Flores (1987) contend that whole language is a set of beliefs, not a set of practices. Whole language theory *becomes* practice as teachers do their work in classrooms.

Lao-Tsu, the ancient Chinese philosopher, is attributed with having said, "Muddy water, let stand, becomes clear." An idea as dynamic as whole language creates its own "muddy water." This is as it should be. Those who gravitate toward whole language often do so with a certain sense of curiosity and ambiguity. Clarity comes with time; time wisely invested in the pursuit of knowledge, classroom inquiry, and reflective thinking.

Case Studies in Whole Language tells the stories of six teachers in various stages of transition who have embraced whole language as a philosophy of education, language, and learning. The teachers we profile didn't "switch" overnight from skills-based teaching to whole language teaching. In telling their stories, we explore the transitions they have gone through in developing a set of beliefs that reflects a whole language philosophy. We try to capture where they are in their thinking about language, literacy, and learning. We also aim for curriculum perspective: How does whole language become practice in each teacher's classroom? What issues, dilemmas, and challenges does each teacher face?

To provide a context in which to better understand their stories, this chapter first explores some of the important principles underlying whole language teaching and learning and then examines the status quo in literacy instruction as it exists today. The status quo represents a skills paradigm. Many teachers today are in the midst of a shift in thinking from skills to whole language. What does the shift involve? Instead of providing a dictionary definition, our intent is to explore some of the common ground that whole language teachers seem to hold, and then to share the stories of teachers who are in the process of "becoming."

SOME PRINCIPLES UNDERLYING WHOLE LANGUAGE

Whole language teachers stand for *something;* they bring together a view of language and literacy that other teachers, whose beliefs are rooted in the status quo, don't. How do whole language teachers define themselves? The answer lies in understanding the underlying beliefs, propositions, and principles that support the work they do in classrooms.

As difficult as it is to reduce a multidimensional concept to a dictionary definition, the process of defining and describing whole language and how it is put to use within a professional context is worthwhile. Whole language means different things to different people. But as the phenomenal grassroots growth of the movement demonstrates, there is widespread fascination with whole language as a *professional theory of education* that weds a teacher's world view with practices that are congruent with it in ways that are predictable and observable in classrooms.

A broad definition reflects the proposition that whole language weaves together "a theoretical view of language, language learning, and learning into an educational stance" (Edelsky, Altwerger, & Flores, 1991). The educational stance has its roots in the *progressive schools* movement (Dewey, 1938), psycholinguistic/sociolinguistic explorations of language and learning, and the humanistically inspired advocacy of children's rights and responsibilities as learners.

In practice, teachers will vary in their working definitions, usually placing emphasis on certain dimensions of their concepts of whole language. If, for example, you were to ask a room full of teachers to associate one or two words that come to mind quickly when thinking about whole language in their classrooms, their responses undoubtedly would vary. Some might use words that associate whole language with child-responsive environments for learning; others, with literature-based instruction; still others, with curriculum integration.

The personal and professional histories of teachers contribute substantially to the way they think about whole language. Teachers grow into their theoretical views as they continue to learn about and experiment with new ideas and classroom practices. Yet, as Dorothy Watson (1989) suggests, although definitions and descriptions of whole language may lack sameness, they remain more often than not within the boundaries of some dimension of a whole language perspective.

Whole language practices are *theory-driven*. The implicit theories that whole language teachers hold influence the kinds and quality of collaboration they have with children, parents, colleagues, and administrators. These theories are supported by principles derived from knowledge and beliefs related to (1) language and language learning; (2) children and learning; and (3) curriculum, teaching, and teachers.

Language and Language Learning

Whole language teachers believe that language serves personal, social, and academic facets of children's lives. Language, therefore, cannot be severed from a child's quest to make sense; language and meaning-making are intertwined. In addition, whole language teachers recognize that oral and written language are *parallel* processes; one is not secondary to the other. Language, whether oral or written, is a complex system of symbols, rules, and subsystems that govern the content and form of language in the context of its use. For the whole language teacher, keeping language "whole" means not breaking it into bits and pieces or isolating the subsystems of language for instructional emphasis.

Language learning isn't difficult when it meets the purposes and functional needs of children. Whole language teachers know that children learn language when they are using language to learn in the context of reading, writing, listening, and speaking. The statements of principle that follow elaborate on these beliefs in more detail:

Language and Meaning-Making Are Inseparable. Language isn't language unless meaning is involved. Oral language, without meaning, represents a string of speech sounds—grunts and groans, at best. Written language, without meaning, is nothing more than a line of irrelevant markings on paper. Language—whether it is oral or written—can best be thought of as a complex system for creating meanings through socially shared conventions (Halliday, 1978). Through language, children learn to reflect upon their own experience, to express themselves symbolically, to make meaning and create knowledge, and to share their meanings with others. Ken Goodman (1986) puts the matter of language learning this way: Learning language is easy when it is relevant and meaningful.

Language is the medium by which humans think and learn. From infancy, children are active participants in their own learning. As they explore their environment—manipulating objects, interacting with their immediate surroundings and with parents, siblings, and significant others in their lives—children interpret and give meaning to the events that they experience. Meaning is central to language, thus prompting M.A.K. Halliday (1978) to comment that children's language development is "a saga in learning to mean."

Little wonder, then, that Gordon Wells (1986) depicts children as "meaning-makers" who in the process of learning language are using language to learn. His fifteen-year longitudinal study of British children's language development from infancy through elementary grades describes patterns of oral and written language development and explains children's individual differences in learning language and literacy. Wells concludes that parents and teachers best serve children's language and literacy development as *collaborators* in learning. He urges that our inter-actions with children demonstrate that what they have to say and write is worthy of attention and response. If we are to help them to achieve their full potentials as makers of meaning and creators of knowledge, then our role is to guide, encourage, and facilitate.

Language Is Language, Whether It's Oral or Written.   An unfortu-nate consequence of conventional reading instruction is the oversimplifi-cation of the idea that the black squiggly marks on a page represent speech written down. This, more often than not, has led to the unwar-ranted assumption that the acquisition of written language proceeds dif-ferently from oral language. When written language is viewed as a coded representation of speech, it creates the expectation that reading and writ-ing are to be learned differently from talking and listening. Whereas oral language is acquired naturally from birth, written language learning, ac-cording to conventional wisdom, needs to be delayed until school en-trance when children are taught formally to read and write.

Such conventional wisdom is indeed unfortunate because it removes learning to read and write from a natural context. As a result, children are put in the difficult position of studying written language in the ab-stract as subjects to be learned from part to whole.

The principle that language is language, whether oral or written, sup-ports the view that oral and written language are parallel modes of lan-guage. As Edelsky (1991) and her colleagues put it, "While each mode . . . has its own set of constraints and opportunities, they all share cer-tain characteristics: (1) they are profoundly social; (2) they contain in-terdependent and inseparable subsystems; and (3) they are predictable" (pp. 9–120). Written language isn't secondary to oral language. Each is a language in its own right and is subject to the same laws and principles of acquisition and learning.

Many children engage in literacy learning, as the research on emergent literacy documents, well before they enter school (Hall, 1987; Harste, Woodward, & Burke, 1984; Heath, 1983; Teale & Sulzby, 1986). They learn reading and writing the way they learn talking and listening—naturally. Whole language teachers use children's emerging knowledge and skill as a starting point to build on their competence and confidence with literacy events in the classroom.

Language Is a Rule-Governed System Made of Subsystems.   Language is a complex system of symbols and the rules for using those symbols. Within this complex system, linguists have identified subsystems that are associated with the symbols and rules of language. They have also described language in terms of its *content, form, and use.* The subsystems of language are always interactive in real instances of communication and give shape and substance to the content and form of language in use. A brief description of the various language subsystems follows:

- *Phonological:* In oral language, one aspect of the form of language is its phonology. The phonological system is concerned with the rules governing the structure, distribution, and sequencing of speech sounds. In written language, the *graphophonic* system is concerned with the rules and conventions associated with sound-letter relationships.

- *Syntactic:* The form of language is also dictated by the syntactic system that allow language users to determine the order of words in sentences. Syntax refers to grammatical relationships and the structure of sentences.

- *Semantic:* The content of language—its meanings—is associated with the semantic system. Semantics is a system of rules governing the meaning of words and word combinations. Semantic knowledge reflects the background knowledge and experiences, concepts, attitudes, values, and skills language users bring to language events such as reading, writing, talking, and listening.

- *Pragmatic:* The pragmatic system is a set of sociolinguistic rules related to language use. Pragmatics is concerned with the way humans use language to communicate. Context is the key to understanding the role pragmatics plays in language use. Context refers to the practical situation in which communication between people takes place. It includes the user's purpose for producing or interpreting language, the sets of relationships between speaker and listener or reader and writer, and the conditions surrounding the speech or literacy event that may influence the way a user produces language and constructs meaning.

UNDERSTANDING . . .

In real speech and literacy events, the subsystems operate simultaneously and are interdependent on one another. Figure 1.1 illustrates the interdependence of language subsystems in a literacy event. Suppose a child is reading a text. The literacy event includes the text itself, the reader, the author of the text, and all of the factors and conditions influencing the context in which the event occurs, for instance, reading the text in school as part of a unit on environmental pollution. The pragmatic context in which the reading takes place affects the way the child interacts with the text. For example, the reader's purpose will influence the quality of the interaction. As Figure 1.1 shows, the pragmatic system encompasses the other subsystems. The child's desire to learn about pollution and its effects on the environment trigger how she will employ the rules of syntax, semantics, and graphophonology to construct meaning. Depending on the context, the child engages in an information search making use of multiple cues from the interacting subsystems.

Figure 1.1
Language Systems in Use During a Literacy Event

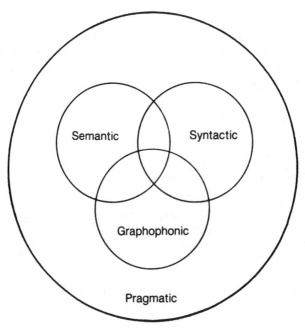

When language is in actual use, the systems are interactive and operate in concert with one another. As a result, a language user relies on the interdependence of the systems to anticipate meaning and make predictions. One eminent characteristic of language is its predictability. The reader in the example just given will use pragmatic, graphophonic, syntactic, and semantic information to make predictions about the text being read. To illustrate: the reader comes to the sentence, "Pollution can be _____ to your health." As a reader, the child can make use of various kinds of language information to anticipate and predict "what comes next" in the sentence. For one thing, the reader can rely on syntactic cues to predict which word must follow the word "be." In addition, one aspect of the pragmatic context—the passage in which the sentence is used—and the semantic knowledge the child brings to the reading may also help to reduce the meaningful possibilities of which word comes next. If the reader were to make use of graphophonic information—the missing word begins with the letter "h" and ends with the suffix "ful"—the possibility of reducing the number of meaningful alternatives for the missing word is even greater.

Language learning is made more abstract than it needs to be when the subsystems of language are separated from one another for instructional purposes. In a whole language classroom, children learn language when they are using all of the subsystems of language to learn.

Because Language Is Inherently Social, Children Learn Language in the Context of Its Use.   Humans could not learn language without other humans. Long before they enter school, children learn what language can do for them. They learn that language is a tool they can use in interactions with others in their environment. In the process of learning language, children are continually using language to describe, explain, and inquire about the world around them and to share their knowledge with others.

Language works because it is purposeful. It functions to help language users to communicate what they have to say or write or to understand and interpret another's communication. Babies, for example, learn early in life to use language as an instrument for their intentions—to satisfy a want or a need: As Edelsky (1991) and her colleagues explain, "The world over babies learn language through actually using it, not through practicing its separate parts until some later date when they assemble the parts and finally use the entire thing" (p. 14). A baby learns language as a way to survive by satisfying functional needs.

Babies not only use language for their own purposes, but they observe demonstrations of language in use by family members and caretakers. They learn from these demonstrations the powerful role language plays as an instrument for self-expression, communication, and meaning-making.

In short, babies learn what language is for through actual use and demonstrations. As they grow and develop, they learn the pragmatics of language in use. By the time they are of kindergarten age, children have learned how to use the conversational context to affect others or to interpret what others have to say. By age five, children have emerged as users of written language as well. Many know what written language is for, use paper and pencil for self-expression, and books as a source of enjoyment and learning. From a functionalist's perspective, a child is tacitly aware that in a particular social context, one's purpose affects the selection of what one says, writes, or reads (content) and how one says, writes, or reads it (form).

Children who know what they want to do with language figure out a way to do it. Form follows function. This is why Ken Goodman (1986) wonders, "Do you have to have control of sounds before you speak, of phonics before you read, of spelling before you write, of vocabulary before you use language? Not really. . . . Kids are universally able to sort out language as they use it to meet their functional needs. If their language use in school is authentic, then they will not find it hard to get control of the language forms they need" (p. 19).

Children and Learning

Whole language teachers hold strong beliefs about children and their ability to learn. In whole language classrooms, respect for the child as a learner is abundantly evident. Whole language teachers believe that children are natural learners who best learn the written form of language—how to read and write—under natural conditions. Because learning to read and write involves trial and error, whole language teachers hold firm to their convictions that children must learn to take risks in classroom contexts. Learning by speculation, discovery, and intuition form the heart of a whole language program. Beliefs such as these are embedded in the following principles.

Children Are Natural Learners. Children have an incredible capacity to learn. Child development experts never cease to be amazed at the learning exploits of young children—so much so that children from birth through age 5 have been characterized as "examiners," "experimenters," "explorers," "exhibitors," and "experts" (Owens, 1988). Often, whole language teachers use the metaphors "community" and "celebration" to describe children's exploits in learning within the context of the classroom. Teacher and students come together as a community of learners to celebrate reading, writing, and other collaborative acts of meaning-making.

Children Learn to Read and Write Easily and Well When the Conditions for Learning Are Informal and Natural. Children learn the written form of language in much the same way that they learn oral language—naturally and informally. The conditions necessary for children to learn language naturally and informally are present in the home environments of preschool children who acquire written language—the ability to read and write—without formal instruction. In schools, one of the most important goals of whole language teaching is to recreate a "home" environment for literacy learning in the classroom.

The conditions described next have been espoused by various whole language theorists and educators such as Goodman (1986), Atwell (1987), Cambourne (1984), and Smith (1989).

Immersion and Authenticity. Children must be immersed in written language. As learners, they need to engage in explorations of a wide range of texts which include those they produce by writing and those they use for reading. They need to be surrounded with all kinds of literature: narrative, poetic, informational, and functional in nature. When they are immersed in literature, children are given numerous occasions to explore real texts to satisfy real needs. These occasions serve as invitations to learners to create meanings and to make sense out of texts.

Authentic texts may include children's actual writings as well as books representing different literary genre. Books may be big or little in size, wordless, predictable, informational, imaginary, biographical, historical, or realistic. Books may include anthologies of poetry or short tales. In addition, genuine texts may also serve the functional, everyday needs of children and may include "environmental print" (for example, street signs, posters, boxtop labels), reference materials, textbooks, newspapers, and magazines.

When children are steeped in written language, the forces of attraction, curiosity, and interest are set into motion. The whole idea behind immersion and authenticity is to create intrinsically motivating, purposeful contexts for learning. A print-rich environment attracts learners to the genuine uses of texts and helps them to make meaningful connections between reading and writing.

Demonstration, Engagement, and Sensitivity. Immersion creates the kind of print-rich environment in classrooms that supports demonstrations related to literacy throughout the school day. Whole language classrooms demonstrate the role literacy plays in children's lives. As the result of various interactions between teacher and children, children and other children, and child with text, demonstrations show how reading and writing can be used to satisfy the user's purposes and functional needs.

Learning occurs in the presence of demonstrations. As Frank Smith (1989) notes, "Learning never takes place in the absence of demonstrations . . . . Demonstrations are continually and inevitably provided by people and by products, by acts and by artifacts" (p. 50). For example, Smith observes that a teacher who is bored by what she or he is teaching demonstrates to children that what is being taught is boring. Likewise, a reading skills workbook containing meaningless exercises demonstrates to children that reading can be meaningless. Smith also notes that demonstrations are self-generating. A young child involved in "pretend reading" by turning pages in a favorite storybook is one kind of self-generated demonstration. Children construct demonstrations in the "privacy of the mind" by using their powers to reflect and to imagine.

In whole language classrooms, children encounter numerous demonstrations of reading and writing in use. These demonstrations are intrinsically motivating to learners: What do children learn when teachers enthusiastically read stories aloud and talk about books throughout each school day? They learn that books can make you wonder, laugh, weep, imagine; that they are an important source of joy and learning. What do children learn when "one of their own" reads a piece of writing to the rest of the class? They learn about the payoffs of sharing writing with a responsive and appreciative audience. What do children learn through self-demonstrations—for example, completing a challenging book or revising a story for a class-inspired publication? They learn the meaning of "sticking with print" and the self-satisfaction that comes from hard, meaningful work.

Every classroom literacy event is a demonstration. Teacher and learners have countless opportunities, through their interactions with one another, to demonstrate the purposes of literacy in use. Sometimes demonstrations are strategic in nature. The teacher, for example, initiates an activity to "model" a learning strategy that shows students how to solve a problem encountered during a reading or writing. Sometimes a teacher provides a demonstration to make students more aware of the purpose of reading and writing.

Smith (1989) explains that engagement and sensitivity are intimately related to literacy demonstrations. Engagement suggests the literacy learner's commitment, mental involvement, and willingness to participate in a demonstration. In whole language environments, children develop an "I'll give it my best shot" attitude toward literacy learning. Once engagement with a demonstration occurs, sensitivity must follow.

Sensitivity suggests a strong expectation that children who are engaged with a literacy demonstration will succeed; learning will take place. Whole language teachers shun the possibility that children will fail at learning to read or write. They create environments which reinforce the expectation that children will be successful and then provide the means by which they will succeed. The teacher encourages risk-taking. In whole language classrooms, there is respect for every child as a reader and a writer; the focus is on successful participation in classroom literacy events.

Ownership, Time, and Response. Becoming literate is an act of empowerment when children are invited by teachers to take over control and ownership for their own learning. The whole language teacher has an important role to play in helping children to assume responsibility for their own learning (Atwell, 1987). In actuality, teachers and children share responsibility in whole language classrooms. For example, teachers plan and gather resources for a thematic unit, but they include their students in setting goals and making decisions about texts, activities, and patterns of participation.

Children achieve power when teachers shift the burden of learning to read and write from their shoulders to students'.

Shifting the burden of learning from teacher to student means putting children in charge of making decisions and exercising options related to what they will read and what they will write; and how they will read it, and how they will write it. Learners must sense that they "own" their work. Teachers serve the vitally important function of guiding students' decisions and choices in the role of coach and facilitator.

The more children are immersed in a print-rich environment that offers countless demonstrations of literacy in action, the greater their expectation becomes for learning literacy, the more they assume ownership and responsibility for their own learning. But literacy learners must also have time and opportunity to use reading and writing in meaningful contexts.

Time to read and write is essential in a literacy learner's environment. Children need time, extended time, to engage in literacy events. In whole language classrooms, opportunities—which whole language teachers call "invitations"—for reading, writing, speaking, and listening occur throughout the day and are not pigeonholed or compartmentalized into periods or time blocks. The oft-heard rallying call for whole language teachers is that "children learn to read by reading and learn to write by writing."

If children are to realize their potentials as makers of meaning and creators of knowledge, they need not only time to read and write, they also need response. Whole language teachers recognize the value of feedback by building systems of response in their classrooms. Signs of a response system are readily evident in whole language classrooms. It is not uncommon, for example, to observe children "in conference" with one another or the teacher as they share writing and receive constructive feedback. It is also not uncommon to watch children as they engage in book talks or use journals to write their personal responses to what they are reading.

Whole language teachers respond positively to students by providing supportive feedback and encouragement. They base feedback on what children can do, not on what they can't do.

Children Learn by Trial and Error. Children learn literacy as they do oral language—by trial and error. According to Cambourne (1987), in learning oral language, no one expects a young child to display adult competence when in the throes of learning to talk. Instead, parents reward a toddler's attempts at oral language with praise, encouragement, and meaningful response. A young child "approximates" oral language by giving it a try. The two-year-old's utterance, "Gimme tigger" is perfectly understood by his father, because it communicates, "Dad, I would like to play with my toy tiger. May I please have it." The utterance communicates—and that's what counts.

Children approximate written language. They experiment with written language as they put literacy to use in purposeful situations. With trial comes error. A whole language teacher prefers a child to write about a "froshus dobrman pensr" instead of a "bad dog." Nonconventional spellings, the child's "inventions," are celebrated as signs of growth as a child develops toward conventional spelling competency. Likewise, oral reading errors, "miscues" if you will, represent a child's attempt to construct meaning during reading.

Errors are welcomed, not frowned upon, in whole language classrooms. Teachers accept errors in writing and reading as part and parcel of a child's development as a user of written language. They encourage children to take risks in order to make discoveries with print. If a child miscues during reading, and the miscue doesn't interfere with meaning-making, the error is viewed as an approximation—it's close; it communicates. The child's teacher will let it stand as is. This does not mean that whole language teachers ignore errors or sweep them under the carpet. Instead, knowing *when* to correct and *why* are important functions of whole language teaching.

Children Learn Literacy by Invitation, Discovery, and Intuition. Whole language teachers create classroom environments for literacy where children learn to read and write by invitation, discovery, and intuition. If we were to view literacy learning in schools as a problem to be solved, solutions to the problem would fall on a continuum as shown in Figure 1.2.

Skill-based programs fall within the "formula" dimension of the problem-solving continuum. Skill hierarchies, represented by scope and sequence charts, suggest that if children learn certain skills, presented in a "logical" order, they will learn to read and write effectively. Teaching from a sequencing of skills provides a prescription for learning.

Lessons, often found in a teacher's manual or guide book, represent recipes for solving the problem of learning literacy skills. One of the classic recipes is the formula for writing a well-developed paragraph. Elementary children are taught that a paragraph has a beginning, a middle,

Figure 1.2
Literacy Learning on a Problem-Solving Continuum

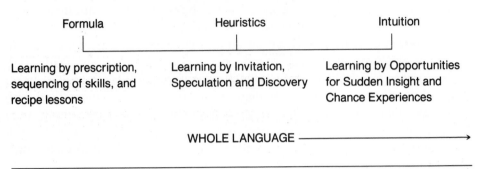

and an end. Often, teachers who teach writing by formula use an analogy, "writing a paragraph is like making a sandwich," to explain the process. The task facing students is to build a paragraph methodically, often on an assigned topic, as they would build a sandwich. The beginning sentence is like a slice of bread; it provides a foundation for the rest of the sandwich by "introducing" the topic. The middle sentences are the meat of the paragraph and serve to "develop" the topic. Children may choose to embellish the topic by adding Dagwoodian touches to sandwich, much like lettuce, tomato. The sandwich is not complete without another slice of bread, the "concluding" sentence that ties the topic together and finishes off the sandwich.

Literacy learning in whole language classrooms, on the other hand, does not rely on formula-driven prescriptions, but rather on "heuristics" and "intuition." Heuristics is another way of saying that children learn by invention, speculation, and discovery. A child, for example, doesn't write by formula in a whole language classroom. Content—exploring what one has to say or what one has strong feelings about—precedes the form and mechanics of writing. Children are invited to choose their own topics. In the process of exploring what they have to say, they find a structure that satisfies the content of the writing. A paragraph is an invention of a child's need for self-expression.

Harste, Short, and Burke (1988) define "invitations" to learning within the framework of choice and hypothesis testing: "Choice is central in curriculum because students test different hypotheses according to their different needs, interests, and experiences. Children should be invited rather than forced to engage in specific literacy activities" (p. 15). Invitations to participate in literacy events allow children to retain ownership of the processes in which they are engaged during a learning activity.

Because they make and test hypotheses about writing and reading, children engage in literacy learning as a search for personal meanings in what they read and write. Discovery involves analytical and inductive thought processes, but also intuitive thinking as well. Whole language learning capitalizes on students' intuitive knowledge about reading and writing. Learners are capable of using reading and writing intuitively to meet their functional needs; they bypass rational thinking to make sudden and immediate insights into how reading and writing work as tools for meaning making. Whole language teachers invite students to investigate what reading and writing are all about by using rational and intuitive thinking to make discoveries about literacy processes.

Curriculum, Teaching, and Teachers

Teachers' implicit theories of whole language reflect the way they view curriculum, teaching, and their roles as teacher. Curriculum is not as much a "course of study" as it is the transactions that occur among learners in a classroom context. Harste likens curriculum to the learner's "mental trip"; it involves everything that goes on in students' heads when they are learning language and using language to learn. A whole language teacher develops curriculum *with* students (Watson, 1989). Together, teacher and students enact and negotiate a whole language curriculum day-by-day throughout the school year.

All of the principles related to language and learning described in previous sections are brought together in a teacher's view of curriculum and teaching. Some of the principles underlying curriculum enactment, whole language teaching, and the role of the teacher follow.

An Integrated Curriculum Is Central for Learning Language and Using Language to Learn. Just as the systems of language should not be separated in language learning, neither should reading, writing, listening, and speaking. In whole language classrooms, language processes support one another and are integrated for instructional purposes.

Teachers preserve the powerful bonds that exist among reading, writing, speaking, and listening by helping children to make connections. When children write regularly, they are reading regularly. Reading, in turn, supports writing development. Often literature serves as a springboard for writing and discussion. As a community of language users, children learn to listen and respond to one another. Integration preserves the wholeness of language events in the classroom.

Not only is language activity integrated, but teachers and children develop curriculum across content areas. Language is for learning. As Watson (1989) puts it, *"The content areas are grist for the literacy mill.* Students listen, speak, write, and read about science, art, music, math, social studies, games and sports, cooking, sewing, nutrition—anything that is important in their lives" (p. 137). No wonder whole language teachers plan curriculum around topics and themes. Thematic unit planning is one of the tools teachers use to integrate the curriculum.

Authenticity Is One of the Essential Features of a Whole Language Curriculum.   In whole language classrooms, students engage in language activities out of genuine communicative intent. They have real reasons for reading, writing, speaking, or listening. When students are engaged in activities that genuinely meet their needs, purposes, interests, and experiences, curriculum is fun, relevant, and meaningful.

Authentic literacy events bring the world outside of school into the classroom. Authenticity bridges the gap between school literacy tasks and real world literacy tasks. As Pearson (1989) surmises, ". . . a school task is regarded as authentic to the degree that it represents the kind of task literate individuals would exercise of their own free will (unfettered by an authority figure to control their behavior)" (234). The "real world criterion," while difficult to achieve in a school setting, is worth striving for in a whole language curriculum. This is why teachers encourage students to read authentic texts and to read and write for real reasons.

Collaboration Permeates the Environment of a Whole Language Classroom.   The whole language classroom is a community of learners who come together in relationship with one another. Children grow and mature personally and socially through language use and interactions that occur in a spirit of collaboration.

Language learners help one another. They talk to each other about what they are writing and what they are reading. They engage in partnerships around projects that evolve out of thematic explorations and content study. They share their understandings of language processes and how they solve problems encountered while reading and writing.

Whole Language Teachers Are Professionals Inside and Outside of the Classroom. Whole language teachers view themselves as professionals. They use their professional knowledge base to make informed decisions that will affect the lives of students for the better. They seek, in collaboration with their principals, a degree of autonomy to plan curriculum and to evaluate students' progress as language learners. They forge partnerships with parents to extend and enrich literacy learning outside the classroom. In their local and professional communities, whole language teachers play an active role as agents of change. As Watson (1989) notes, inside of classrooms teachers are coaches, researchers, participants, learners, and resources; outside of classrooms, they are activists and advocates for students, curriculum, and themselves.

WHOLE LANGUAGE AND THE STATUS QUO

Whole language constitutes a view of curriculum, language, and learning that is challenging the status quo. It is now under scrutiny and critical evaluation by educators and researchers outside of the movement. Some of these critics have a vested interest in maintaining the status quo. P. David Pearson (1989), for example, is one of the most influential literacy educators of the past decade, but he is also one of the senior authors of a leading basal reading program. He notes that there is much to like about whole language and acknowledges the strides the movement has made in changing the face of literacy instruction.

Whole language, Pearson observes, is founded on such worthy principles as preserving the wholeness of literacy events, integrating reading, writing, speaking, and listening, and supporting learners through the use of authentic texts and authentic reasons for engaging in literacy activities. But Pearson questions the lack of clear description and an explicit definition of whole language. He expresses concern for what he considers the political naivete of the movement and wonders what its legacy will be twenty years from now.

Walter MacGinitie (1991) echoes Pearson's concerns. He is the major author of a widely used standardized reading test, a past president of the International Reading Association, and a scholar whose work spans several decades. MacGinitie warns that whole language is destined to fail if it is carried to extremes. The champions of whole language, he argues, would do well to heed the mistakes of previous educational movements—for example, the open classroom movement of a few short years ago. If not, he predicts that whole language as a curriculum reform will be oversold, misunderstood, overdone, and ultimately, overwhelmed by excesses: "Naively eager, and oblivious of the past, we recreate not only enlightened curriculums but the very conditions that doom them" (p. 55).

From a research perspective, Michael McKenna and his associates (1990) argue for a comprehensive agenda to assess the effectiveness of whole language practices. To this, Carole Edelsky (1990), a leader in the whole language movement, responds rather forcefully, suggesting that McKenna and his associates do not know what whole language is, fail to acknowledge an existing body of research, and are "blinded" by their own conceptual shortcomings and theoretical perspectives.

Whole language is, in the best sense of the expression, an anti-establishment movement that has called into question the way children and youth are taught to read and write in our nation's schools. As a philosophy of language, learning, and curriculum, whole language cuts across the grain of conventional wisdom in the teaching of reading and writing.

From a whole language perspective, language is language, whether it is oral or written. When language is splintered into its parts, and the parts are isolated from one another for instructional purposes, learning to read or write becomes more difficult than it needs to be. As Ken Goodman (1986) points out, "Many school traditions seem to have actually hindered language development. In our zeal to make it easy, we've made it hard. How? Primarily by breaking whole (natural) language up into bite-size, but abstract little pieces" (p. 7).

A "part-to-whole" logic has been the guiding principle in the design of reading programs in American schools since colonial days. With the publication of the *The New England Primer* in 1683, the children of American colonists were taught to read by first learning the alphabet, then vowels, consonants, double letters, italics, capitals, syllables, and so on in that order (Vacca, Vacca, & Gove, 1991). A part-to-whole logic persists today and is firmly rooted in the status quo of literacy instruction. Goodman (1986) describes the predominance of part-to-whole instruction this way: "It seemed so logical to think that little children could best learn simple little things. We took apart the language and turned it into words, syllables, and isolated sounds. Unfortunately, we also postponed its natural purpose—the communication of meaning—and turned it into a set of abstractions, unrelated to the needs and experiences of the children we sought to help" (p. 7).

Not only is language segmented into bite-sized pieces for instructional purposes, but also *the processes by which children learn language* have been splintered into bits of alleged behavior called "skills." Teachers whose implicit theories of literacy and language embody a skills perspective believe that reading and writing development require the mastery of skills arranged in a hierarchical progression often called a "scope and sequence." In schools, the status quo is maintained when children are required to learn certain skills before they are taught other skills. Skills hierarchies, however, vary considerably from school district to school district and from one commercially prepared reading program to another.

Are skill hierarchies based on fact or fiction? When scope and sequence charts from various commercially prepared reading programs are compared to one another, it becomes apparent that the hierarchy of skills involved in learning to read is both contrived and arbitrary. Scope and sequence charts listing and ordering reading skills varies from program to program. No wonder S. Jay Samuels (1976), a noted educational psychologist and researcher, admits, "Despite the fact that . . . commercial reading series, with their scope and sequence charts, order the reading tasks (skills) as if we did know the nature of the learning hierarchy in reading, the sad truth is that the task is so complex that a validated reading hierarchy does not exist" (p. 174).

Not only has the hierarchy of skills been called into question, but reading skills as separate entities with their own psychological reality have been challenged. Are reading skills more apocryphal than real? John Downing (1982), a prominent psychologist and reading researcher, concludes from his analysis of research on actual reading behavior that the "so-called reading skills" are largely mythical. Jerome Harste (1989) puts the matter of skills more bluntly by stating, "The skills taught are for the most part hallucinated by basal authors for the purpose of sequencing lessons" (p. 265). He suggests that a skills perspective does not take into account what readers naturally do to comprehend texts or how they develop literate behavior.

If reading skills do exist, it is likely that they are so highly interactive during reading that they are impossible to separate. Probably Yetta Goodman and Carolyn Burke (1972) best express the role of skills in any process when they argue: "You cannot know a process by listing its ingredients or labeling its parts; you must observe the effect of the parts as they interact with each other. Acting together, the parts compose an entity which is uniquely different from the identity of any of the separate parts" (p. 95). Goodman and Burke use an analogy, that of baking a cake, to make their point. Flour, sugar, eggs, baking soda, and water are some of the ingredients of a cake. Yet the actual cake itself cannot be related directly to any one of the ingredients. It can only be related to the quality and result of the interaction among the ingredients.

The teaching of skills is a predominant practice in the existing state of affairs of literacy instruction today. Three symbols, if you will, of the status quo are highly visible in the culture of American education and the technology of conventional reading instruction as it is practiced in many schools across the country.

Readiness

For more than sixty years, reading readiness programs have been the predominant technology used to introduce kindergarten and first grade children to the world of reading instruction. Reading readiness has been institutionalized by schools, curricula, and commercial publishers of instructional programs and tests (Teale & Sulzby, 1986). For most children, readiness programs mark the passage of time from school entrance to the point where they are deemed ready to benefit from reading instruction.

Readiness to read is a concept that originated with the belief that children must reach a certain level of physical, mental, and emotional maturity to profit from teaching. The prevailing thought behind the readiness concept was that there is a "best time" to learn to read. In many school districts from the 1930s through the 1960s, children were delayed from participating in reading until they reached a mental age of 6.5, an age where they were considered "ripe" for teaching them to read (Morphett & Washburne, 1931). Such practice resulted in the proliferation of readiness workbooks where children were exposed to activities that had little to do with reading or learning to read.

Today, however, the readiness concept has evolved into the belief that early instructional experiences are essential before engaging children in the reading of texts. The earlier children learn the prerequisite skills of reading, the better. The shift from a maturational to an instructional emphasis has resulted in the development of formal, prescribed sequences of instruction focused on *prereading skills.*

Today's reading readiness programs have changed little in the past twenty years. They include activities to develop prerequisite skills such as auditory memory and discrimination, and visual memory and discrimination. Children are expected to master the smallest units of written language in most readiness programs—for example, naming and recognizing letters and sounds associated with letters—before progressing to letter combinations and words. Scope and sequence charts depict the order of skills through which children progress.

Marie Clay (1966, 1979), a New Zealander whose research with early readers and writers has contributed substantially to whole language theory and practice, coined the term *emergent literacy* to describe the literacy development of young children. She is one of the first literacy educators to refute the concept of reading readiness. According to Clay, readiness supports the notion that children gradually change from nonreaders to beginning readers. The readiness concept leads to the misleading conclusion that children bring little, if anything, to school in the way of knowledge about and experience with print.

Emergent literacy, on the other hand, represents an important construct in whole language theory because it underscores the role natural learning plays in the acquisition of literacy. Children are in the process of becoming literate from birth. They are as predisposed to learn to read and write naturally as they are to learn to speak, because they are immersed in oral and written language. Table 1.1 contrasts reading readiness with a whole language/emergent literacy perspective.

Not all children come to school with the same background knowledge and experiences with print, the same reading and reading-like behaviors, or the same interests in reading or learning to read. Yet from a whole language perspective, a teacher of young children builds on their language competence and incorporates the principles of natural learning into literacy lessons.

Table 1.1
Differences Between Reading Readiness and Whole Language*

	Whole Language	Reading Readiness
Theoretical Perspective	Children are in the process of becoming literate from birth and are capable of learning what it means to be a user of written language before entering school.	Children must master a set of basic skills before they can learn to read. Learning to read is an outcome of school-based instruction.
Acquisition of Literacy Skills and Strategies	Children learn to use written language and develop as readers and writers through active engagement with their world. Literacy develops in real-life settings in purposeful ways.	Children learn to read by mastering skills arranged and sequenced in a hierarchy according to their level of difficulty.
Relationship of Reading to Writing	Children progress as readers and writers. Reading and writing (as well as speaking and listening) are interrelated and develop concurrently.	Children learn to read first. The skills of reading must be developed before introducing written composition.
Functional/Formal Learning	Children learn informally through interactions with and demonstrating from literate significant others and from explorations with written language.	Children learn through formal teaching and monitoring (periodic assessment) of skills.
Individual Development	Children learn to be literate in different ways and at different rates of development.	Children progress as readers by moving through a "scope and sequence" of skills.

*Adapted with permission from Vacca, J.L., Vacca, R.T., and Gove, M.K. (1991), *Reading and Learning to Read (2nd Ed.)*, New York: Harper Collins.

Phonics

Whole language advocates argue that in the status quo of reading instruction, phonics has been elevated to an exalted, but unwarranted, position. Phonics involves teaching the relationships between speech sounds and letters. Whole language is sometimes interpreted as an anti-phonics movement. It is . . . and it isn't. *It is* only in the sense that whole language teachers are diametrically opposed to the way children learn sound-letter relationships in today's conventional classroom. However, whole language advocates recognize that children must develop and refine a knowledge of the *alphabetic principle*, the principle that reflects how spoken language is coded in written language.

Critics such as MacGinitie (1991) worry that whole language, if taken to extremes, will result in teachers ignoring the alphabetic principle and, therefore, neglecting phonics instruction. Whole language teachers, on the other hand, are quick to acknowledge that they rail against the status quo wherein children spend inordinate amounts of time on phonics "skill and drill" lessons that are isolated from authentic, meaningful texts. They reject phonics outright when it is reduced to matching letters to sounds or filling-in-the-blanks on worksheets.

Yet whole language teachers recognize that children must discover and rediscover their own phonic "rules" and generalizations. The whole language teacher's job is to help learners develop and refine a working knowledge of how oral language is coded in writing and to assist them, when it is appropriate to do so, in using this knowledge to construct meaning during reading. So phonics is taught in the whole language classroom, within the context of real reading and writing situations, but in ways vastly different from the conventional classroom.

Basals

The most visible, dominant practice of conventional reading instruction involves the use of basal readers. More than 90 percent of elementary classrooms today use basal readers as the major approach to reading instruction. A basal reading program is a comprehensive, integrated set of books, workbooks, teacher's manuals and ancillary materials designed to provide children in elementary and middle grades with developmental instruction. The *raison d'etre* of basal programs is to teach the skills of reading. To this end, basal publishers incorporate into their programs comprehensive scope and sequence schemes that include provisions for readiness, phonics, word identification, comprehension, and study skills development within the framework of textbooks, workbooks, ancillary materials, and a management system/assessment program.

The pervasive use of basal programs in schools has been described by Harste (1989) as the "basalization" of American reading instruction. A "basal reader mentality," according to Harste, affects the way teachers and children think about reading comprehension. In basals, comprehension is thought of and taught as a set of skills rather than as something (a language process) readers actually do to make sense of text.

The National Council of Teachers of English (NCTE), through its Commission on Reading, reports that basal reading programs perpetuate a number of misconceptions about reading and learning to read. Table 1.2 depicts these misconceptions and show how they lead to instructional practices that may pose threats to children's literacy development and teachers' empowerment.

Goodman, Shannon, and Freeman (1988) assign basal readers a failing grade and call for their abandonment in schools. In their book, *Report Card on Basal Readers*, they argue that reading, like other language processes, develops easily and well in the context of its use. Basals work against

Table 1.2
Issues, Misconceptions, and Threats Posed by Basal Readers*

Issues	Misconceptions Promoted by Basals	Threats to Learning and Teaching
Nature of Learning	Reading is learned from part to whole.	Learning to read is made more difficult than it needs to be.
Logistics of Instruction	The sequencing of skills in the context of a complete system of textbooks, workbooks, and ancillary materials supports the teaching of lessons day after day, week after week, year after year.	An inordinate amount of time is spent on teaching and practicing the skills of reading rather than on engaging learners in actual reading.
Comprehension	The ability to verbalize or locate an answer is evidence of understanding and learning.	Basals do not show students how to make sense from text or think with print.
Assessment	Periodic testing of isolated skills facilitates reading development.	Mastery of skills in isolation does not ensure transfer to actual reading situations.
Empowerment	Detailed lesson plans tell teachers what to do and say, thus facilitating children's reading development.	Teachers are deprived of the responsibility and authority to make decisions and informed professional judgments

*Table 1.2 developed from information provided by: The Commission on Reading, National Council of Teachers of English (1989). Basal readers and the state of American reading instruction: A call for action. *Language Arts, 66,* 896–898.

children's literacy development because the basal exercises tight control on literacy lessons. A crucial question raised deals with the empowerment of children as literacy learners and of teachers as professionals, "Who owns the literacy lesson?" Not the child. Not the teacher.

Basal programs are not child-responsive, but are based on adult part-to-whole logical notions of learning to read. Children have no choice in the selection of texts, responsibility in planning lessons or pursuing what is to be learned. Basal authors make assumptions about children's experiences, interests, and needs and plan a program of skills development accordingly. In the struggle for control of literacy lessons, Shannon (1989) argues that the basal authors and publishers maintain tight control. Not only do they control what is to be learned (the sequence of skills), but also how (through the sequence of lessons in the teacher's manual). As a result, basal reading programs disempower teachers by depriving them the responsibility to make informed professional judgments as to what is instructionally appropriate for literacy learners.

In whole language classrooms, teachers and children assume the responsibility for literacy lessons, and they negotiate and enact the curriculum together. The broad instructional goal is to help learners become *skillful* as language users—readers, writers, speakers, and listeners. Children develop language processes when they have good reasons to put these processes to use in meaningful situations.

SEARCH FOR COMMON GROUND

Some of the principles of whole language we outlined earlier provide, at best, a baseline understanding of the common ground that whole language teachers share. But a search for common ground does not end here. The principles we described provide some insight into what whole language teachers and whole language classrooms are all about. The more one studies the literature and theoretical bases for whole language, the richer one's conceptual understanding becomes.

Yet we are inclined to agree with Dorothy Watson (1989), "A single visit in a whole-language classroom is worth more than a hundred definitions, for it is in the classroom that the definitions, the theory, and the stated practices come alive" (p. 134). An important way to ensure that you are on *terra firma* with the concept of whole language is to get into classrooms to study what whole language teachers do and why.

And so we come to the purpose of this book. Case studies are one way of getting you into the minds of teachers and into their classrooms. Your entry, of course, is vicarious. However, by sharing in the stories of the six teachers whose classrooms you are about to visit, you will develop another way of relating to the joys, dilemmas, and challenges associated with whole language teaching and learning. No two whole language teachers are alike, although they share many of the same ideas and concerns. Each whole language classroom is different, because the teachers are different. Their personal and professional histories have brought them to the point in their development that they are now going to share with you.

Enjoy the visits. Learn from the stories.

REFERENCES

Altwerger, B., Edelsky, C., & Flores, B. (1987). Whole language: What's New? *Reading Teacher 41*, 144–55.

Atwell, N. (1987). *In the middle: Writing, reading and learning with adolescents.* Portsmouth, NH: Boynton/Cook/Heinemann.

Cambourne, B. (1984). Language, learning, and literacy. In Butler, A. & Turbill, J. *Towards a reading/writing classroom.* Portsmouth, NH: Heinemann.

Clay, M. M. (1966). *Emergent reading behaviour.* Unpublished doctoral dissertation, University of Auckland, New Zealand.

Clay, M. M. (1979). Reading: The patterning of complex behavior (2nd ed.). Auckland, New Zealand: Heinemann Educational.

Dewey, J. (1939). *Experience in education.* New York: Collier.

Downing, J. (1982). Reading: Skill or skills? *Reading Teacher, 35,* 534–537.

Edelsky, C. (1990). Whose agenda is this anyway? A response to McKenna, Robinson, and Miller. *Educational Researcher, 19,* 7–11.

Edelsky, C., Altwerger, B., & Flores, B. (1991). *Whole language: What's the difference?* Portsmouth, NH: Heinemann.

Goodman, K. (1986). *What's whole in whole language?* Portsmouth, NH: Heinemann.

Goodman, K., Shannon, P., Freeman, Y., & Murphy, S. (1988). *Report card on basal readers.* Katonah, NY: Richard C. Owens.

Goodman, Y., & Burke, C. (1972). *Reading miscue inventory manual: Procedure for diagnosis and evaluation.* New York: MacMillan.

Hall, N. (1987). *The emergence of literacy.* Portsmouth, NH: Heinemann.

Halliday, M. A. K. (1975). *Learning how to mean: Exploration in the development of language.* London: Arnold.

Harste, J. C. (1989). The basalization of American Reading Instruction: One researcher responds. *Theory Into Practice, 27,* 265–273.

Harste, J. C., Woodward, V. A., & Burke, C. L. (1984). Language stories and literacy lessons. Portsmouth, NH: Heinemann.

Heath, S. B. (1983). *Ways with words.* Cambride: Cambridge University Press.

MacGinitie, W. H. (1991). Reading instruction: Plus ça change . . . . *Educational Leadership. 48,* 55–58.

McKenna, M. C., Robinson, R. D., & Miller, J. W. (1990). Whole language: A research agenda for the nineties. *Educational Researcher. 19,* 3–6.

Morphett, M. V., & Washburne, C. (1931). When should children begin to read? *Elementary School Journal, 31,* 496–503.

Owens, R. E. (1988). *Language development,* 2nd ed. Columbus, OH: Merrill.

Pearson, D. P. (1989). Reading the whole-language movement. *The Elementary School Journal. 90,* 231–241.

Samuels, S. J. (1976). Hierarchical subskills in the reading acquisition process. In J. T. Gutherie (Ed.). *Aspects of reading acquisition.* Baltimore, MD: Johns Hopkins University Press.

Smith, F. (1989). Demonstrations, engagement and sensitivity: The choice between people and programs. In G. Manning & M. Manning (Eds.), *Whole language: Beliefs and practices, K-8.* Washington, DC: National Education Association.

Teale, W. H., & Sulzby, E. (1986). *Emergent literacy: Writing and reading.* Norwood, NJ: Ablex.

Vacca, J. L., Vacca, R. T., & Gove, M. (1991). *Reading and learning to read,* 2nd edition. New York: Harper Collins.

Watson, D. (1989). Defining and describing whole language. *The Elementary School Journal. 90,* 129–141.

Weaver, C., & Watson, D. (1989). *Report on basal readers.* A statement of the National Council of Teachers of English, Urbana, IL: National Council of Teachers of English.

II
EMERGING . . .

The first few years of school are the most critical time in the literacy development of children. Children enter the formal world of learning excited and full of anticipation about learning to read and write. In many cases, however, that vitality is replaced by literacy instruction and is marked by contrived and uninteresting encounters with print.

In whole language literacy instruction, authentic uses of reading and writing replace the artificial texts and drills of traditional approaches. When literacy serves the real purposes and needs of children, youngsters will reciprocate by plunging deeper and more vigorously into written language. In the three case studies that follow, you will read about three teachers who work hard to make emergent literacy meaningful and enjoyable for preschool and primary grade children. As you read the stories of these teachers, reflect on the ways in which they enact curriculum and create classroom environments that allow children to continually emerge more fully into real life and real literacy.

Chapter 2

WHOLE LANGUAGE
IN THE PRESCHOOL

"My children are reading, writing and communicating in a variety of ways."

Conventional and traditional wisdom says that most young children cannot engage in literate behavior prior to entering kindergarten. Encouraging children toward authentic reading and writing is futile for the teacher or parent, frustrating for the child, and potentially harmful for later growth in literacy.

Dona Greene Bolton's preschool classes challenges such wisdom directly. Children in her room successfully engage in all sorts of reading and writing behavior. Children attend to and discuss stories, poems, and articles that she reads to them. They enthusiastically dramatize other stories that they have read and dictate new versions and new endings to memorable stories. They read familiar books to one another and to Dona and receive just praise and encouragement in return. They express their deepest thoughts in their own writing and write notes to Dona and their parents.

In short, Dona has a class of active readers and writers. Children in her class describe themselves as readers and writers and use reading and writing for the same purposes that adults use literacy-to enjoy a story or poem, to communicate with someone, to learn new things, to remember things, to help think about important issues, to get things done. Clearly, these youngsters, in their own literate community, are on the road to becoming fully functioning members in the larger literate society.

Dona implements a whole language curriculum in an early childhood (pre-kindergarten) setting. As a veteran teacher, Dona has subscribed to holistic teaching since entering the education field. She admits that her involvement has become more intense over the past seven years as this type of approach has become more accepted in professional circles.

Dona's interest and involvement in whole language began as an undergraduate at Cornell University. "It was natural to be a whole language teacher at the pre-school level," she notes "because the program focused on children's acquisition of language and literacy through rich environments for play, drama, talk, and literature." Her initial involvement and interest in whole language was reinforced as she took graduate courses in children's literature at Kent State.

WHAT DONA THINKS ABOUT WHOLE LANGUAGE

Dona maintains three beliefs that are central to her philosophy of instruction. First, she believes that instruction needs to meet the individual needs of her students. Many of her children speak English as their second language. Some come from a limited experiential background while others have traveled widely and have had many opportunities for varied experiences: Even at the preschool the diversity between students can be tremendous. Dona is sensitive to this and tries to design her instruction to satisfy the individual needs and interests of her students.

A child recently arrived in her classroom from Korea and is not familiar with English. Dona meets this child's needs for safety and reassurance through nonverbal communication that her room is indeed a safe, secure, and nurturing environment during the play curriculum. Nurturance comes from a hug given spontaneously by the teacher or whenever the child feels a need. Acceptance is developed through constant low key encouragement of new activities and recognition of accomplishments. Dona noted that it was the children in the class who called her attention to Wong Yong's first words in English—"Clean Up." This was cause for praise and celebration.

Another child in the class uses an adult vocabulary and talks about the nightly news with Peter Jennings. Dona works to stimulate this child with maps, globes, stimulating books, easy reference materials and unusual props to augment her imaginative role play.

Dona centers her curriculum on communication. Yet she interprets communication in broad terms, to include music, art, drama, play, as well as talk and written texts. "To me communication is any way to express one's thoughts, feelings, and experiences." Her curriculum, then, is designed to provide rich opportunities to communicate in a variety of media.

A favorite unit of study is the circus. When the Barnum and Bailey train pulls into a nearby train station every fall, the children are on hand to see how big an elephant really is. Children can smell the animals and hear a lion roar. These direct experiences lead to a re-enactment of a full blown circus back in the classroom with acts for every child's individual interest involving music, dance, large muscle activities, drama, art, and role play.

Finally, Dona sees good literature for children as the common element that ties together the whole program. Books and stories can be used to meet individual needs and interests as well as introduce and connect activities in drama, art, music, and so on. Dona uses children's books as a springboard to the lessons she develops. They are used as concept books for science and math, to introduce discussion on topics in social studies, and to nurture children's play, imagination, and drama. In addition to her own use of books, she ensures that children have ready access to a rich and changing assortment of books. There are many books that provide opportunities for dramatization in the classroom. Some all time favorites include *Caps for Sale* by Esphyr Slobodkina, *Mr. Gumpy's Outing* by John Birmingham, *The Three Billy Goats Gruff* by Paul Galdone, and *Sun Grumble* by Claudia Fregosi. Nursery tales of *Little Red Riding Hood, The Three Little Pigs,* and *The Three Bears* are also favorite dramatizations of predictability, use of dramatic voice, and destruction of evil in the plot.

In the class's dramatization of *Caps for Sale,* a blonde-haired girl calls out "Caps for sale, Caps for sale. Fifty cents a cap" as she adjusts a pile of assorted hats from the dress up corner sitting on her head. Grinning at her, perched on a row of chairs, are seven little monkeys just waiting for her to rest under their tree so they can grab the caps.

"You monkeys you give me back my caps!" she yells shaking her fist at them.

They counter with "Tse Tse Tse Tse" shaking their fists right back in imitative fashion. A little girl from Poland with no English smiles with understanding from underneath her cap, as does the boy from Brazil and a girl from Germany. Non-English speaking children are learning by imitation in a nonthreatening part of their play. Dramatic play based upon a book encourages children to learn and play about stories without having to have an extensive vocabulary. Instant dramatic success is achieved! Though the initial production was guided by the teacher, the children, on their own, dramatized this story many times through the year. Moreover, their play led them back to the original book over and over.

INSIDE DONA'S CLASSROOM

The Environment

Dona's classroom is actually made up of two connected yet separate rooms. (See Figure 2.1.) In each room are several activity areas or learning centers to which children are free to go during self-selected activity time. In one room is a kitchen/restaurant and home living area which contains toys, artifacts, and furniture related to home life. Nearby is a dress up area which contains a variety of clothes and props that children can use in their dramatic play. A common area is also a part of this room. It is here that the class congregates for group lessons, discussions, sharing, and story time. Off to one side is a phonograph and record

Figure 2.1
Dona's Classrooms

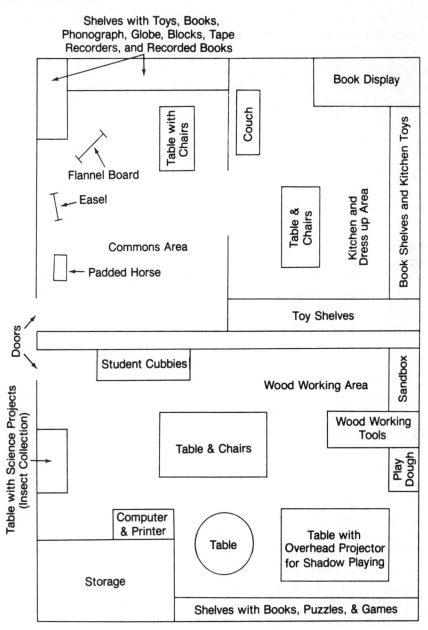

collection and the class library. The books are displayed so that their fronts can be seen by students. Tape-recorded books and cassette tape recorders are also available. These are especially helpful for children learning English as a second language. Students are free to choose books at their leisure. On a nearby bulletin are posted book jackets of favorite books that the class has shared.

The room contains an assortment of other toys, artifacts, and materials that the children are free to play with, explore, and observe. These include a large block collection, a globe, more books on shelves, a stuffed riding horse, two gerbils in a cage, an easel with blank chart paper and markers, a flannel board with cut out figures, a second bulletin board on which children's work is displayed ("Things I Like to Do . . ."), and several puppets. Children are free to play at any of the areas. The most popular areas include the home living area, the floor of the common area, the stuffed riding horse, and a writing table with accompanying chairs and a typewriter.

The second room contains a variety of other centers. These include an easel with paints, a wood-working center containing pieces of wood and working tools, an overhead projector with a cloth screen that students use for shadow plays, a sandbox and modeling clay area, a holding area for in-progress projects, a place for students to keep their personal belongings, a computer, and more shelves containing games, puzzles, and over 400 books. An exhibit area is also present at which children have on display insects that they have collected on a recent nature walk. In both rooms, a variety of children's art projects are hung from the ceiling.

The room is not particularly neat. It is apparent that this is a place for children. Children continually play in the various areas, using the toys, tools, games, and instruments that are available to them. It is obvious that the children make use of the rich and stimulating environment. Dona and her aide circulate among the class challenging, explaining, and assisting children in their explorations.

The environment is flexible as well as varied. Dona says that the centers are in a state of "continual evolution." New items are brought in and new centers are created throughout the year.

The sand and water table contain soap bubbles, hunks of clay, water, beans, seeds, soil, sawdust, and styrofoam. Instruments include measuring devices, scales, scoops, a water wheel, micro-play small animals, buildings, and transportation vehicles. Other items are added throughout the year.

The science center is filled with hands-on rock collections, tree and plant textures and seeds, insects, shells, bones, kaleidoscopes, magnifying glasses, a microscope, binoculars, prisms, magnets, flashlights, an oil and water wave machine, and a water-filled tornado tube. Concepts of big and little, that everything changes, heavy and light, metamorphosis, growth, camouflage, and physics principles are explored at this center and become invitations for students to add to and arrange the collections according to the concepts under study.

The art table is always filled with self-selected, open-ended projects that stress process rather than product. The children can explore what Jupiter's gaseous swirls might look like in various colored fingerpaints on the round table as a group activity. Rich conversations about color mixing, storms, Jupiter's "red eye," and aliens evolve as four children swirl finger, hands, and even arms through the paint while classical music provides an aural backdrop.

In the dramatic play area, a study of Native Americans is underway. A teepee is constructed from poles found in nearby woods and dragged into the school. The children construct a canoe from large hollow blocks and have a pretend fire built with sticks and corn husks. Some children role play beavers and bears, others are hunters or builders. Animal pelts and other props are nearby to enhance the role play. Each child interacts according to her ability and understanding. A Chinese girl is cooking on her stove in the back of the canoe. One shy hunter stays close to the teacher and just keeps paddling, another skins the stuffed bears with a wooden Cree Indian knife. Later, Dona (and the children) will add and subtract props from the room as new areas of interest and exploration emerge.

At snack time (and at the end of the day) children clean up the rooms and help in rearranging tables and chairs so that they may enjoy their snacks as a group.

Beginning the School Year: Learning about the Children

Beginning a school year is always a challenge for teachers. Early childhood education is no exception. Dona explains that first on her agenda at the beginning of the year is learning about the children, their needs, and interests. She talks with them and their parents discovering where they come from, what experiences they have had and enjoyed, and what experiences they would like to have.

Through requested home visits, one-on-one intake conferences, personal history sheets, and informal family gatherings, picnics, swims, and ice skating, Dona learns about her children and their families in a variety of authentic contexts.

With this information in mind, she brainstorms themes to explore with the class, plans activities that develop the themes, and goes to the library to find books at various levels of difficulty that are related to the theme and can be connected to social studies, music, drama, science, or math. As early as possible, Dona moves the class into projects and explorations on themes that she knows the class has an interest in.

A Typical Day

Dona has two class sessions (morning and afternoon) for approximately 17 preschool children, ages three through five for each session. Each session runs for two-and-one-half hours. A definite yet flexible routine is readily apparent in Dona's classroom. The first hour of class is spent on self-selected exploratory activities. Children are encouraged to investigate the classroom and engage in activities at one or more centers. Children come to the areas and play by themselves, with a friend, or in groups. Children are free to move from one area to another and the social make-up of the center continually changes.

The workbench is alive with hammering and sawing with real tools under the close supervision of Dona or an aide. Only two children are allowed here at a time, but the noise from a four-year-old pounding nails in a soft pine log and a three-year-old sawing a board in the vice suggest more. Jessica is planning to glue the board she is sawing to a house she is constructing. Ryan asks for some rubber bands. He will attach the bands to the nails he has pounded to make a mouse trap.

The wood-working center provides a creative outlet for inventive children. It provides a nonthreatening outlet for children to take out frustrations in a constructive physical way of sawing or hammering, providing an emotional outlet. Conversation, planning, and cooperation on a one-to-one basis is a large part of this center. For those children needing to take something home, a piece of wood that they sawed is very important for self-esteem and pride. The drawn and written plans children develop and share with the teacher and classmates mark early and real uses of reading and writing.

On another day, Dona and the class roll out a large roll of heavyweight paper. Sitting nearby is a dishpan filled with warm water, soap, and bath towels. Children remove their shoes and socks, roll up their pants, and step into three dishpans filled with sponges soaked in tempera and soap. The three primary colors change to orange, green, and violet as the "Dance of the Snowflakes" from *The Nutcracker* plays. The finished cooperative mural is alive with the twirling, squishing, and blending of colors and footprints. Warm water and soap whisk away the paint from small feet, but the experience will be remembered for a long time.

The next day Dona discusses the experience with the class. She asks children to call out words that describe the experience. "Squishy, rainbows, funny, messy, happy" and others are contributed. Dona writes these words on a large sheet of paper that will become the title for the children's creation.

Talk is an important feature of this period. Children can be heard explaining things to themselves or others, discussing their various activities with other children or the teacher, "reading" books, being read to, singing songs, or carrying on conversations in dramatic play activities. Throughout this cacophony of exploration and talk, Dona and her aide mingle with the children, encourage exploration and conversation, and monitor the classroom activities. At any one time, Dona (or her aide) could be reading to a child on her lap (or to a group of four or five seated on the floor), playing the part of audience for a group's skit, asking children to explain or describe their creations in the block, art, or wood-work areas, encouraging children who are not getting along to explain their feelings, comforting a child who is not feeling well, participating with a group in a song or dance, or helping a child who is having difficulty on the computer.

Dona does not direct children to any one center or activity. She picks up on what the child has chosen on his or her own and works to facilitate, enrich, and support that activity. For example, a child might be trying to build a birdhouse in the work bench area. Rather than attempt to direct the child to an easier project, she will show her how to use the various tools, provide her with appropriate material, ask her to explain how she envisions the house and how she intends to construct it, and provide help when the child seeks or requires it. In several observations of Dona's classroom, we were struck by the ease she displays in allowing, even encouraging, children to choose their own activities and to go beyond themselves in trying out new ideas and projects. Dona sees her role in the first hour as an observer, facilitator, and challenger. She challenges children to risk new adventures, to play with children they haven't played with in the past, and to explain their thoughts, plans, and feelings honesty and clearly.

During the recent Persian Gulf war, the children were filled with anxieties. It was hard for them to understand or explain their feelings. This became apparent with the increased acting out by several children.

Two boys began to dramatize karate contenders. Dona recognized the physical need for the children to act this out but had to guide the activity by helping them choose a safe place in the classroom environment. One boy threw out his arms in a typical karate pose. "Give me your best shot," he challenged. Dona being unfamiliar with karate, asked them to first demonstrate the moves for her. This helped to set up the activity and establish "safe" fighting with rules. Soon the contenders were joined by a cheering audience of their peers who also entered into the drama as referees, trainers, and audience. The fighting turned to boxing and wrestling with both boys and girls participating, acting out the role play according to the way they had seen it on television. As the children switched roles, winners were announced and when feelings were running high over winning, many ties were declared. One referee announced the winner and placed a "peace" hat (a black velvet Mexican sombrero from the dress-up corner) on the winner's head. Dona acted as facilitator, weaving new children into the action, commenting on the children's feelings, and keeping an eye on safety. At clean-up time, she experienced the class' collective feeling of satisfaction in channeled physical acting out of "fighting" as it related to their own world.

The next segment of Dona's classroom routine runs about 20 to 30 minutes. The teacher-directed circle time involves the whole class in a discussion of a current theme involving social studies, science, math, music, or language. During this time, children are seated around the teacher who challenges them to listen, think, and respond to important issues. Literature is often a key element in these discussions. In one circle time, Dona read Leo Lionni's *Tico and the Golden Wings* to an assembled circle of children. The children listed in rapt attention as they felt the plight of the handicapped bird and how he gains feathered wings through good deeds for those in need.

Dona brings out a collection of feathers she has gathered and a bird body and head made of styrofoam. She explains that this is poor Tico

without any feathers. "Our job is to help Tico get feathers. Each time any of you is helpful to others in the classroom you will come up, select a feather, and put it on Tico."

This literature extension activity helped children work as a group and individuals as they tie shoes for a friend, hold a door, or share a sought-after toy. Tico's feathers kept increasing until one day toward the end of the year Tico was airborne (suspended from invisible fishing line from the ceiling). The rewards of placing the feathers on Tico are individual, but it is group cooperation and commitment to the bird that led to his flight. Through *Tico* and the activity that followed, children developed a greater sensitivity to the needs and limitations of themselves as well as others.

During another circle time, Dona decided to invite the children to explore issues related to living and dying. She chose this in response to the recent death of a child's grandfather and as a continuation of a discussion on fear that also was begun as a result of her observation that the children were fearful in different situations. Dona began the session by reading the book *Lifetimes* to the class. The book deals with life/cycles and the inevitability of death. During the reading, the children were attentive and responsive as Dona read the book with expression and paused at appropriate points to ask a question or allow responses.

After the book was read, Dona asked the class to think of any relatives, friends, or pets who have died. Then she asked the children to consider how they themselves felt when they became aware of their relative's, friend's, or pet's death. She also asked the students to think of why a particular person or pet was special to them. Students responded to the teacher's questions and to each other's comments. When Robbie told the class that his great grandpa died, Dona asked him, "How did you feel? Did you do anything special with him?" Robbie responded, "I had breakfast with him." This led to a discussion of pets who had died and a comment by a girl and affirmed by the teacher, that, "It's scary to look at dead things sometimes."

Following this comment, Dona drew the class' attention to a book authored by the class and entitled, "I'm Afraid When." She noted that experiencing the death of a loved one could be a fearful experience. In the book, each child had drawn a picture depicting something he or she feared. Fears included bears, smoke, shadows, nightmares, and Tom's big brother. After drawing their pictures, students either dictated a brief caption or wrote their own captions, usually in invented form. These were often little more than scribbles or random letters, but they had real meaning for the students.

Circle time is followed by a short break that includes bathroom, snack, and social time. While enjoying their snacks, students are encouraged to talk to one another or one of their teachers about events at home or school. Dona and her aide visit with several students during this period, attempting to draw out and encourage the more reticent.

At snack time, the children delight in telling jokes of which the "knock-knock" jokes are a favorite.

"Knock Knock"

"Who's there?"

"Banana"

The child repeats this as many times as the teacher can stand and then

"Orange"

"Orange who?"

"Orange you glad I didn't say banana."

Various new jokes using the same format surface as the children play with language and what might be funny. Funny, to the children, usually means ridiculous and they will laugh the hardest as they seek reaction from their table full of snacking peers and teachers.

Large muscle activity time occurs next for about 20 minutes. It is either held on the playground or in a room intended for physical activity. Children engage in teacher-directed or self-selected activities, often in the form of movement activities or games.

In one activity, Dona lays a parachute on the ground. The children gather around and grab hold of the cloth. While the children walk in a circle and lift the parachute up and down, Dona asks where shall we go today. Various places are called out from Cleveland to the Planet Zukaplumia. Maintaining their hold on the parachute, the class travels to a destination singing the "Wheels on the Bus" song or calling out what they see on their outer space travel. Once they arrive at their destination the children huddle under the cloth and continue their verbal and imaginary trip. Children talk about what they see and meet in these new and strange places.

The final segment of the day is story and finger-play time. A variety of activities occur at this time, all centered around the sharing of stories. During this period, the teacher tells or reads (or retells and rereads) favorite stories. Flannel board stories are told (sometimes by the children). Dramatizations of appropriate stories are made by the class. Individual students can also paint pictures that go with favorite stories, read their own books (often in groups of two, three, or four and also in the form of one child reading to another or a group). Children also have access to a number of stories recorded on tape which they can listen to at their leisure. The specific activities change from day-to-day but through it all is woven the common thread of sharing, enjoying, and responding to a wide variety of stories.

Dona's teaching is certainly not prescriptive. She does not follow a highly structured or scripted approach to early childhood education. She creates a general framework for her class in which children are given wide latitude in choosing what to do and with whom. Within this framework Dona encourages her children to take risks, to try new activities and projects, and to work with different children in pairs, groups, and individually. She encourages talk as a way of developing social cohesiveness in the class, clarifying and expressing thought, and communicating one's needs and desires. Children's literature and stories are used by Dona to allow children to enjoy and delight in the world of narrative to help children consider important issues in their lives, to develop in the class a sensitivity to their culture and the culture of others, and to nurture a community of listeners and readers. Language, both oral and written, are at the center of Dona's class.

Puppets are a way of being one step removed from a situation and so are very useful in helping children to explore their world in a nonthreatening way. They help build imagination and alternative perspective.

There is a grandpa puppet in Dona's class. He is retired and comes to be with the children because he is lonely. He loves to tell stories about when he was young. He loves children to "read" to him because his eyes aren't so good.

A mouse puppet bites children's shoes when they aren't looking. The children deny him cheese when he has been especially naughty but they care for him, carry him around, and talk to him.

There is also a raccoon puppet in the class who borrows things from the room whenever something can't be found. The children search until they find the item and then scold Bandit for hiding things.

Dona feels that it is important to give each puppet an identifiable characteristic that is predictable. She says that the children can identify with, enjoy, and talk about the pretend puppet episodes that deal with everyday events, fears, and emotions.

Organization and Management

The daily routine forms the general framework around which instruction is organized. Class time is divided into specific segments during which different activities are organized.

Dona attempts to help students develop an internal sense of control and responsibility for themselves and for the entire classroom community. She does this by respecting each child as a person, becoming aware of their feelings, fears, and vulnerabilities, and communicating with them at their level. It is not unusual to see Dona kneeling at a child's eye level, exploring with the child the reasons behind his or her behavior and collaborating in discovering alternative behaviors. Dona tries to make children aware of and responsible for their own actions.

During group time, the class often discusses problems and brainstorms solutions. As a group, the class makes choices and develops plans to overcome classroom problems. When the weather is marginal, some members of the group like to go outside to play while others would prefer to play in the room. The use of voting and majority rule is often used to help the children understand the democratic process. At first the students who are in the minority feel cheated. But after using this process they will invariably say, "Let's talk about it and vote," when class decisions and discussions come to an impasse.

Dona tries to instill in the class a sense of family. Cooperative games and activities are used whenever possible. Dona talks with the class about working together and helping one another. Competitive activities are not part of the class routine. The sense of family or community is further developed in the way Dona calls on students. She always tries to call children by their given names and rarely uses impersonal words such as "you," "class," or "children" to address the class.

Dona uses other activities to give a class a sense of unity. Since pizza seems to be the favored dish of the class (it is the food of the Teen-age Mutant Ninja Turtles), Dona has the children form a circle where three and four-year-olds sit on the floor putting all their toes together at the center. Each becomes a slice of pizza, an important part of the whole. Along comes a pizza-eating dinosaur. Dona says each child's name as the dinosaur came to that wedge of pizza. One by one the children disappeared around the room divider where they could witness the pizza growing smaller as another piece disappeared until all was gone. The children were delighted with the activity and asked to play it again and again.

During one play period, two girls were observed calling Glen a name. Glen was visibly hurt and came to the teacher for comfort. Dona and Glen talked for awhile, exploring why he felt badly and how he might respond. He then walked back to the offending girls and told them that they hurt his feelings by calling him a name and asked them not to do it again. The girls agreed. Later in the period, Dona spoke with the girls about how easy it is to hurt someone through words and actions. The girls appeared remorseful and were later seen playing cooperatively with Glen.

Strategies

Dona's teaching has a disciplined yet informal nature. Upon first observation, it may seem unplanned and unconnected. However, it doesn't take long to realize that Dona's teaching is very carefully considered and implemented. During the self-selected activities period, she attempts to meet with every student. This can mean discussing a wood-working project with one child, having a puppet talk with another, helping to inspire a drama theme with three children working with blocks, involving a shy child in a discussion or story group, stopping by the computer to comment on a game two children are playing, listening to an explanation of an art piece, making pretend pizza with a child at the clay table, being sure to discuss ingredients, buying items at a child's play store, and many other activities that respond to the children's initiatives and work to deepen and extend their involvement.

During group times, Dona works to encourage all children to share their ideas. She validates their contributions by responding to them thoughtfully and with encouragement and by frequently writing the ideas down on chart paper and putting the child's name with the idea.

Dona's approach to preschool education encourages exploration through physical activity and oral language. In her interactions with students, she makes it a point to try to connect reading and writing with activities and talk. For example, during self-selected activities, any student can choose a book to be read to her or him individually by the teacher aide or adult visitor. Writing materials (including a typewriter) are available to students on a table near the book center at all times. Children make signs, labels, menus, and other written artifacts as part of their dramatic play. They write instructions for inventions. They sign, label, and caption their

art work. And they are read to *every day* by the teacher, aide, and/or other adult visitors. This one activity itself has extended in several interesting directions. After several weeks of read aloud, students begin to choose favorite books of their own to read to the teacher, fellow class members, or dolls and puppets. Many students use stories read to them to create their own dramatic interpretation of the story which is later presented to the class. All students choose books to take home to read to their parents or for their parents to read to them every day.

In their writing, children are encouraged to try writing using their own knowledge of writing and writing conventions. Some students become very comfortable with invented spelling while others need assistance from the teacher, who gives it generously while at the same time encouraging children's own experimentation with written symbols.

Children need models for their own writing. Dona does this through extensive use of the language experience approach. Class experiences, discussions, responses to books, group story compositions, and the like are turned into activities in which children dictate their thoughts, feelings, or

---

Reading Strategy: Read-Aloud

Dona shares literature with her students through read-aloud. Each day she reads several books to the class. Dona notes that most of her children are read to at home. For them read-aloud makes for a smooth transition to preschool. For those children who haven't been read to at home, read-aloud serves as an inviting initiation to the world of literacy. Dona chooses a variety of the very best picture books to share with her class. "I try to expose children to different genre, different cultures, different characters, and different stories." She notes that children will often beg to hear favorite stories again and again. She willing accedes to these requests knowing that children will get something new out of each rereading and that her students are developing literary tastes.

Read-aloud is not difficult, but Dona does prepare for it. "I make sure I read the story at least a couple times before reading it to the class. I want to make it my own first." When she reads, she has students sit comfortably on the carpeted floor. She makes sure she reads in a clear and expressive voice and she allows children a chance after each reading to respond to what they heard. The stories often elicit thoughtful and emotion-filled comments from students and lead to related projects and activities.

---

story lines to the teacher who transforms their oral speech into written language by writing their utterances on chart paper for the class to see. This text is read by the teacher (pointing to words as well as demonstrating the directional flow of the print), by groups of student chorally, and by individual students.

This approach is also used by Dona with individual students as she visits with students throughout the day. They may wish to dictate a note for mom, dad, or a friend, or have the teacher write out the caption for an art project as they say it orally. In all these activities, children see their utterances transformed into permanent written texts that they can read again and again.

ISSUES

Individual Differences

In Dona's class, students come with a wide variety of abilities as well as backgrounds. In every class, there are usually some children from another

---

Reading Strategy: Language Experience

Children in Dona's class partake in many and varied experiences. Dona takes advantage of these experiences by working with the children to turn them into literacy events. After a class experience such as a field trip, a walk in the neighborhood, or art activity, Dona will talk about the experience with the class. What did the children see and hear? How did the experience make them feel? What did they like most or least about the activity? When all students have had an opportunity to respond, Dona invites the children to transform their oral language into written form on chart paper.

Sometimes she will ask for and write individual words in list form that describe the experience. At other times, students will dictate sentences that summarize the experience, express their feelings, or tell a story about the experience. Once written, the text becomes a permanent record of the experience that teachers and students will read and talk about for days to come. Dona realizes that most students cannot read these stories in the conventional sense. Still she feels they are valuable. "Even if students can't read they're picking up something, maybe their making the connection between oral and written language, or they could be developing a sense of directionality or a notion about what a word is through our writing and reading. The most important thing is all the children are involved in real reading experiences connected to their own life events in a nonthreatening and enjoyable way."

---

country. Some children have little difficulty picking up new concepts while other children struggle.

Dona reads often to children who show little interest in reading or have a poor understanding of reading. Many books she reads several times through so that students will later be able to read the same books on their own. Dona believes that at this age the most important thing an adult can do with children who are struggling with reading is to instill in them a love of stories, a desire to read, and model of how reading is done. This is largely done by reading to students and having the children borrow a book every day which their parents or older siblings read to them.

Several of the students in Dona's class are already able to read. She encourages these children to try more advanced projects such as making an animal encyclopedia or writing a book based upon a story previously read. She feels that it is also important for gifted children to become aware of other children and their feelings. She may ask a more advanced child to help another with spelling, to read to others, or to take another child's dictation.

Evaluation

Dona assesses her students' progress informally. Students are never tested. Dona keeps a journal in which she records her observations of individual students. Her observations focus on oral expression, socialization, task persistence, willingness to share or participate in group activities, reading and writing behavior, risk taking, and creativity. She records her observations during class when possible. Dona notes that teachers have to have good memories and she uses hers to record observations of students after school has ended.

In observing children, Dona mentally records important progress and will jot down specific quotes to be remembered. A brief note stuck in each child's folder that is dated becomes helpful at parent conference time. Dona recaps the day to her husband in the evening by talking of events, which makes the memory a more lasting one. She often tape records circle and discussion time so that she can re-examine responses and individual participation or interest. This helps in planning other curricular experiences.

The rich contextualization of her observations presents a narrative of progress that is more informative than any set of test scores or grades. Dona often reviews her notes to help her in planning and modifying her instruction.

Home Connections

In Dona's class, the school is an extension of the home. Thus she encourages parents to do things at home with their children that complement the school activities. She provides parents with booklists and requests that they read to their children daily. Children go home each day with books (and cassette recorders and books on tapes) to share with their parents. She writes a regular newsletter that includes activities for and information about books that parents and children will enjoy. Dona talks with parents daily and tries to instill in them an awareness of the importance of reading to children and an enthusiasm for children's books. She believes that her own enthusiasm for books is caught by many parents.

Dona notes that there is usually some concern among parents that the children are not learning their skills (for example, alphabet, shapes, colors, and numbers) in a formal and systematic manner. However, parents find out, early on, that their children *are* learning. Moreover, Dona feels that the number of parents who have come back to tell her about how well their children are doing in elementary school and how they have become such avid readers provides strong validation for her whole language approach to preschool education. Nathan, a former student now in second grade, is an avid reader. His mother reports that he can be found reading books for several hours a night until she insists on "lights out." Arthur, also a second grader and former student, regularly reads to his younger sister who is enrolled in nursery school. Jordan's mother reports that her first grader picks up his seventh grade sister's books to read when she comes home from school.

These parents and others, have told Dona that it is the early and enthusiastic introduction to the world of stories and reading that has made the difference with their children.

School Connections

Dona enjoys very positive and supportive relations with her fellow teachers and the school director. She has given workshops on literacy in early childhood education for colleagues and, on a more informal basis, she shares ideas on books that might work with themes other teachers are in the process of developing. Dona has an extensive collection of literature for preschoolers and shares these with her colleagues. Similarly, Dona finds that her colleagues are always willing to "lend an ear" or share an idea, book, or material with her. Dona recognizes that there is limited time in the school day for communication and collaboration. However, the school does have regular in-service faculty meetings in which whole language or related topics are presented, usually by other members of the faculty.

Keeping Current

Dona recognizes the importance of maintaining her professional knowledge in holistic preschool education. She has taken graduate courses in early childhood, education, literacy education, psychology, and children's literature at Kent State. Moreover she regularly accepts interns in early childhood education from Kent State. She finds that she is constantly learning from the ideas that these students bring to her class.

Dona takes several professional journals and reads everything she "can get her hands on" to help her as a teacher. Her professional library includes *Young Children, Language Arts,* and *Childhood Education.*

Dona is asked frequently to give workshops at the local, state, and regional level on developing holistic early childhood programs. She finds these professionally stimulating. She notes that they force her to organize and consolidate her thinking on her own teaching. Dona has also accepted opportunities to work with university faculty on research projects. Most recently she worked on a project dealing with the effects of literature on young children's literacy development.

Challenges

Time is a major constraint on Dona's doing the things she wants to do in her classroom. She says that developing programs that meet the individual needs of children and allow them to emerge into the world of reading and writing in naturalistic and authentic ways takes a great awareness of teaching resources. And this means time. Dona says that she spends a considerable amount of time in the library reading book reviews and browsing through professional journals to which she does not subscribe. "I need creative time when I can let my ideas flow free. Sometimes, there is simply too much organizational busy work."

Developing and maintaining a whole language curriculum requires time for research and thoughtful planning. Dona sees helping teachers find this time by reducing their bureaucratic requirements essential in encouraging new teachers to try whole language, and existing whole language teachers to continue to experiment and innovate.

SUMMING UP

Some people may believe that implementing whole language in a prekindergarten setting is not possible. After all, it might be argued, formal reading and writing instruction doesn't begin before elementary school.

That may be true, but research has demonstrated quite clearly that what happens to children in the way of literacy activities before the elementary grades is crucial to children's success in learning to read and write. If children are successful at learning to read and are avid readers, chances are they were provided positive experiences related to reading and writing before they started formal school.

This is what Dona's approach to reading and writing is all about. She realizes that most of her children cannot read and write in the conventional sense. Yet, she views the process of becoming literate as one that begins early, even before conventional reading begins. She encourages growth in literacy by providing a rich literate environment, by giving children real opportunities to read and write, by modeling reading and writing, by exposing children to the richness of literature, and by giving children many opportunities to respond to reading and writing to themselves and one another in a variety of ways. These activities involve real literacy for real purposes—the heart of whole language.

Children do not generally leave Dona's room knowing how to read. However, they do leave with a good understanding of what reading and writing are about, with a willingness to experiment with reading and writing, with a desire to learn to read and write, and with a confidence in their abilities to become literate persons. Certainly these children are on their way to becoming life-long and active readers and writers.

Chapter 3

WHOLE LANGUAGE IN A MULTI-GRADE PRIMARY CLASSROOM

"Schools should be more than places where children learn to read and write. Schools should be places where children learn to become concerned and caring citizens of the world."

Upon entering the classroom, one is nearly overwhelmed by the seeming cacophony of sight, sound and children of various size and age. Kindergartners and first- and second-graders are in every part of the room, working in groups, pairs, and alone. Everyone seems to be talking and doing at the same time. Children's work is displayed on the walls, from the ceiling, on tables and the floor. Everything seems a blur.

However, after taking this scene in for a minute or two, one begins to see that beneath this hurricane of activity lies a thoughtful organization and environment for learning. Students are actively engaged in authentic and educationally stimulating activity. They are using what they have learned to plan and execute learning projects that are meaningful to themselves, the teacher, and the class as a whole. One group of children is writing a shared story; another group is practicing a script they had written; a third group is building a model of a city recycling center. A pair of students in a comfortable corner of the room are taking turns reading to one another. In the other corner, a student is interviewing a classmate for a survey she had developed. And near a bookshelf, the teacher is conferencing with three students about a book they are in the middle of reading. Welcome to the world of whole language in a multi-grade primary classroom.

Sylvia Jackson teaches in an elementary school that has been known as a center for informal, child-centered education for nearly two decades. The faculty is made up of teachers dedicated to the conceptualization and creative implementation of a curriculum that has as its central focus children's affective and cognitive development, interests, and needs.

The school is located in the middle of a large urban area. Students come to the school from all parts of the city. Because there are more parents who seek placement for their children then there are available places for students, a district-wide lottery takes place every year in which children whose parents applied for admission are randomly selected. The lottery is designed so that the racial composition of the school matches that of the school district itself.

Sylvia teaches a multi-grade class of kindergarten, first and second grade students. She has been a teacher for thirteen years and has been evolving as a whole language teacher since beginning her teaching career. Sylvia says that she has employed a whole language curriculum before such a name was applied to a particular kind of curriculum. Much of her growth as a whole language teacher is attributable to her participation in continuing staff development programs on whole language curriculum, some of which have featured speakers from New Zealand who have practiced whole language in their own country. In addition, as a teacher in a school dedicated to whole language education, Sylvia has grown through her interaction and collaboration with her colleagues. Informally and through planned staff meetings, Sylvia and her colleagues share information, ideas, and insights about whole language.

WHAT SYLVIA THINKS ABOUT WHOLE LANGUAGE

Sylvia believes that whole language is more than a method for teaching literacy. It is "a way of thinking and being that permeates all your teaching and carries with it a responsibility to have knowledge about current trends in education, research findings, children's interests, attitudes, cultural diversity, behaviors, how children learn, and above all an intense respect for the competence and rights of children."

Sylvia is aware of the increasing emphasis on measuring learning through objective testing and the trend to allow the testing to influence, even dictate, the curriculum and teaching that children receive. She contrasts this approach to whole language by suggesting that it is like "taking a natural herb rather than a powerful synthetic drug." She says the results of the more natural approach may be slower but they are more thorough, long lasting, and with fewer of the damaging side effects that are often part of a quicker more "expedient" approach.

Whole language focuses more on the entire child. In traditional, skill-oriented approaches, the cognitive sides of children are developed at the expense of the human affective sides. A whole language approach, Sylvia notes, encourages children to develop sensitivities to others, to develop viewpoints other than their own, to realize the freedom to express themselves, to develop internal values and standards, and to allow those values to guide their actions and choices, rather than values that may be imposed on them without the opportunity for reflection.

According to Sylvia, whole language is a way to change society. She asks, "Do we want people who will think before they act, who will have empathy and altruism for others, who will care for others and for the planet?" She believes that teachers have the power to change the future by how they teach and not just by what they teach. Children learn by how they are treated and how they are taught to treat themselves and others, as well as by the content they are presented in school. Whole language is a pedagogy that seeks to treat children in ways that allow children to become reflective, caring, and activist citizens of the world.

INSIDE SYLVIA'S CLASSROOM

The Environment

Sylvia's classroom is on the bottom (below ground) floor of the K-5 school. On first entering the room, one is struck by the lack of individual student desks. (See Figure 3.1.) The room does not give the appearance of a typical classroom. There are neither neat rows nor clusters of desks in this room.

Sylvia's aim in room arrangement is to involve the children in the decisions regarding the environment. This is a way to give students ownership of their classroom. Given the goals of fostering learning, communication, and community, the class discusses ways to create a classroom environment that meets these goals. For example, early in the school year Sylvia holds a class meeting. She asks the children what they need in order to feel safe and happy in the classroom and at school. She writes down their thoughts, restates them in terms of class "norms" or expectations and possible ways to restructure the classroom environment (for example, creating a quiet area in the room for students who need such a place to read and work on their own) and presents them to the class at a later meeting for consideration. At that time, the ideas are refined and adopted by the class. Sylvia states that this approach, used throughout the year, gives children "a stake or a sense of ownership in their classroom and a personal and collective responsibility for the maintenance of a safe and enjoyable classroom atmosphere.

The centerpiece of the learning environment is a common area that is located in the middle of the classroom. Here Sylvia meets with the whole class to share and discuss books, writing, student projects, and issues of importance. The common area is an open space on which a rug has been laid. At one end of the rug is a teacher's chair and nearby is an easel with chart paper. Sylvia has strategically placed bookshelves, filled with books and materials directly related to the current unit of study to define this common area.

Figure 3.1
Map of Sylvia's Room

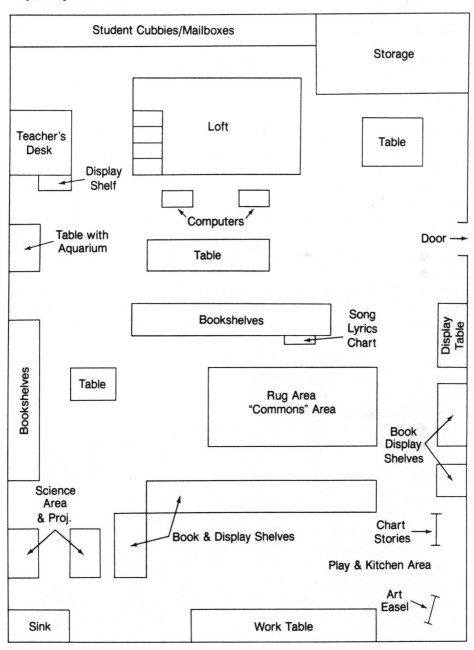

Off to one side of the common area is a wooden loft that children use for independent reading or study. Also included at this end of the room are a bookshelf, a class mail center, a round table with chairs, and two computers.

On the other side of the common area are tables at which students work. There is also a play area nearby that contains a play kitchen. Children's in-progress projects are kept on shelves, cupboards, and tables in this area.

Children do not have assigned seats in Sylvia's classroom. They are free to move about and to sit at unoccupied spaces. This encourages a sense of community and class ownership of all areas within the room.

A central part of the classroom environment are the bountiful displays of children's work that are evident around the room and in the adjacent hall. Children hang notes, signs, art projects, written texts, songs, and stories on the walls in the room and hall. During a unit of study on ecology, a variety of completed projects and texts were on display in the hall for visitors and other students to see. Nick's "Recycling Plan" was hanging on the wall as was a report on an earthworm experiment. Nick had visited a recycling center and had written a book on the experience. This was on a display table. Included on the table were several dioramas on the water cycle, a model solar cooker, clay models of endangered animals of the rain

forest, and art work depicting polluting factories. Nearby a sign entitled "Don't Kill the Animals" was on display. Several group chart stories were also hanging on the walls (see Figure 3.2). Many persuasive signs were hung on the walls in the hall (see Figure 3.3). On another wall was a bar graph which depicted the number of bags of trash students' families put out in a week. A recycled model house made of cardboard from boxes stood in the hall. It even had a model solar roof. The only constraint on what was displayed was that the work must have relevance to what had been studied in class. For a short period of time after each language arts session, Sylvia has a "read around the room" time. During the time, students circulate around the room reading, admiring, and sharing the work of their classmates.

A critical part of Sylvia's curriculum is her extensive use of trade books. She has a large permanent library in the classroom. Books are arranged by author with special volumes such as big books and pop-up books in their own area. Sylvia also keeps a unit library in the classroom. This is a set of

Figure 3.2
Chart Stories

Earthworms

Earthworms make soil
better. They don't like
light. They like certain
kinds of leaves. They
also eat bugs.

Pollution Hurts Animals

Once there was a duck
that was going for a swim.
She flew into an oil spill.
She looked black and yucky.
She started to sink. An
ecologist came and picked
her up. He cleaned the
oil off and she was happy.

Figure 3.3
Students' Signs

"Noise Pollutes"

"Don't Use Styrofoam"

"Litter Makes the World a Mess"

"Do not Take Elephant Tusks"

"Do not Use Rabbit Fur"

"Do not Litter"

"Don't Kill Whales"

books that she borrows from the school and public libraries that are related to the unit of study that the class is currently investigating. The unit library changes as unit themes change. Teacher and student-made books complete the classroom library which the students themselves maintain.

Media equipment such as records, audiotapes, filmstrips, and video-tapes are available and used frequently, as are globes and maps. Since the children enjoy creative drama, Sylvia has a wide variety of puppets, dress-up clothes, playhouses, and figures, as well as a sand table in the room.

Chart paper is available. It is used extensively to document students' dictated texts. In addition, Sylvia keeps an assortment of blank books available for the students. These are book covers between which she has stapled paper. Students use these to make their own books. A large assortment of paper and markers are a must. In addition, old magazines and photographs, envelopes, tape, scissors, glitter, stickers, stars, and bookmaking supplies facilitate and entice children into writing and experimenting with texts.

Although the room contains many items and does not have a specific organization to constrain student placement and movement, the room is not messy. Early in the year as items are introduced to the class, students devise a plan to maintain order among the equipment and material in the room. Moreover, since children are in Sylvia's classroom for more than one year, there is continuity in classroom organization that is passed on from older students to younger ones.

Beginning the School Year: Building a Sense of Community

Sylvia says that one of the major tasks to accomplish in the first few days of school is to get children to change the way they may think about school. She says that she wants students to realize that "their play in school is work and that there is a learning purpose for everything they do in her classroom, even when it is sitting and laughing together." Students need to develop an attitude that learning can occur in everything students do. Children need to develop an awareness of their own learning. Throughout the day, Sylvia can be seen asking students to talk about what they have learned; to reflect on their activities and learning experiences.

At a more pragmatic level, Sylvia tries to establish a routine of activities in the classroom so that students will understand (are able to predict), early on, the sequential and integrated nature of classroom activities. Since the class is made up of kindergarten through second-graders, returning students are familiar with the routine and are able to help the new ones become acquainted.

Many of the activities done during the early weeks of school are designed to establish a sense of community in the classroom. Sylvia chooses activities and plans discussions that cause class members to share about themselves with each other. The emphasis is on having fun together. This is done through activities such as learning songs and lyrics together during rugtime, exploring different areas in the classroom, and writing about what was done in each area. For example, one student might write or dictate an essay on "I was a mom in the playhouse." These activities help establish routines, focus students' attention on the type of activity appropriate for each class time and classroom area, and help students develop familiarity with the classroom, the teacher, and their classmates.

As students begin to interact with one another and become acquainted with the areas and features of the classroom, teachable moments occur in which Sylvia leads the class and individual students in discussions related to the norms and expectations of student behavior and classroom use. For example, early in the year a first-grader and a kindergarten student were seen arguing over blocks in the wooden block area. Sylvia went to these students and quietly talked with them about her expectations for students working together. Later, during rugtime, she brought this event up to illustrate points about personal conduct and to discuss alternatives to fighting and disruptive arguing.

The first weeks of school are also used for assessment. Sylvia uses this time to observe students and make notes on their behavior and academic progress. She may informally assess new students by asking them to identify letters, to read a short selection, to write, to count, or to do a few math problems. Again, she uses written anecdotal records to describe student performance and to make note of appropriate instructional activities.

One of the many positive aspects of having a multi-grade classroom is that more than half the students return to Sylvia's class every year. Not only are these children familiar with Sylvia's class routine, she is familiar with these students. She knows where to begin to assess academically and socially and can begin more immediately to have these students engage in appropriate instructional activity.

A Typical Day

There are many manifestations of whole language in Sylvia's classroom. She sees her own interpretation of whole language as distinctive from others in several ways. First, Sylvia believes that whole language weaves itself throughout all subject areas. Thus, math, science, and social studies are fertile ground for literacy teaching and learning. For example, in math she uses literature extensively to introduce important concepts and contextualize problems. Drama is used to demonstrate and experience math concepts and relationships. Students' written stories containing math concepts are used to express understanding and application.

Music is also an important part of Sylvia's pedagogy. Sylvia introduces the class to many songs throughout the year. For each song, students see the printed lyrics. Each week Sylvia prints the words to a song on large chart paper and tapes it to the back of an exposed bookcase. Every morning during the week, the class sings the song and does a different activity related to the song (for example, acting out the lyrics, discussing the meaning, seeing solo performances). The songs themselves are motivating and lead to repeated singings and readings. In this way, students learn to recognize words in songs by sight and to develop fluency in reading through the rhythms and patterns of the music. The songs are often related to topics that the class is currently studying.

A typical day in Sylvia's primary classroom begins with journal writing. Students reflect on events of the previous or present day and jot their thoughts in their journals. Sylvia asks for at least one sentence per day. For students who cannot write in a conventional sense, pictures or unconventional writing (invented spellings, scribbles) are accepted. Older students and the teacher also take dictation from younger ones. Children are given the opportunity to share their journals with the group or with individual students. Sylvia makes weekly journals for students by stapling together five pages of unlined paper and a cover. (See Figure 3.4.) On the cover students write a title, date, and their name. Sylvia collects the journals weekly and uses them to help assess students' progress in writing. At the end of each month journals are sent home for parents to see.

After writing in and sharing their journals, students meet with Sylvia in the commons area for about 45 minutes. She calls this period "rugtime." During rugtime, students learn new songs and sing past favorites. The lyrics to the songs are presented on large chart paper on the back of a bookshelf so that all children can see the words. Often the songs relate to a current unit of study such as pollution. However, Sylvia starts the year with traditional songs that most children are familiar with such as "Twinkle Twinkle Little Star," "Miss Lucy Had a Baby," and holiday favorites. Sylvia doesn't play a musical instrument but makes exceptional use of records and tapes. Sylvia directs the children's attention to various aspects of the lyrics such as interesting sentences and words and repeated words and letter combinations. During rugtime, Sylvia leads the class through a discussion of the current date, time, and weather. Any interesting current events are discussed at this time as well.

Figure 3.4
Journal Entries

Josh

> (Kindergarten)
> I Jist CAM BIK FRAM MY DaDs I got a Tom Gordon (Baseball card) I have lose teeth

> (Kindergarten)
> I am going to BRINS my RELL MEdicAL KIT.

Alan   (Retained first grader diagnosed as learning disabled)
> I Got A RTABT (Robot)

Matt   (first grade)

> in for Days Me and J.J. our Going to have our fist TeeBall Game

---

Reading Strategy: Reading and Singing

Sylvia has found that the regular use of songs in the classroom is an excellent and enjoyable way to introduce children to reading. Most young children come to school familiar with many songs and rhymes. Sylvia capitalizes on this past experience in her reading instruction. She says, "Children know lots of songs when they begin school and want to learn more. They love to sing and learn new songs. And, our group singing helps them build community and spirit in the class." Sylvia notes that the songs she uses have very predictable lyrics. Moreover, the rhythm and music surrounding the lyrics add another layer of context that makes the lyrics even more memorable.

Each week Sylvia writes the words to a song on chart paper and displays it in a prominent part of the commons area. Many songs are familiar to the students. Others are chosen because of their connection to a thematic unit of study, holiday, or other important event or activity in the class. Throughout the week the class sings and reads the lyrics. As the class begins to master (memorize) the lyrics, Sylvia gradually draws students' attention to individual lines, words, rhymes, letters, and sounds in the song. In this way, children begin to see how written language works in different contexts. Words, word structures, and phonics are taught from a text that is thoroughly familiar, understood, and enjoyed. Although a new song is introduced each week, the class likes to return to old favorites often throughout the year.

Sylvia uses the time, also, to share new and previously read trade books with the class. She reads the stories with clarity and expression so that students can hear the story and learn what good reading is like. She tries to choose books that students will pick up later and attempt to read on their own. Class favorites include Dr. Seuss, books by James Stevenson, Eric Carle, Arnold Lobel, and William Steig. She adds that students especially like unusual books such as pop-up books and pattern books that stimulate students' own writing and bookmaking. Discussion often occurs during and after stories as Sylvia elicits verbal responses from the students. Sylvia notes that book experiences and discussion contribute to students' developing sense of story that is reflected in their own written and dictated stories. Language experience activities are part of rugtime. Students dictate a text to Sylvia who transcribes it on a sheet of chart paper that rests on the nearby easel. The enlarged written text is read several times by the class as a group and by individual students. The nature of the text can vary. It could be a response to the story that was read or to the class discussion on current events, it could be students' reflections on the previous day's experiences, it could be a story or song that the class writes as a group, it could be used to brainstorm and plan a unit of exploration, or it could be students' anticipatory thoughts about the coming day or week.

Early in the year the children dictated a story on cleaning up the school. This text was read throughout the school year by individuals and small and large groups as the class returned often to themes of environmental and ecological awareness and action.

Rugtime is followed by a class work period. Students are not to be found at their seats doing worksheets or copy activities at this time. During the 45-minute work period, students choose activities to engage in related to the unit that the class is currently studying. Activities/projects are chosen in different ways depending on the topic and the level of knowledge the children possess on the topic. They can range from individually chosen and researched projects on the effect of oil spills on the environment to small group projects (usually developed with the aid of the teacher) on pollution in the home. Students get their ideas from their immersion in the topic through books, speakers, field trips, learning centers in the classroom, and so on. Many activities are inspired by the previous day's discussions. As Sylvia encourages students to reflect on what had been talked about in class, students often discover interesting topics or methods for exploring a topic. For instance, after a discussion on solar energy, a girl decided to design a house on paper that took advantage of energy from the sun.

The unit of study is a broad topic area that Sylvia has chosen in consultation with the students and that is related to interests expressed by the class. Units chosen included Careers, Ecology (Save the Earth), and African Folk Tales. Students read selections about the topics, both fiction and nonfiction, develop projects related to their reading and understanding, then write about the project. The writing can focus either on the subject of the project itself or on the process of planning and making the project.

Before beginning their projects, students and Sylvia "web the unit." In webbing, students brainstorm topics, ideas, activities, and resources related to the central theme of the unit of study. Webs are never the same. Some may focus on the subject of study itself. Others, called project idea webs, allow students to brainstorm the types of projects and activities they may wish to engage in as they explore the topic. From the list of brainstormed topics, students choose one to focus on. Then, on their own or in groups, they plan a course of action to learn more about their topics. They identify further resources related to their specific topics. They read books and articles and take notes, view films and filmstrips and write reviews; they interview key people and take trips to observe, firsthand, things related to their topics and to talk with experts. The students' investigations end with some sort of product, usually a report or a book, accompanied by artwork, in the form of drawings, photographs, models, or dioramas. Sometimes the product takes the form of a dramatic production, puppet play, or an event. For example, a class circus ended the class's study of various aspects of the circus while a cultural festival concluded a study of Africa and folktales.

Careers and ecology were studied at the same time. Several students created projects that combined both topics choosing careers that were designed to have an ecological impact. One student wanted to be a professional baseball player. He developed a set of baseball cards that contained "tips" for saving the earth. Two girls who wanted to become dancers created an ecology dance and several students made outwork on the theme "saving the earth." Two children who saw themselves as movie stars and directors wrote and produced a script on saving the earth. A budding songwriter wrote and performed songs in the movie. Three children who wanted to become doctors made a filmstrip on taking care of the body through nutrition.

During the work period, Sylvia occasionally poses a story situation with the children in which students develop the concept of the story provided by Sylvia. This is transformed into a dramatic play as well as reading and writing activities. During the study of scientists and the scientific process, Sylvia presented the class with the story of a trip into space for scientific purposes. Sylvia set the stage for the drama by developing the background and interest in the work of scientists through filmstrips, videotapes, bulletin boards, books, and discussion. She introduced the drama by telling students the story of the discovery of a new planet in the universe. Over the course of the next several days, students played out this drama with Sylvia. Each child took on the role of a specific type of scientist, from astronomers to zoologists. As the children played out their space trip, they conducted scientific projects and met alien life forms. The chemists developed a solar cooker and studied air pollution. Geologists explored caves and found artifacts on a visited planet. The biologists made clay models of body parts of life forms found on the planet, named them, and developed an X-ray machine. Botanists planted seeds and observed their growth in the different conditions presented by the planet. They also classified and charted plant life found on the planet. Language activities abounded in the dramatic play as the scientists recorded their findings, discussed with other scientists their experiments and problems encountered (and solutions) in their travels, and communicated with aliens and colleagues on earth. In Sylvia's class, children encounter new worlds through dramatic play. They enter those worlds with anticipation, excitement, and a willingness to learn, use what they know, and over-come problems as they occur.

The work period is followed by recess. Before going outside, students often tell Sylvia something they have learned. For example, on one occa-sion each student had to name one way to save the earth. "Ride a bike" and "use cloth diapers" were some of the responses. After recess, is a short "quiet relaxation" time. Here Sylvia works to develop students' imaging ability through creative visualization activities. Children sit with legs crossed, hands on knees. She has the students close their eyes and she dims the lights as she creates a scene for them to visualize such as "you are entering a house set on top of a hill. There are trees around the house . . ." or "you are walking down the street one morning and you see a bright red and yellow rock. You pick it up and discover that when you do it . . ." or "imagine yourself in a rain forest. You encounter one animal. What does he say to you?" Many times the visualizations are related to the units of study or to a book that Sylvia will share later in the day. Sylvia usually asks for students to share their images, noting the differences and similarities in students' image construction. Deep breaths before and after the visualization help students relax.

A large group instruction period follows in which shared language ac-tivities are the focus. Students listen to stories read by Sylvia. They also read big books and chart stories that students have authored. Students are continually exposed to previously read texts so that familiarity and automatic processing of the texts develops in an environment that is warm, nonthreatening, yet stimulating. After students have read a text several times and have developed some mastery over individual sen-tences, words, word parts, and letters, she tries to draw their attention to common elements in the text so that students can make generalizations about text features. For example, she might draw students' attention to words in an enlarged story that begin with the same letter or consonant blend. She challenges students to see that such letter constructions repre-sent a particular sound. Similarly, she might ask students to find and identify words that appear more than once in a text, or that rhyme, or that have the same endings. These issues become brief and informal points of discussion, but intensive mini-lessons on words and phonics.

The final part of the morning is devoted to math or writing. The subjects alternate to insure that the kindergartners, who attend school for half days, are provided a complete curriculum in the mornings. Sylvia uses a writing process approach in writing. During the writing workshop, students work at different stages on their own writing. Sylvia emphasizes that in the workshop students write what they want to write. Some students draw, some dictate their texts to a teacher, aide, or fellow student. Some students feel comfortable with invented spelling while others aim for more conventional spelling. At any time during the workshop, some students will be brainstorming topics while others are writing a first draft or sharing the draft with a peer or teacher in order to get feedback. Still other students may be revising an earlier draft, editing for mechanical difficulties such as spelling and grammar, or publishing the writing by presenting it to the class, putting it on display in the classroom, or putting it into book form. Only second graders are asked to edit their work. Sylvia wants younger writers to focus exclusively on communication of content.

Throughout the writing workshop, students can be seen working alone or in small groups. Often the writing that the students work on are part of their thematic unit of study. Sylvia goes from student to student to offer help, encouragement, and instruction. Students receive feedback in conferences during the workshop with the teacher or during a sharing time at the end of the workshop. Near the end of this period, and especially on Fridays, Sylvia calls the students together to talk about what has been accomplished during the period and to share work that has been completed or is still is progress. After each sharing, students in the audience give positive feedback and suggestions for improvement. On one recent visit, two students performed a puppet play that they had written.

It usually takes students several days to complete a story or book. Most stories are written by the students but some are dictated depending on the ability and confidence level of the child. A great deal of students' writing is connected to their units of study. Some typical titles of student stories demonstrate the students' wide range of interests—"What happens in Spring," "The First Four Leaf Clover," "Spring Butterflies," "The

Rainbow Fish, Part 1," "The Shoe Book," "The Dog," "My clothes," "Good Things and Bad Things," "Parts of Machines," "Baseball Stars," "All about Sylvia," and "Robo Cop." Student work is published in book form, hung on walls and from ceilings in the classroom and throughout the school.

Sylvia hesitates when asked if she provides direct instruction in writing, "Mainly I set the stage for writing and offer encouragement and feedback for what students are doing." But it is clear that Sylvia is not passive during writing. Throughout the day, she suggests ideas for students' writing, talks about how books can inspire writing, and provides micro lessons in her writing conferences with individuals and small groups.

After lunch and recess, Sylvia's class engages in silent and partner reading. For ten minutes, students read self-selected material by themselves. Then, for the next fifteen minutes, students read with a partner. They choose a comfortable place in the room to read. When students are with their cross-age partners, one student reads to the other or they will talk softly about the stories they have shared. During this time, Sylvia also reads—acting as a model for her students.

Another rugtime follows in which students and teacher talk about math or writing. Math and writing alternate from morning to afternoon depending on the day of the week. On days in which math follows, Sylvia often uses rugtime to explore math issues through literature with the class.

Stories are used to illustrate and introduce math concepts and to contextualize math problems. For example, Sylvia uses Eric Carle's *Grouchy Lady Bug* and Mitumasa Anno's *All in a Day* and *Anno's Sundial* to introduce the concept of time and time measurement. Norman Bridwell's *Count on Clifford*, Norma Faber's *Up the Down Elevator*, and Dick Gackenbach's *A Bag Full of Pups* are used to introduce addition and subtraction to students. Sylvia maintains a well-organized bibliography of over 230 books that deal with various mathematical concepts and operations. Sylvia uses a math series that employs many manipulatives to help students concretely work through and explore basic concepts in math. Math also finds its way into the thematic units of study as students survey, graph, chart, measure, and estimate with great frequency.

The final part of the day for Sylvia's class includes clean up, reading a portion of a book to the class, and dismissal. Before or after the reading, Sylvia will ask the class to predict the events of the upcoming chapter.

Organization and Management

Sylvia organizes her class by the types of instructional activities she employs. She has large group instruction times which she calls "rugtimes," small group instruction times, often used for mini-lessons on topics of interest and/or need, and individual conference times during which she talks with students about their current reading, projects, ideas, and concerns. Sylvia normally leads students in these activities. In addition, there are work periods during which students are able to choose the nature and form of their work and writing periods during which students have time to work quietly (not silently) on various aspects of their writing.

Sylvia uses these periods as a way of thinking about instruction in her class. The range of instructional activities demonstrate balance in locus of control and in social constitution of the activity groups. Sylvia tries to ensure that all types of activities are represented in students' instructional day.

Classroom management begins with developing a sense of community in the class and of self-esteem in individual students through activities that require cooperation and lead to success. In one activity, each student is given a piece of a puzzle. The children must work together to put the puzzle together. Sylvia finds that dramatic play also helps to encourage a sense of common purpose and community in the class. In this way, students feel a sense of responsibility toward the class and one another. Students learn to consider the consequences of their actions on the classroom community.

In addition, early in the school year, Sylvia and the class develop a set of norms and expectations for members of the classroom community. These include being respectful, listening carefully, not gossiping or putdowns, keeping the room neat, helping one another. All students learn the norms as well as the rationale behind them. Regular class meetings are times to talk about management issues. Behavior by students that consistently goes beyond class expectations is discussed as are any additions or modifications to the classroom code of conduct.

Through all this, Sylvia consciously tries to treat each student with respect and gentleness. She works constantly to nurture mutual respect among students. This is done through the respectful way she interacts with students and through gentle reminders and words of encouragement.

Sylvia realizes that some students, for whatever reason, need to be away from the class at times. She provides a place where students can go to take a break outside the classroom. She emphasizes that this is not a punishment. Many students go to the area at their own volition as well as on the recommendation of the teacher. Students are free to return when they feel ready to continue in class activities in an appropriate manner. The fact that many students use the time-out center on their own suggests that they are developing an internalized system to monitor and control their behavior. Students see themselves as being responsible for their own actions. The multi-grade classroom format expedites this process as younger students observe first hand how their older classmates have developed and use their inner system of control.

Sylvia also uses elements of the *Tribes* program in her classroom. Tribes is a cooperative learning program designed for drug abuse education and prevention. Sylvia has customized the program for her own class. During morning rugtime, she poses a question to the class, such as "what are you afraid of?" and asks students to share. Through this type of sharing, she hopes to develop greater interpersonal sensitivity among students and a stronger sense of community in the class.

Strategies

Balance describes Sylvia's approach to instruction; she tries to balance large groups, small groups, and individual instruction. She provides children with opportunities to explore on their own and balances this with periods of more direct instruction.

Another principle that guides her instruction is the notion of models. She believes that it is important to provide students with models of proficient performance and appropriate behavior. Sylvia models fluent reading for her class through read-aloud. She realizes the powerful model that good literature provides for students' writing. She models good reading behavior through her own regular silent reading. She models how to discuss and work through problems with students. And, she models the humane treatment of others that she feels is a critical element of schooling that is often lost in the current fascination with academic performance and achievement.

Certainly the use of children's literature, language events tied to real experiences, and quality discussions are essential parts of Sylvia's instruction. In addition, Sylvia likes to use the performing arts as ways to get children into reading and the other curricular areas. Children sing everyday in her class. They author their own songs and perform them for the class. Similarly, class members are frequently involved in role play, skits, dramatic play, readers theater, and story theater activities as ways of exploring or responding to a text that was read or an issue that faced the class. The acting out helps students see things differently, in greater depth, and brings about more fruitful discussions.

Integration is pervasive in Sylvia's classroom. Not only does Sylvia attempt to integrate horizontally across subject areas but also vertically across grade levels. By recognizing individual students' talents and abilities, she can group students of different ages in ways that permit all students to contribute to the success of the learning activities.

Sylvia adheres to several personal principles to guide her coverage of the curriculum. First, she feels that, with few exceptions, there is no knowledge that is essential for everyone at a particular point in time. Second, learning how to learn on one's own is more important than what one learns. Third, the memorization of facts does not constitute learning. Fourth, how one structures knowledge is personal and a function of an individual's culture and experience with the world. And, fifth, the best measure of a child's work is his or her own purposeful work itself. These principles allow Sylvia considerable flexibility in designing educational experiences that are instructionally varied and curricularly rich.

The units of study in which students explore various subtopics of the unit are the major way in which instruction is integrated across subject areas. In her units, she tries to balance issues in science, health, and social studies. After the class webs and plans a unit of study, Sylvia assesses which curricular objectives will be met. She may choose to add activities to broaden the scope or depth of the unit in its curricular coverage. Nevertheless, Sylvia's first concern is with the quality and process of students' learning over the coverage of any particular part of the curriculum.

Literature also plays an important role in the integration of subject areas. For every unit of study, Sylvia finds a set of books to complement the unit. Students use these books as resources to explore their own particular part of the unit. The books that Sylvia chooses for read-aloud represent variety in genre and also touch on various parts of the curriculum. For example, Sylvia uses books to illustrate important concepts in math.

Other books can find application through content discussion and/or response, in social studies, science, physical education, art, music, and, of course, writing.

Students often use the books they are exposed to as models for their own writing. Unusual books such as pop-up books and other manipulative books provide ideas for creative formats. Patterned and repetitive phrase books provide ideas for texts. Also, through their work in the writing process workshop, the content of students' writing can usually be tied to an important part of the subject curriculum.

One unit study combined Africa and folktales. Students read and listened to all types of folktales, especially folktales from Africa. Using dramatic play, students took trips to Africa and explored various aspects of African culture. The unit concluded with an African folk festival in which students read or told their own African folktales and parents brought in artifacts, pictures, and foods from Africa. It was a grand celebration.

Sylvia's class is somewhat unique in comparison with other elementary classrooms in the United States in that the students represent three grade levels. Sylvia uses small group and individual conference times to deal with important concepts in math and reading specific to each grade level or student need. However, through most of the day, the children work in multi-grade groups.

Work on the unit of study, read aloud and discussion, rugtime, and writing time involve all students. Sylvia assumes that all children will work at their own level of competence and interest. She constantly encourages and challenges students to go beyond themselves, to see things differently, and to respond to what they learn, see, and hear in different ways. Comprehension of shared stories is at different levels for different age students. Moreover, the multi-grade nature of the classroom offers some unique advantages over traditional one-grade classrooms. Older children are able to help younger students in all areas. Younger children see their older classmates as models of appropriate learning behavior and older children benefit from having to explain concepts and procedures in ways that are understandable for children up to two years younger than they. It is not unusual to find older students reading or listening to younger students in a corner of the classroom. Above all, the multi-grade concept creates an ideal environment for learning about responsibility for others and the development of community.

Reading-Writing Strategy: Drama in the Classroom

Children like to play in new and exciting worlds. Sylvia has used this observation to help children learn about their world and to help children learn to read and write. Throughout the year, Sylvia gathers the children around her and tells stories about different lands and people, new adventures, and interesting problems. The story is often connected to the thematic unit of study and creates a context in which the children explore, learn, read, write, and collaborate. When studying scientists and the scientific process, Sylvia created a new planet that the "student-scientists" had to learn about. African culture was explored through folktales and students became writers of folktales. In the study of pollution, children became residents of a polluted land. They had to devise ways to reduce pollution in their land.

These dramatic play scenarios usually last several days and in each day Sylvia recreates and adds to the world with the help of her students. New information is added. New stories are told. Reading and writing become important tools in students' explorations. Students need to learn about their play world and its problems through reading—tradebooks, encyclopedias, and texts written by the teacher. Writing is used for planning activities, for documenting observations, inventions and solutions, and for expressing students' thoughts and stories about their experiences. Students' reading and writing become parts of the teacher's ongoing story and their written work is eventually displayed on the room walls as artifacts of their explorations.

ISSUES

Individual Differences

With an age span of three years represented in her classroom, Sylvia must certainly attend to individual differences among her students. Individual assessment is the starting place. Sylvia uses running records, a type of informal reading inventory, to determine the strategies students use while reading. She also uses individual conferences with students to develop an understanding of them as learners as well as of their interests in reading and school.

For students who manifest significant difficulties in learning to read Sylvia employs a variety of strategies, even some that may not fit within her philosophy of instruction. However, the highly structured activities that she may employ are always only a small part of the entire curriculum for children with difficulties and are always balanced against purposeful and holistic approaches to learning. Moreover, such instruction lasts only as long as students have a need. Among the activities and materials that Sylvia employs with children who have difficulties in learning to read are: (1) short stories that can be completed in one setting; (2) stories with repetitive phrases; (3) having students read their own stories and stories of their peers; (4) discussing, developing, dictating, writing, and reading group chart stories; (5) analyze sentences and phrases from students' own stories; (6) discuss selections *before* having students read; (7) examine strategies each child is employing and failing to employ in his or her reading, and work with each child individually to develop effective reading strategies; (8) consistent and daily reading activity.

The central feature to Sylvia's instruction of children with difficulties is daily and consistent individualized instruction. She chooses books and materials that meet students' interests. Interests are assessed through interest surveys given to students and parents at the beginning of the year. Sylvia also gets a sense of students' reading interests through close observation of students in various contexts and talking with students about their likes and interests. Inasmuch as most students' difficulties in reading are in word recognition and fluency, she finds books and materials that are highly predictable and which have repetitive in phrases and sentences. Through repeated readings, done in real contexts (for example, to practice for reading to the class, parent, or principal), students gradually develop fluency and confidence in their reading. One first-grader named Kevin experienced considerable difficulty in developing fluent word recognition. From January to June, Sylvia arranged for Kevin to read repeatedly to her, parent volunteers, other students, the school principal, and others willing to listen and give praise. Kevin's fluency and confidence soared in the last half of the school year. Self-made books and other texts are also often used in individualized reading instruction. Sylvia is quick to point out that the use of genuine praise is an essential part of any attempt to meet individual needs.

Sylvia does not fully agree with the concept of "giftedness" as it is operationalized in schools. She believes all children are gifted in their own way and all areas of exceptionality should be fostered. Nevertheless, Sylvia's classroom can easily accommodate more advanced students. In her class, children work at their own level. More able students take on more advanced projects. They do a wider range of research, reporting, and response. Three students whose interests were captured by the class' study of ecology wrote, produced, and performed their own readers theater play on pollution in the city. Two other students developed and implemented a recycling program for the class. More advanced students can choose to read more advanced literature. This includes meeting in book discussion groups appropriate to the level of the literature and becoming involved in higher level analysis of and response to the literature.

More able students are often asked to share their gifts in helping other students in the class. This works toward the development of responsibility and self-esteem in these students and of community in the classroom.

Evaluation

Evaluation of students' progress in reading and writing is done informally. At the beginning of the school year, Sylvia does an informal assessment of students. This may include having students read a few short paragraphs of various difficulty, identify letters, demonstrate knowledge of conventions of print, such as the concept of word or directionality, demonstrate understanding of a passage read by or to a student, and complete a brief writing sample. Sylvia uses the information gathered here to place students in loosely organized and immensely flexible instructional groups.

Similar informal assessments are given at midyear and at the end of the year in order to document progress and refine instruction and instructional groups. A running record, a more detailed assessment of students' oral reading, is used for students who are experiencing difficulty in reading. In her running record, Sylvia notes any deviations from the text that a student makes in oral reading. Later she analyzes these "errors" to determine the extent to which students are employing letter-sound, word structure, and contextual (passage meaning) information to identify words. She also makes an impressionistic judgment of students' level of fluency while reading. This information is then used to guide instruction.

Direct observation is Sylvia's most important evaluation tool. She keeps records of the books students read, their responses in individual book conferences, and activities completed in reading, writing, and language arts. Sylvia records her observations on note cards that are kept in a file for each child. She keeps examples of students' written work. As she watches students in class, she makes notes about their level of involvement and the level of sophistication of the activity. She comments on the "skills and strategies" students seem to have acquired and indicates areas in which further instruction is required.

Making sense out of the multitude of observations, notes, and artifacts can be an overwhelming task. Sylvia notes that the varied information usually converge in making general and specific assessments of students. She also notes that commitment to observational assessment is a long-term process. Over time, a teacher hones his or her skills in determining what to observe and how to interpret it. Efficiency and proficiency improve over time. What may seem like an incredibly complex task for the uninitiated is, in reality, an organized, powerful, contextually appropriate, and efficient way to assess children's reading and writing.

Home Connections

Sylvia views parental involvement in reading as essential for students' continued growth in reading and writing. She admits that communication with parents can be difficult at times. Part of the problem lies in the fact that students come to her school from all parts of the city. It can be difficult for parents to come to the school for programs and conferences. Nevertheless, Sylvia works at increasing parental involvement and notes that most parents work with their children, at some level, on reading and writing.

Sylvia has developed a Home Reading Program that has been well-received by parents. The program encourages parents to become involved in reading and language activities with their children at home and in school. During the careers unit of study, several parents talked with the class about what it is like to be a newspaper reporter, a business manager, a mechanic, and other types of work. The centerpiece to the program is daily read aloud to the children and discussion. Other activities are designed to strengthen students' performance and interest in reading and writing. These activities are outlined in Figure 3.5. Several parents have dropped by to tell Sylvia how much their children have improved in reading since they began some of the activities with their children. Moreover, several have indicated that doing the activities together has actually improved the relationship between parent and child.

For the home involvement program, Sylvia has coded books in her room by level of difficulty. A one-dot book is easy while a three-dot book is more challenging. Sylvia has students take books home to share with their parents. Parents are expected to read to or with their children or listen to their children read. Families can keep the books for a week or more.

Figure 3.5
Activities in the Home Reading Program

- Daily read-aloud and discussion
- Vast and varied family experiences
- Parents listen to children read and follow-up with specific activities
- Regular library use
- Books sent home for parents and children to read
- Have children keep summer journals and have a quiet reading time each day during the summer
- Pass letters between parents and children

Parents are given a comment sheet on which they list the books that they are exploring with their children and make comments about each session.

Sylvia communicates her Home Reading Program to parents through regular and informal class newsletters (typed and sometimes handwritten), formal conferences, and many informal chats as parents stop by the school to drop off or pick up their children. The newsletters contain news about the class and provide information on ways parents can explore books and other reading with their children. Sylvia also notes that she often calls parents in the evenings to keep them informed of their children's progress.

School Connections

Sylvia works at a school dedicated to whole language approaches to literacy education. Thus, Sylvia's teaching colleagues share her vision of education. This means that at her school there is a community of teachers who support one another in developing curricula and instruction. There is a lot of sharing. Some of it occurs at formal staff-run inservice sessions. The inservice sessions are usually on specific topics, such as using drama in the classroom or creating environmental awareness through an integrated curricular approach. Some of it is informal, occurring in the teachers' lounge or in conversations before or after school. Teachers seem always to be talking about new children's books they have read and how they can introduce them into their classes. Sylvia's school attracts many student teachers. In this school, student teachers are given opportunity not only to learn from seasoned and master teachers, but also to share what they have learned and thought about in their on-campus courses. One teacher mentioned that she learns about books and teaching strategies from her student teachers and also has the chance to reflect on and discuss her own teaching with the student teacher.

New teachers to the school, not thoroughly knowledgeable of holistic approaches, are given considerable help by their more experienced colleagues. Most new teachers, however, do have some idea of whole language because the faculty is highly involved in the recruitment, interview, and hiring of new teachers.

In whole language, teachers are empowered to develop and implement curricula. Sylvia acknowledges that this empowerment is fostered by the school principal who encourages teachers to learn more about and explore whole language. She sees the role of the principal as a facilitator, one who supports teachers in their teaching, is open to new ideas, and creates conditions that make whole language viable at the school level, and keeps up-to-date with trends and research in education. The principal works with teachers in bringing in speakers to talk about various aspects of whole language and learning and book authors to talk about books. She informs parents about what is happening in the school and encourages them to become involved in their children's reading education and the school. She coordinates operation of the school bookstore. She works to involve the surrounding community in the life of the school and supports field trips and other community explorations that individual classrooms may undertake. School-wide activities are based on notions of whole language education, from the school bookstore to school assemblies that are based upon topics of study in individual classrooms. The school has great appreciation for the arts. The principal takes a leading role in maintaining an on-going, school-wide arts program with special events, performances, and exhibits throughout the year. Teachers work to weave the arts program into their own units of study at all grade levels. Teacher brainstorming and discussion groups help facilitate this integration.

Keeping Current

Whole language education implies a commitment to learning about teaching and children. In addition to school inservice meetings, Sylvia reads professional journals and books that deal with literacy education and whole language teaching. She belongs to several professional education organizations and regularly attends meetings of interest. She works hard to keep up to date on children's literature. This is done by reading books, talking about new books with colleagues and the school librarian, and reading reviews of books in professional journals such as *Language Arts* and *The Reading Teacher.*

Keeping current also means changing the curriculum. Sylvia says that change is constant in her classroom. She constantly tries new trade books, new approaches, and new topics of study. Her thematic unit approach allows her to teach the same basic curricula is significantly different ways. She never teaches the same units in the same way or with the same materials. Each year she does things a bit differently. Commercial teaching guides that formalize the curriculum would not be of great help to her. Sylvia notes that change keeps her interest in the topics and activities that she and children explore and engage in. Change allows her opportunities to be creative and makes teaching a personally challenging activity.

Challenges

Sylvia argues that whole language, by its very nature is more organic than other literacy curricula. That is, it is more than the sum of its parts. Its impact is on the social and emotional dimensions of students' lives as well as the cognitive. Because of the organic nature of whole language, it resists testing and measurement that is analytic and categorical. Students' scores on tests of vocabulary or reading comprehension do not provide a complete picture of the impact or effectiveness of whole language instruction.

One of challenges, then, that Sylvia sees in whole language is developing holistic measures of the curriculum's effect on students that are accepted as valid and are reasonably easy to administer and interpret. What is called for are more sophisticated methods of curricular evaluation that assess process as well as product, teacher as well as students, and affective and social aspects of schooling as well as academic.

Until whole language advocates can objectively "prove" the effectiveness of their approach, opposition will remain. Sylvia recognizes that, regardless of what can be "proven" about whole language, there will always be opposition to it. There will always be advocates of other approaches with their own claims of effectiveness in student learning.

Sylvia knows that whole language "works." Students in her class enjoy school and they learn to read and write. Moreover, they learn to enjoy reading and writing to such an extent that they want to read and write recreationally, when it is not required. Sylvia's students continue to do well in school when they leave her class. Although compelling for some, this is not the kind of objective proof, however, that others will easily accept.

Thus, whole language face opposition from proponents of the status quo. One of the greatest challenges for whole language advocates is to remain true to the principles about teaching and learning that underlie holistic approaches. It is easy to try to compromise or find common ground with other approaches. Buy, Sylvia recognizes that excessive compromise will drastically alter the very nature of whole language. Whole language advocates need to be firm in their convictions about the value and nature of their approach.

SUMMING UP

Sylvia's class is unusual by several of today's standards. Children from three grade levels are in one class. Sylvia uses no textbooks to teach reading or the language arts. Yet, in her class, children learn to read and write successfully. They learn to work well with children of different abilities, ages, and cultural groups and they learn to enjoy reading and writing at school and home. The key ingredient in Sylvia's teaching is a fundamental respect and caring attitude for each child in her classroom. She feels that a whole language curriculum is the best vehicle for implementing this attitude.

Like other whole language classrooms, Sylvia's implementation of whole language features the liberal use of literature for children. She is flexible in how students are grouped for instruction. And, she works to integrate meaningful reading and writing activities into all areas of the curriculum.

What is distinctive about Sylvia's implementation of whole language is her multi-grade classroom and her focus on social and affective dimensions of schooling. Sylvia's classroom demonstrates that whole language not only works well in multi-grade settings, in many respects, multi-grade classrooms are ideal for whole language. Multi-grade classrooms are more nearly like real families and communities, the social groups that whole language tries to emulate and for which children are prepared.

In multi-grade classrooms, there are wonderful opportunities for children to work with one another in different ways. In Sylvia's classroom, children are not just students, they learn to act as teacher and concerned family member for each other. They learn to explain, to help, and to be accepting of help.

All good teachers recognize and foster affective and social growth in their classrooms. In Sylvia's whole language curriculum, these are the centerpieces. Sylvia believes that schools are places where children learn to become caring human beings as well as learned people. In nearly every classroom activity, whether it is reading, writing, or recess, Sylvia tries to help children learn to develop emotionally and socially. Her whole language curriculum is aimed specifically and directly at these rather unmeasurable but, nevertheless, critical goals of schooling. Sylvia's classroom demonstrates that it is possible to successfully combine affective, social, and cognitive aspects of learning.

Chapter 4

WHOLE LANGUAGE IN FIRST GRADE

"Whole language appealed to my intuitive sense of good teaching. I decided, then, that I wanted to become a whole language teacher."

The morning bell rings and children begin to enter the first-grade class of Betsy Pryor. They come in alone, in pairs, and sometimes in groups of three or four. Some are quiet, others noisily offer greetings to friends and teacher. Yet, students seem to come in the room with a single-minded purpose.

After hanging up their coats and putting away their belongings, each student finds a book or magazine and a place to read. Several students remain at their desks. Others find their own special places within the room. Two girls sit next to each other in a corner. Another girl sits in the rocking chair in the classroom common area. A pair of boys lay on their stomachs under a table. Betsy sets her clock and announces that Sustained Silent Reading will last for twenty minutes. A hush quickly falls over the room as students (and teacher) begin to read. Another day has begun in first grade.

Betsy Pryor teaches first grade in a semi-rural, suburban primary grade school. She has 23 students in her class. Betsy has taught for eighteen years and for the past six years she has been implementing a whole language curriculum.

Betsy's move toward a more holistic approach began with her concern about her students' poor comprehension scores on basal and standardized reading tests. Despite her best efforts in following the teaching guide in the basal, her students did not perform up to her expectations. At the same time, Betsy wanted her students to be able to write their own stories, rather than respond to questions on worksheets or write stories based on artificial prompts given by the teacher.

Her first move toward whole language began when she attended a workshop on journal writing and invented spelling at a workshop for teachers. Learning about these new ideas began a gradual but continuous process of growth and change in Betsy as a teacher. Betsy was excited by the ideas presented at the workshop. She asked her principal if she could try journals and encourage invented spelling in her classroom. The principal apparently saw the spark in Betsy's eyes. Not only did she endorse Betsy's proposal to alter her curriculum, she asked her to make a presentation to the other teachers in the building on what she had learned. The presentation got others interested in literacy learning. Since that presentation, a core group of teachers interested in whole language has developed and the entire school has made a gradual yet definite shift toward a whole language curriculum.

Betsy has made gradual but steady progress in her commitment to whole language literacy. Over the past six years, she has attended and presented papers on whole language at professional meetings, taught college level courses on the teaching of reading and writing, and entered a doctoral program in literacy education. Developing a whole language perspective has enabled Betsy to take risks in her teaching, to try new strategies, and to become a scholar of literacy education

WHAT BETSY THINKS ABOUT WHOLE LANGUAGE

Betsy's approach to teaching is based upon a set of personal and fundamental principles about instruction. First, Betsy believes that, as in learning oral language, all children have the ability to learn to read and write. Second, learning to read and write occurs best in an atmosphere that encourages children to take risks and make approximations of conventional literate behavior. Betsy believes that student errors are best used to guide instruction, encourage rather than stifle risk taking, and to help the learner take charge of his or her own learning. Third, the best environment for encouraging literate behavior is one that is filled with a wide variety of printed materials where students have daily opportunities to read and write for their own purposes. Students need to realize that they have a responsibility for their own learning and that responsibility implies a certain amount of personal control or direction over their own learning.

Finally, Betsy believes that the proper role of a whole language teacher is to facilitate, coach, and encourage students in their own explorations and learning of reading and writing. Excessive amounts of teacher direction and coercion can lead students to take a passive and timid role in their learning.

Over the past several years, Betsy has worked to gradually implement these principles in her own teaching. She has been pleased with the results. Students are more active in and excited about their own learning. Even at the first-grade level, they are willing to follow up their own ideas, turning them into projects that involve reading, writing, and learning content knowledge. Students are eager to write and put on plays based on stories they have read and their own experiences. They regularly make puppets and dioramas, write books and reports, create mobiles, draw maps, write letters and poems, and do other projects that extend their exploration of a topic and deepen their levels of comprehension and learning. Students leave her classroom enthusiastic about school and eager to continue their own learning.

Betsy states that whole language teaching is "a process that is never finished, never static, always involving growth, development, and change of both students *and* teacher!" She notes that her own approach is unique because she is unique. She has "tailor-made" her curriculum to her own students' needs and interests and to her own ideas of what is important about teaching, learning, and children.

INSIDE BETSY'S CLASSROOM

The Environment

Betsy's first-grade class is located in a spacious room in a school built in the early 1960s. The room is not unlike thousands of classrooms constructed in the late 1950s and 1960s to serve the baby boom generation. The walls are painted cinderblock. One wall is completely dominated by a set of windows under which are built-in cabinets and shelves. Along the other three walls are chalkboards and bulletin boards.

Like all the other rooms in the building, Betsy's is equipped with individual desks for each student. Betsy tries to be creative in her seating arrangements while adhering to the principle of maximizing opportunities for student interaction—visually and verbally. At the beginning of the school year, Betsy arranged 15 desks so that they formed a U-shape. Within the open end of the U she placed the remaining eight seats in a 2 by 4 grid so that all seats touched and the two rows faced each other. When students get "too comfortable" with a seating arrangement, Betsy changes it. At one time she may have students sitting in pairs and at other times she places them in groups of three to five. These groups are often asked to work together on classroom projects and activities. Changing children's perspective of the room and having them interact with new students are the two principles that guide Betsy's room arrangements.

Betsy's desk is in one corner of the room, at the bottom of the U. (See Figure 4.1.) In another corner is the class common area. Although the classroom had a tile floor, Betsy brought in her own rug to ensure that this important corner was warm and comfortable. Betsy put two bookshelves along the edge of the common area to separate it from the rest of the room

and to allow the area to be transformed into an independent reading center when it was not used for class activities. Betsy has designed her room so that there are nooks and crannies throughout the room that readers can "snuggle" into. The common area is equipped with a large wooden rocking chair and an easel on which is perched a variety of big books. The rocking chair serves as a reader's/author chair when students share their own compositions and current reading. Several stacks of books—both conventionally sized and enlarged—as well as a tape recorder and listening equipment can be found near the rocker and easel.

At different areas of the room are learning/exploration centers and equipment. Along one wall are shelves containing blocks, toys, and games. A computer is near another corner. A science center is near the classroom sink and counter. Placed here are science artifacts that students had

Figure 4.1
Betsy's Classroom

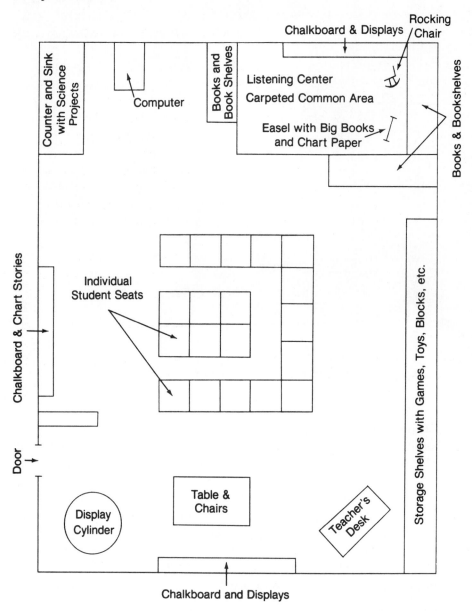

brought for sharing and observation. Rocks, leaves, insects, a wasp nest, flowers, and a bird's nest share space on the counter. Students regularly come by to look at, touch, and talk about the items. Some students even write about the artifacts in the journals, speculating on where something was found or how it was used.

Near one corner, Betsy secured several stacked cylindrical potato chip boxes. On this she displayed students' work. Evidence of students' art, literacy, and science projects was apparent from early in the school year. Several chart stories were posted on the wall. (See Figure 4.2.)

On another wall, the results of a watermelon science project were displayed. Students had each been given a piece of watermelon and asked to predict the number of seeds in their piece. Once the predictions were recorded students ate their piece and determined the exact number of seeds in it. For each student, both the predicted and the actual number of seeds were listed and displayed in bar graph form. The watermelon seeds were glued on the chart to form the bar graph.

Books and magazines dot the entire classroom environment. They are in all parts of the classroom, students' desks, in various centers, on chalk ledges, at Betsy's desk, and in a variety of shelves. Students had great access to books.

Near the common area is the class writing center that contains a wide variety of paper, writing tools, story starters, pictures, art materials for illustrations, and dictionaries. Utensils for making various types and shapes of books as well as blank books are also available.

Figure 4.2
A Chart Story Displayed on A Wall in Betsy's Room

Mooncake

Little Bear wanted to take a bite out of the moon. He built a rocket ship. He fell asleep in it. The wind blew his rocket ship over. He thought he was on the moon. He scooped up some snow and make a mooncake. He thought his own footprints were made by a moon monster. He fell asleep in his rocket ship. Little Bird woke him up. Little Bear said mooncake tasted delicious.

Betsy believes that the appropriate atmosphere is critical to the development of a literate classroom environment. Her goal in fashioning her classroom environment is to provide students with a safe and supportive atmosphere that encourages students to use their strengths and take risks. This means more than simply the arrangement of desks and the development of learning centers. Atmosphere refers to the teacher's attitude and actions that pervade the classroom. Betsy respects each student as a person and a learner. She tries to nurture in students a recognition that they are in control of their own learning. She wants her students to learn how to learn on their own and she provides time for them to read, write, and explore topics of their own choosing. Betsy avoids criticism. She feels that, more than anything, teacher criticism keeps students from recognizing their own abilities and becoming active learners. Instead, she uses encouragement and praise to nurture students' feelings of self-esteem and confidence in their own abilities.

Beginning the School Year: Immersed in Print

In the first week of school, Betsy works to establish a classroom routine, familiarize students with the classroom and her approach to teaching, and make the students feel welcome and comfortable in the room. The first days are filled with many whole group activities in the carpeted common area. Many patterned big books are read and reread by Betsy and the class. Class discussions about the books and other issues related to classroom expectations and routines are held. Students tells stories and share artifacts collected during the summer months. During the early weeks of school, the class takes a tour of the school and the school grounds. Students interview each other and the class talks about important school rules and student expectations. These experiences are transformed into language experience activities as students dictate their observations and comments to Betsy who writes the dictation on chart paper. These chart stories are read and reread throughout the first month.

Betsy passes out an individual journal to each student, talks about the purpose of the journals and how they are used, and invites students to begin making daily entries in them. Betsy models journal writing in her own journal and shares her own entries with the class.

The beginning of the school year is a good time to find out about her students. Betsy prepares an interest inventory for parents to complete for their children. The inventory asks parents to identify the children's interests, hobbies, and family experiences including the types of literacy experience found at home.

A Typical Day

Betsy's class begins each school day with sustained silent reading (SSR). This begins on the first day of school, when most children are not reading in the conventional sense, and continues to the very last. When students enter the room, their first task is to find a book—either one in their desk, one they have brought from home, or one they find in the classroom library. Even visitors to the class are asked to find something to read.

In the beginning of the school year, Betsy has the students remain in their seats during sustained silent reading. Later, as students become familiar with the format and expectations for SSR, they are encouraged to find their own preferred place in the classroom to read. Betsy sets a timer (ten minutes at the beginning of the year, thirty minutes by the end) and SSR is underway. Students who are unable to read at the beginning of the year are encouraged to look at the illustrations in books and try to figure out the story.

Betsy's rules for SSR are that students must remain where they are during the duration of SSR and they should not talk. She believes that a quiet atmosphere sets the stage for SSR and distinguishes it from other, more vocal, times of the school day. Students are given time to share what they are reading at the end of the period.

After students become familiar with the SSR routine, Betsy gives each student a blank notebook. She asks the children to respond in writing to what they have read and thought about after each SSR period. Students do their response logs while Betsy works with small groups in reading. At first most children write the title and author of the book or draw a picture. However, after modeling by Betsy and sharing students' entries, the responses become more thoughtful and elaborate. Betsy (or a parent volunteer) tries to respond in writing to the students' entries.

Following SSR is a whole group time in the classroom common area. This time is used to orient the class to the coming day, review events from the previous day, and continue to make literacy the centerpiece of the class' day.

First, Betsy talks with the class about the weather and students complete the weather chart and calendar that is attached to the nearby wall.

Each day students add one number to the number line that will eventually stretch across two walls. At the beginning of the year, Betsy asks students to speculate on the number of days in the school year. The class returns to the predictions as the number line continues to grow. Betsy also keeps three jars and a pile of straws. One jar is labeled ones, another tens, and the third, hundreds. Each day another straw is added. The regrouping that occurs on every tenth and hundredth day helps students understand how the number system works.

Next, students are given an opportunity to share any special news or artifact that they have brought from home, One child brought a bird's nest and an egg that she had found in her yard. Betsy asks if she knows what kind of bird lived in the nest. Alicia said it was a blue jay because the egg was blue. Another child, Chris, suggests that it might be a robin. When asked by Betsy to explain, Chris says, "because it's small." Another child adds, "and because it's blue. I know robins have blue eggs." Another child has a cicada that he caught. This sparks several rounds of comment and discussion. Finally, a girl tells the class about the birthday party she plans to have that afternoon.

After sharing, the class reads a few big books that they had previously read, poems that Betsy had written on chart paper, and dictated texts that the class had authored on previous days. The class chorally read *The King's Pudding,* a text they read with confidence and expression since they had read it several times through on previous occasions. Betsy supports the children's reading with her own voice and points to the words as they are read. (Betsy explained later that through her pointing and demonstration of fluency, she is tacitly reinforcing basic concepts of reading such as directionality and wordedness.) After the reading, she asks the students to look at the word "cold" in the big book. She asks students to think of all the words that can be made by changing the first letter and sound of the word. Students volunteer mold, fold, and told. Betsy writes these words on the chalk board after students indicate the letters that represent the new beginning sound. Then, Betsy covers up the "C" in "cold" with her hand and asks if students know what new word remains. In addition to exploring a few other words in this way, Betsy asks students to compare the meanings of word pairs, "What's the difference between smell and taste?" The reading and discussion take several minutes.

Next, Betsy reads the *Bear in the Frigidaire* and *Cat and Mouse* to the class. Both are patterned books, and after Betsy reads each text the first time, the class is able to read the stories chorally with fluency in the second and third passes through each story. This is followed by the class standing, singing, and acting "The Wheels on the Bus." Betsy holds up phrase cards ("the wheels," "on the bus") to cue the class into each verse.

Betsy then tells the class that she is going to read two regular-sized books to the class and then discuss how the stories are the same and different. The first book is *In a Dark Dark Wood* and the second is *A Dark Dark Tale.* The class is delighted and surprised by both stories. After the reading, students share that the stories are similar in how they lead up to a surprise ending and different in what that ending consists of. Students also note the repetition of the words "dark dark" in both stories. Another student notes that one story ends with a ghost while the other with a mouse. Betsy asks students to think of other scary things that could have been found at the end of the story. She also focuses students' attention on how both stories are constructed, moving progressively from a location outside the house, to the house, up the stairs, into a room, and so on. She has the class think of ways they could progressively move from the school playground to their classroom, and from the school to their homes. She graphically maps several of these sequences on the chalkboard for students to see.

Finally, after thoroughly exploring the structure of the two stories, Betsy tells the class that since Halloween is near they will be writing their own dark dark story. She leads a brief discussion with students on planning and mapping their own story ideas and how their stories can be different from the two presented. Betsy has the students choose a partner and asks them to talk about the story they envisage, take notes, and begin to map out the direction of the story.

After the whole group time in the class common area, students engage in independent work and learning center activities while Betsy works with individual reading groups. She makes sure students know what is expected of them in their independent work. This usually involves working on one or more projects that were talked about previously or which students choose to do on their own. Students can also write in their journals at this time. During this time, students are encouraged to work with others at places of their own choosing. While working on their own version of the dark dark stories students could be found in nearly every conceivable nook and cranny in the classroom.

Reading groups are best characterized as flexible groups of students reading books and poems of interest. Betsy has multiple copies of many

---

Reading-Writing Strategy: Copy-Change

Children's literature holds center stage in Betsy's classroom. Throughout the year, students listen to, read, and talk about a wide variety of stories and poetry. Literature for children plays a key role in the writing curriculum as well. Betsy finds that children's literature is an excellent model for her students' writing. Sometimes she plans lessons in which children model their own writing after an exemplary piece of writing. Other times children spontaneously choose to write their own version of a well-liked story or poem.

When Betsy plans a copy-change lesson, she makes sure students are thoroughly familiar with the story. This occurs through repeated presentations and readings of the story. Betsy talks about the story with the class, noting important characters, events, and stylistic elements employed by the author. She leads a discussion of ways children can make the story their own while retaining basic plot and/or the style of the author. Often she will map the story with the class in order to help students get a graphic sense of the story development.

Once students feel comfortable with the story, she lets them write. The results are impressive—children's stories such as *Josh and Super Cool Awesome Totally Excellent Day* and *Laurie and the Magic Rock* are read aloud, talked about, and reread for weeks.

---

books such as *Ferdinand, Caps for Sale, Sylvester and the Magic Pebble,* and many folk and fairy tales available in her room. She also chooses stories she knows that children enjoy from the basal reading series. Stories are introduced by accessing student background knowledge and eliciting predictions about the story. Before reading *Ferdinand,* Betsy talked with the group about Spain and bull fights. Once students speculate on the nature of the story, characters, or even words that they might expect to encounter in the story, the book is read. Sometimes Betsy reads the story to the group and then asks students to read the story again silently. Other times she reads the first page and asks students to continue reading. Choral reading and radio reading are often used as well in reading groups. Betsy's aim is for students to reread stories for real purposes in order to build fluency and confidence, improve word and phrase recognition, and ensure comprehension.

During and after reading and rereading the text, which may take several days, the group talks about what was read. Students are encouraged to share what struck them as they read or how the story made them feel. Betsy's role in story discussions is as a participant rather than a leader.

She shares her own feelings and encourages students to ask questions of one another. Betsy challenges students to compare current stories with ones read previously. Often students will list significant differences and similarities between stories. Betsy tries to get students to think about the general structure of stories. She uses metaphors to help students understand different types of stories. For example, domino stories describe cause and effect and problem-solution texts. Group story mapping on the chalkboard helps students see visually how stories are played out.

If a story is enjoyed, many students will try writing their own version. Special books such as shape books, pop-up books, and flap books add variety and invite emulation. Other times students enjoy practicing the story or performing it for another group of students, a parent volunteer, or for a parent at home.

Betsy does teach phonics and word analysis skills to her students. This is done in the mini-lessons she conducts during reading or during other times of the day. She pulls words from the stories read and demonstrates word families or phonics generalizations. Occasionally, Betsy will ask students to complete a workbook page that deals with word analysis. Although she feels somewhat uneasy about this practice, she feels that since students are tested on these skills they do need some instruction on them. It would be a disservice to the students to ignore a specified area of the curriculum that is explicitly tested.

Betsy tries to create variety in her reading groups. No lesson is ever the same. She finds many ways for stories to be read, talked about, and responded to in ways that are cognitively challenging and satisfying. She does this by varying the size of the group (individuals to whole class), mode of reading (oral and silent), purpose for reading, and response to reading. Often Betsy will forego reading groups entirely in favor of extended periods of whole group reading of big books, experience texts, favorite stories, and poems. Mini-lessons are also conducted on other various aspects of reading such as vocabulary building and comprehension strategies.

In one lesson, Betsy displayed the cover picture of a picture book to a group. Then she asked if students could predict what the story would be about and what words students might expect to hear. Betsy read the story to the group, stopping periodically to talk about what had been read. At the end of the story, she wrote the word parts "oat" and "an," which had been repeatedly used in the story, on a piece of chart paper and talked about and wrote on the chart the variety of words that can be developed from these two parts. Later, this chart was put on display on a wall of the room.

During reading group time, Betsy does a considerable amount of individual conferencing with students. During conferences, which occur at least once a week for each child, she talks with students about what they are reading at home and school and she asks about how they are feeling about reading and what progress they see themselves making. Betsy also has children read for her. She uses this as a way of evaluating students' progress and to show students how repeated readings leads to greater fluency, better word recognition, and improved understanding. Betsy takes about five minutes with each student. When finished, she sends each student off to practice reading with a friend, jots down a few notes about the student's performance and progress, and calls another student.

At the end of the morning, the class gathers again as a whole group to share their writing and reading. Students talk about what they accomplished during the morning, some sharing what they had done in the group writing activity. Betsy completes the morning session by reading to the class and, if time allows, having the class chorally read some favorite big books.

Subject areas are presented in the afternoons. However, literacy activities continue to play a significant role. After lunch Betsy calls the class together again for another read-aloud session. Individual students are given the opportunity to read to the class or to share an interesting experience or artifact with the group. Students must sign up in advance for this activity. Readers are expected to have practiced/rehearsed their reading prior to sharing with the class so that their oral reading performance is given with fluency and confidence.

In the afternoon, time is reserved for writing. Students work on ongoing writing projects or write in their journals. During this period,

Reading Strategy: Repeated Readings

Repetition of whole texts is an important part Betsy's instruction. She tries to create situations which have natural opportunities to read short passages. Betsy feels that repeated readings help her students improve in word recognition, fluency, and comprehension. "You can just see them take control of their reading with practice of this type. Increases in confidence are obvious as the children embed expression, intonation, and phrasing in their reading. At first I thought the children might not like repeated readings. However, just the opposite has occurred. They see the value in it and enjoy practicing and performing their reading."

Betsy says that the most challenging part of repeated readings is being aware of and creating situations for which repeated readings can be employed. Betsy tells students good stories are meant to be reread, "They are like old friends. You don't visit an old friend once in your life. No, you go back to your friends now and then to relive their stories and enjoy their company."

The class repeatedly reads experience stories and big books across several days and weeks. In radio reading, each student practices a portion of a text silently before performing it for a listening group. During conferences with students, Betsy will ask a student to read a section of text several times and then talk with the student about the progress that was made during the repetitions. At other times she will pair students and ask them to practice reading a text to one another two, three, or four times. Betsy herself will reread favorite stories to the class. She is struck by the deeper levels of understanding that accompany each rereading.

Reading Strategy: Conferencing

Betsy conferences with students throughout the day. Sometimes the conferences last several minutes, often they last only a few seconds. Betsy uses conferences for a variety of purposes. She assesses students' reading by having individuals read to her and retell what they have read. She talks with students about what they have been reading and writing, offering suggestions as needed. Most of all, she uses her conferences to offer encouragement, give praise, and display enthusiasm for reading. "Children like to know that I think so highly of them and their reading that I want to talk with them about their reading every day."

---

students can be seen drafting, conferencing, and publishing their writing. Betsy monitors student activity during the writing workshop, conferences and offers encouragement to individual students, and provides large and small group instruction on an as-needed basis. Instructional topics range from brainstorming ideas for writing to providing substantive feedback during peer conferencing to learning how to publish their work in book form, display or other manner. Betsy also writes during the writing period. She demonstrates for students how she chooses topics from things she has read, experienced, seen, or talked about with others. She shows students how she plans her own compositions, sketching maps that help her organize the major ideas she wishes to present.

Students' writing usually finds its source in a need to communicate, or in stories and poems they have read or heard, or in their own personal experience. Family, friends, and familiar locations are often written about. When the puppy she had received as a gift died a few weeks later, Whitney was crushed. Betsy and Whitney talked about her feelings on several occasions. Betsy suggested that Whitney may wish to write about her feelings and about her puppy. The resulting composition, *Whitney's Dog*, was written at school and home with the help of Whitney's mother. The process of exploring her feelings through writing and sharing her loss with others seemed to help Whitney overcome her hurt.

In the remainder of the afternoon, Betsy teaches math and alternates social studies, health, and science. Betsy teaches these areas through thematic units. In science the class has done in-depth studies of insects, plants, trees, animals, and dinosaurs, while in social studies the class has studied friends, the elderly, and different cultures. Betsy tries to make reading and writing an integral part of each unit. When a theme is selected, she finds and brings to school related books from her personal collection, the public library, and the school library. The public library has a wonderful program to aid teachers in finding and using library books in the classroom. The books are shared in a variety of ways and the writing activities are equally diverse. Students write letters to newspapers and government officials. They make signs and posters. They write poems and stories. They write reports and essays on related issues. They record their thoughts in their journals.

One day in social studies, the class read and discussed an article on Barbara Bush's volunteer efforts for important causes. The class discussion lead to the role of the parent volunteers in their own classroom. One student noted how unappreciated the classroom volunteers were by the students. Other students mentioned how hard working and fun to be with they were. As a result of reading and talking about this article, the class decided to write notes of thanks and appreciation to the classroom volunteers. The notes were warmly received by the parents who developed regular correspondence with the students.

Organization and Management

Betsy conceptualizes the organization of her classroom in terms of groups. She employs a variety of grouping practices. Because one of her teaching goals is the development of a classroom community and students developing responsibility and for one another, she uses many whole group activities. Opening exercises, reading aloud, sharing, shared reading of big books and poems, and class discussions are typical of the whole class activities that are focused yet comfortable and informal. Betsy does provide reading instruction in small and flexible groups. Teacher-student pairings are used for reading and writing conferences as well as for personal discussions of issues that Betsy or a student may wish to raise. Students also spend a considerable amount of time working in small peer groups and student partner activities. Peer groups are used for activities such as group study and exploration and peer writing conferences. Students are often paired for partner writing, partner reading, and sharing. Throughout every school day, students work in a variety of groups and have opportunities to interact with a variety of peers as well as the teacher in a number of activities.

Because children enter Betsy's first-grade class with different levels of experience in a school culture, Betsy acknowledges the need to help students understand her expectations for student behavior in the class. She recognizes the importance of setting up classroom management procedures that will create optimal conditions for academic learning and social development.

Prior to the first day of school, Betsy posts a few class rules on a classroom wall. On the first school day, she reads the rules to the class and leads the class in a discussion of the rationale for the rules. For several following days and sporadically thereafter, she reviews her expectations with the class. As the year continues and new problems arise, Betsy and the class talk about the situations and negotiate new rules. During the school year, several students began throwing things in class. In a class discussion, students noted the danger involved in carelessly pitching objects in the room. The class developed a rule prohibiting throwing objects in the classroom.

Betsy uses a marble jar to monitor and reward appropriate behavior. When Betsy observes positive behavior among students, she places a marble in a jar that sits on her desk. When the jar is filled, the whole class receives a treat, extra recess, or some other reward. Betsy notes that the jar is very effective, "the sound of a marble going in the jar is like magic to students." However, the most important aspect of the marble jar is that it reminds Betsy to look for positive behavior in students.

To help children monitor their own classroom behavior, Betsy posts a pocket envelope for each child in her class. In each pocket is a blue index card which indicates that all is well with the child's behavior. When the blue card is replaced by a yellow one, the student realizes that a warning has been issued. Pink and green cards indicate a loss of some recess time and a note to parents, respectively. Students realize that they control the color of the card through their own behavior. Betsy also conferences frequently with individual students about their behavior and the need to be considerate of others.

It is not unusual for students at this age to have problems with one another. When such problems arise, after assuring that both students are not physically injured, Betsy tries to get students to "talk it out," to tell their stories. Betsy listens, encouraging students to talk to each other, not to her. Through sharing their feelings and points of view, most student problems can be resolved without the teacher having to impose a solution. When the problem is satisfactorily resolved, the students go on about their business. Betsy's goal in this type of crisis management is to get students to see the other's point of view and to develop internal strategies for self-control and interpersonal problem resolution.

During recess, Mike complained to Betsy that Nick tried to choke him. After first ensuring that Mike was not physically injured, Betsy brought the two boys together. Mike told his side of the story to Nick. Nick explained that he wasn't trying to hurt Mike, he just got carried away in the excitement of the game. Nick apologized to Mike and the friendship was renewed.

Because Betsy encourages students to use reading and writing for real purposes, she should not have been surprised when a group of boys were employing reading and writing to resolve an interpersonal conflict. But she was. Todd had caused disruptions in the classroom and playground throughout the year. Four boys had had enough of it. One spring day, Betsy saw the boys diligently working in a corner. She went over to the corner and saw the boys writing in a notebook entitled *Plan Book*. She looked through the book and found that it contained detailed plans for cornering Todd (not his real name) during a future recess and beating him up. The book outlined the roles to be played by each boy, coordinated times for carrying out elements of the plan, and labeled maps of the playground. As Betsy said later, "The book was amazing for its clarity, detail, and purpose." She convinced the boys to abort their plan.

Later, however, other children became so irritated by Todd's antics that they wrote notes to his mother (see Figure 4.3). Betsy shared the letters with the principal and the mother. Todd later was referred for special counseling.

Several books that Betsy shares with the class contain interpersonal conflicts. She uses these books as calm and peaceful opportunities to talk with the class about getting along with others and strategies for resolving problems when they arise.

Strategies

Betsy uses good books for children as the centerpiece to her instruction as well as the common thread in her efforts to integrate reading and writing in her classroom.

On any given day, Betsy will read several books to her class. Some books are new to the class. Others are old favorites. Class favorites include all Eric Carle books, Peggy Parrish's *Amelia Bedelia* books, *Charlotte's Web*,

Figure 4.3
Letters to Todd's Mother

Dear Mrs. _____,
   Todd always wen he come in the room he fights me

Dear Mrs. _____,
   Todd has ben bad. - like asking me everything and he put the stamp pad on Anne
B.'s shirt
        Love,

      _____
        I'm from Todd's class

Dear Mrs. _____,
   Todd has been vary bad in school do not let him bring toys to school chek his pockits
befor he goes to school everyday

        from _____

Dear Mrs. _____,
   Todd has bin bad always. he says cuss words.

Nate the Great by Marjorie Charmat, the *Frog and Toad* series by Arnold Lobel, books by Tomie DePaola, especially the Strega Nona books, and *Little Bear* by L. C. Minarek. Each read-aloud is followed by class discussion and opportunities for children to respond orally to books. Many times books read aloud find their way into students' hands during SSR. After reading a book to the class, Betsy places it where students can gain easy access. Betsy finds that students enjoy learning about the authors and illustrators of the books she reads. When she finds background material on an author or illustrator, she shares it with the class. One children's book club has sent her taped interviews of authors. Children enjoy listening to these after hearing some of the author's work. Read-aloud is a great way to nurture children's interest in reading, a goal that Betsy feels is a crucial part of the reading curriculum. By spring, Betsy is reading books with chapters to the class.

   Recreational reading offers other opportunities for students to develop an enjoyment of and desire for reading. Each day in Betsy's class begins with a period of sustained silent reading, even at the beginning of the year when most students are nonreaders. Betsy uses the sustained silent reading time to give expression to her goal of developing an interest in reading in her students.

Betsy believes in the importance of modeling appropriate behavior for students. Modeling is a wonderful way to encourage students to read. Students learn not only from what their teachers say but from what they do. Betsy reads with her class during sustained silent reading and any visitor to the class during this time is asked to read as well. Betsy says that she reads a variety of materials during SSR from professional books and adult novels to children's books and even the local newspaper. Betsy talks to her class about the books and other materials she has been reading for her own enjoyment and for the graduate classes she is enrolled in.

Betsy has come to view writing as a key part of any literacy program and students write often in Betsy's class. Every day students are given opportunities to write in their personal journals. For some students, the entry may be drawing. For others, only a word or two will be written in the journal. Nevertheless, Betsy responds enthusiastically to all students' attempts to record their thoughts and feelings on paper.

Books that Betsy shares with the class offer chances for students' writing as she encourages students to use those books as models for their own writing. Students write their own stories and reports during a time of the day devoted to writing. The writing workshop is designed to allow students to explore the writing process, from topic selection to conferencing, sharing, and revising, as well as publishing the products of their efforts.

Betsy's instructional strategy can be summarized as an attempt to immerse students in the enjoyable and beckoning world of literacy. Children use reading and writing throughout their school days, by themselves and in groups of various sizes and make up. They have access to a wide variety of materials from books to paper. And they are given constant support, encouragement, and examples of literate behavior from a teacher who herself is genuinely excited about books and reading and writing.

Betsy tries to make content area study interesting and relevant for students through the use of thematic units of study that are connected to the school curriculum and to students' identified areas of interest.

Betsy's approach to these units is to immerse the class in the subject. This immersion is largely done through books. Betsy finds as many books and other appropriate materials as she can about a particular subject and brings them into class for students to read and share.

Students' are immersed in the subject area through read-aloud, sharing, independent reading, and independent and group activities. Betsy expects students to respond to the learning experience in some way. This can be a short report or poem on an aspect of the subject, a letter, sign, or poster, the creation of a piece of art or puppets, development and production of a skit or play to be performed for the class, making of a diorama or model, or some other meaningful response. One girl created a mobile as a way to explore what she will be when she grows up. On the large main section she wrote "Someday." On smaller sections extending from it she wrote, "I'l Lrn to Dans," "I wil Bee 7," "I'l gro up," "I will hav my own pup," "I'l grow up an hav a Howse." Betsy gives students a great deal of freedom in choosing their mode and type of response. However, she provides continual advice and guidance through her frequent and informal conferences with students throughout the school day.

Betsy prefers short units, usually lasting no longer than a week. This allows the class to cover a variety of topics, explore different types of children's literature, involve themselves in a wide range of projects, and work with different students in groups of various sizes.

Betsy likes the different kinds of connections she (and students) can make with books. Before reading *Charlotte's Web* to the class, the class embarked on a study of farms and pigs. Included in the study was a variety of stories about pigs from Lobel's *Oliver and Amanda Pig* series to his *Pigericks*, a collection of limericks devoted to pigs. The class visited a nearby farm and interviewed farmers. Some students developed a plan for a farm while others wrote their own pigericks.

ISSUES

Individual Differences

Even in first grade, Betsy has children who represent a wide variety of progress and potential in learning to read. Continuous assessment of children's progress is one key to Betsy's approach to helping children with special needs. Through her assessment program, students are able to benefit from specialized instruction as early as possible. When she notes a potential learning difficulty, Betsy contacts the parents to determine if the parents have noted similar difficulties at home and to get parents' suggestions for helping the child at home and school.

Difficulties that seem severe are referred to the appropriate specialist for further evaluation and potential placement in special instructional settings. Most reading difficulties, however, are treated in the classroom itself. Betsy has developed a strong parent volunteer program in her classroom. Most of the volunteers work one-to-one with children having some difficulty. For many of the children simply having the opportunity to be successful in reading and to receive support and encouragement from a caring adult is all that is needed. Betsy works with the parent volunteers in helping them learn how to choose reading material that children can be successful in and in helping parents support, encourage, and respond to children's reading. Betsy, herself, finds time to work individually with several students who can use the extra help.

Betsy also works with children who appear to excel in reading. One strategy is simply to guide such children to appropriate books for their level of interest and development in reading. Her extensive knowledge of books for primary grade children allows her to make instant recommendations of books to children during individual and group conferences. Betsy also arranges for special lessons to help the more gifted readers develop greater independence in their reading. For example, several brief lessons were developed to help this group find books to match their interests and development in reading.

Many of the regular activities in the classroom permit all readers to develop greater independence in reading and writing. For example, sustained silent reading and the writing process workshop allow children to read and write at their own pace and level of interest and development. More able readers use this time to continue their personal exploration of literacy and the world.

Betsy believes in the need for students to share their gifts. Thus she regularly asks the more capable students to help others and to explain to others how they have thought out problems and discovered solutions. Betsy makes the student matches spontaneously and changes them often in order to give students many opportunities to work with others. Such heterogeneous partnerships help to develop a sense of common purpose in the class as well as developing the academic and social skills of both students in the partnerships. One student wrote three books with three different partners over the course of two weeks. The books were entitled

Wrestling, Ninja Turtles, and *Scary Stories to Tell in the Dark.* The pair that wrote *Scary Stories* collaborated again on a sequel entitled *Better Scary Stories to Tell in the Dark.* In addition to writing, student pairs read and listen to one another, check papers, work on projects, and work at the computer together.

Evaluation

Rather than rely on one or two product-oriented measures (such as test scores) to assess students' progress in reading and writing, Betsy uses multiple indicators of performance in literacy activities to develop a "mental picture" of each child's overall performance in reading and writing as well as to identify specific areas of concern that are directly amenable to instruction.

Among the indicators she employs are multiple reading miscue analyses of students' rehearsed and unrehearsed oral reading conducted at various points throughout the school year, interviews of children about reading, students' behavior during sustained silent reading, performance in small and large group reading and writing activities, demonstrated interest in reading and books, book discussions, book choices, reading log entries, completed written stories and reports, and journal entries. Betsy records her informal observations of SSR, book discussions, and reading and writing activities on notes that she dates and files for each child. She also keeps samples of student work over time. She uses this to demonstrate progress to students and parents and to look for patterns of behavior that may impair progress in literacy learning. Students' journal writing is an excellent vehicle for demonstrating progress in literacy. Bart, a student enrolled in Chapter I corrective reading, made only drawings and tic-tac-toe symbols in his journal in December. By January, he copied the title and author of a picture book he was reading in his journal. By April and June, his entries were much more thoughtful and elaborate (see Figure 4.4). A girl reading slightly above average at the end of the year also demonstrated considerable progress (see Figure 4.5). Finally, another slower progress reader used his journal to express himself in poetry (see Figure 4.6).

Betsy tries to use this information holistically in reporting student progress. As she reads her annotations, reviews oral reading performance, and studies the other indicators of student performance, Betsy tries

Figure 4.4

The Best teacher in the whole World.

by
Bernice Chardiet

Bunny was takeing a note to Mrs. Walker but She didn't know where Mrs. Walker's room.

It is a good Book.

EMERGING . . .

Figure 4.5

the Wheels
on the Bus,
by Harriet
Ziefert,
I Like the
Book Becus
I Like how
it sings a soig

Figure 4.6

I Read where
the sidewalk
Ends

and it has
pomes' in it
and my
favorit one is
the unicorns I
like this one
becous it has
unicorn in it.

to develop a complete "mental image" of each child as a literate member of the classroom community. She poses questions of each child's portfolio that focus on specific and important aspects of reading. Does this child like to read? Does the child respond well to instruction? Does the child understand the functions of reading? Does the child read for meaning? Does the child read a variety of genre and types of materials? Can the child read without substantial help from others? Can the child work and read productively in groups? Does the child freely choose to read outside of school? Consideration of such questions helps Betsy develop evaluations that track progress and that are meaningful to teachers and parents in understanding and helping the child as a reader.

Betsy is required by school policy to administer standardized tests to her class. Rather than disregard the results, Betsy uses the information as one "piece of the puzzle." She notes that her class has performed very well on these tests.

Home Connections

Parents of students in Betsy's class have been overwhelmingly positive toward the whole language curriculum she has developed. Parents like the idea of their children reading real books and writing for authentic purposes. They appreciate the personal attention she is able to provide each student. If there is one area of the curriculum parents voice a concern about, it is invented spellings. Many parents have difficulty accepting the notion the spelling is a developmental process and that students' spelling will inevitably approximate more conventional spelling as they have opportunities to read and write in functional environments, to talk with the teacher about spelling, and to be provided with models of correct spelling. Betsy sees this as an area to which she needs to devote greater attention in communicating to parents her philosophy and rationale for treating spelling in this manner.

Betsy makes a concerted effort to get parents involved in the literacy learning of their children. She does this through continuous communication beginning early and continuing throughout the school year. Betsy sends home professional articles on ways parents can support the literacy growth of their children. She finds articles from the International Reading Association's publications, *Reading Today* and the *Reading Teacher* as well as from *Teaching K–8* to be particularly helpful to and readable for parents. Family activities such as read-aloud, regular trips to the library, writing and exchanging notes and letters are emphasized in Betsy's communications. She tries to stress to parents the importance of valuing and celebrating the things that children know. During Open House, Parent-Teacher conferences, and throughout the year Betsy reinforces the suggestions implied by the articles she had earlier sent home. In addition, regular notes and phone calls keep parents up-to-date on what the children are studying and serve as vehicles for reminding parents what they can do to support their children's growth as readers and writers.

In addition to soliciting parental involvement at home, Betsy runs her own parent volunteer tutoring program in her class. Early in the school year, she invites parents to work as tutors in her classroom for whatever amount of time they can spare. Betsy runs several after-school training sessions to familiarize parents with her instructional philosophy, classroom routine, and approaches for helping individual children. This is followed by weekly planning times with parents. Included among the repertoire of activities that parents can engage in with children are reading aloud, listening to children read, responding to and discussing children's reading and journals, paired reading, taking dictation, grading papers, conducting writing conferences, helping students edit and type their compositions, and assisting students in bookmaking and publishing. Parents are encouraged to do what they enjoy most. One parent received particular satisfaction from making big books. She made several throughout the school year. As parents become comfortable with the classroom routine and their interactions with students, they fit in nicely and unobtrusively with the classroom literacy curriculum. Students thoroughly enjoy the special time they have with the parent tutors. Betsy has found that the parent tutors have a singularly positive impact on many students' cognitive and attitudinal development in reading and writing. "They absolutely do make a difference." Moreover, the work of parents frees Betsy to spend time with individual children.

Betsy says that it is the personal contact with parents, the time spent acclimating parents to the classroom routine and procedures, and the substantiveness of the work parents do with children that makes the program a success. "Parents really want to help children, they want to know their child's teacher, and they want to see their own child in the context of classroom life. Getting them in the classroom and making them feel welcome and needed creates incredible support for myself as a teacher and the school."

Not all parents can volunteer on a regular basis. Those that can't, participate on special occasions such as parties and field trips. Parents with unusual occupations or skills are often invited into the room. One parent who has experience as a bookmaker came to class near the end of the school year. He helped students make nonglue books and talked about how students might use the books during the summer. Several students said they would use their book as a journal, another wanted to use it as an autograph book, still others promised to write stories that they would present to their own dads on Father's Day. The parent finished by reading *Georgia Music* to the class, a story about how a young girl spent her summer with her grandfather.

School Connections

Betsy describes her working relations with fellow teachers and the school principal as excellent. However, she notes that the school schedule limits the opportunities and times she has to interact with colleagues. In her school, the first-grade teachers share materials, ideas, and plans even though they maintain somewhat different orientations to curriculum and instruction. "The main thing," Betsy says, "is that my first-grade teaching colleagues are very accepting of and respectful toward one another. We can be different in the way we approach our teaching, but we all realize that we can learn from each other." At the present time, the first-grade teachers are donating one lunch hour a week to collaborate on the design of big book ideas and activities.

The current principal in Betsy's school is in her first year. Betsy feels very comfortable with the way the principal has fit in with the school. Betsy appreciates the encouragement and support she has received from her principal to try innovative approaches to teaching. The principal has given teachers considerable freedom in modifying their own curriculum to match their own styles of teaching and their children's needs. Recently, the first-grade teachers chose a series of books to replace the existing basal series. The principal has been a strong defender of this choice. Betsy also notes that the principal has supported a variety of professional growth opportunities proposed by teachers and has worked to inform central office administrators and parents about whole language.

Keeping Current

In addition to her teaching position, Betsy is a part-time doctoral student in literacy education. She notes that this forces her to keep current in the field. "I read professional books and journals on reading and the language arts. I also am active in the local TAWL (Teachers Applying Whole Language) group, the local, state, and international levels of IRA (International Reading Association), NCTE (National Council of Teachers of English), CRA (College Reading Association), and NRC (National Reading Conference)." Betsy is a regular attendee and presenter at conferences of these groups. She also teaches courses and workshops on literacy education at the local university. Betsy finds that she learns much from other teachers. She asks other teachers many questions about what they're doing. This sharing helps to validate her own feelings about whole language.

Finally, Betsy notes that she learns and grows as a teacher through self-evaluation and reflection of her own teaching and her students' learning. "Sometimes I just have to sit down at the end of the morning or the end of the day and think about what transpired. Sometimes I put my thoughts on paper. These reflections help me to clarify what I know and do as a whole language teacher. They help me adjust my teaching. I think I see the importance of being a reflective teacher."

Challenges

Betsy is thoroughly committed to whole language. Unlike basal instruction, whole language not only appeals to her sense of good and appropriate instruction for children, it works. She has observed children blossom in a whole language environment whom, she is certain, would have been stifled under a more rigid and analytic system.

Betsy, however, sees several areas of concern and potential difficulty in her own implementation of whole language. One concern is the school bureaucracy from administrators to legislators who, despite talk of curriculum and instructional innovation and reform, seem tied to the old methods and ideas. Grassroots attempts at reform and innovation are frustrated by mandated bottom-up curricula, skill-based materials, and analytic and standardized testing policies. Creative and dedicated teachers often feel frustrated in their own attempts to make schooling more responsive to the needs of children.

Betsy sees other factors that threaten the implementation of whole language. Among these are the lack of appropriate materials. Betsy has indicated that she has spent "a lot of money on books and materials for my room." The attitudes of teachers who have not kept up with the research or who refuse to even consider change are another concern. Scheduling problems often result in the breakup of the morning into short time blocks which makes it difficult to plan for lengthy periods of study. The overcrowded curriculum and the simple lack of time to cover the various aspects of the curriculum make implementing a whole language curriculum extremely difficult.

But perhaps the greatest challenge to Betsy's further growth as a whole language teacher is herself. She recognizes that it is her own fear of failure and her own reluctance to give up complete control of the classroom as the greatest threat to further implementation of a whole language curriculum. She realizes she has come a long way from her tradition-bound approach to teaching reading and she recognizes she still has room to grow. She says that she feels pulled in two directions—by what is expected of her and by her desire to do what she believes is right for her students. Such conflict is real and must be dealt with every day. Betsy even feels that her occasional "laziness" ("whole language is hard work"), her lack of confidence in herself as a capable teacher, and a personal feeling of disorganization tend to weaken her resolve for whole language.

Betsy doubts that she will ever become a complete whole language teacher. She sees herself as being on a journey toward a whole language orientation. And, even though she continues to grow toward that orientation, she feels and expects that she will never stop changing, growing, and learning as a teacher and a person.

SUMMING UP

Betsy is a concerned, caring, and competent teacher who, like most elementary teachers, has used a basal reading series as the focal point to her reading curriculum. She wasn't always a whole language teacher. Yet, over time and through thoughtful reflection, she came to the conclusion that the approach she was employing was not meeting the needs of her students nor the goals of the school curriculum.

Betsy's is a story of a teacher who made a conscious and very personal decision to alter fundamentally her orientation and approach to reading and writing education. She is not a born whole language teacher. As such, she is familiar with change and views change as a necessary part of her instructional philosophy.

Betsy acknowledges that she may not be as whole language oriented as other teachers. Indeed, she still employs basal readers for some lessons. However, when measuring her development as a whole language teacher, she sees how far she has come and how far she has yet to go. Her commitment to whole language is not based primarily on philosophical or theoretical issues but rather it is rooted in her pragmatic desire to provide the very best instruction for her students.

Betsy's movement toward whole language is perhaps the most common way teachers come to whole language. Dissatisfaction with the status quo leads teachers to question the assumptions upon which the traditional approaches rest and to consider more promising alternatives.

To become a teacher like Betsy requires courage to change and dedication, perseverance, and hard work to see the change through. But, most of all, teachers like Betsy are reflective. They constantly monitor their own performance and seek answers to questions that arise from their reflection. Reflective teachers recognize when and where change is required. Change is not made for change's sake: It is made to improve teaching and learning in the classroom.

QUESTIONS FOR REFLECTION AND DISCUSSION: EARLY CHILDHOOD CLASSROOMS

1. Working in an early childhood setting is different from regular elementary schools. How does Dona's teaching compare with traditional and whole language teaching done in the primary grades? What is similar and what are the major differences? What are the major themes or concepts that Dona attempts to nurture and develop in her students?

2. In early childhood classes, most children are not reading in the conventional sense. How does Dona explore, nurture, and promote literacy learning with her students? Do all her literacy related activities deal with books and/or printed texts? Describe ways in which she promotes literacy development without the use of print?

Multi-Grade Primary Classroom

3. Sylvia sees her teaching as a way to make a better world. In what ways does Sylvia connect to the world outside the school? How does Sylvia help students become better persons?

4. In what ways does Sylvia use drama and dramatic play in the classroom? What does drama foster in students in addition to an appreciation of drama itself? What other ways might it be used that have not been discussed in this case?

First-Grade Classroom

5. Betsy makes a conscious attempt to be sensitive to the needs, concerns, and interests of her students. In what ways does Betsy make this desire a reality? To what extent do you feel she is successful in being a sensitive teacher? What else might she do?

6. Betsy sees herself as "still becoming" the whole language teacher she wants to be. What else does she need to do or accomplish in order to become a complete whole language teacher? Will she ever reach a point where she will consider her development complete? Why?

Comparisons Across the Primary and Early Childhood Grades

1. Compare and contrast the instruction offered by the three primary teachers? How are they alike? How do they differ? And, as a group, how do they differ from traditional literacy instruction? In your opinion, which is closest to the ideal of a whole language teacher? Why?

2. Teachers come to whole language in different ways. Review the ways the primary teachers described in the previous cases were drawn to whole language. Consider your own journey into whole language. How did you first learn about whole language? What do you think is the next step in your development? Share your responses in a group of three or four colleagues.

3. Critically analyze the teaching strategies of teachers in the previous cases. For each of the teachers list potential areas of instructional strength and concern? How might each teacher modify her instruction to overcome the perceived concerns?

4. Compare and contrast the philosophies of instruction held by each teacher? On what does each teacher focus? How do the philosophies described in the preceding cases compare with what you value in education?

5. Each teacher makes a concerted effort to involve parents in her students' literacy development. What principles guide each teacher's home-school literacy efforts? What would your ideal home-school program look like? What principle would it be based on?

III

MATURING . . .

Whole language teaching transcends primary education in the elementary school, even though emphasis in articles and books often is on the emerging development of writing and reading beginners. As young literacy learners develop fluency, competence, and confidence with written language, there are increasing demands to use literacy toward purposeful ends. They are in a process of maturing as readers and writers.

How do whole language teachers work with maturing readers and writers? The cases that follow tell the stories of third-, fourth-, and fifth-grade teachers who ply their craft in similar but different ways as they help children to grow in their ability to use language effectively. As you read the stories of these teachers, reflect on the ways in which they enact curriculum and create classroom environments that allow children to continue maturing as literate individuals.

Chapter 5

WHOLE LANGUAGE IN THIRD GRADE

"I'm Not Yet Where I Want To Be."

Eight-thirty Monday morning: Dusty, one of twenty-nine children in Gay Fawcett's third-grade class, walks quietly into the classroom before the start of school. Gay is busy getting ready for the day, her back to the child, as she writes a poem on a large sheet of paper at the chart stand. She doesn't hear Dusty enter the room as he walks quietly toward her. With an enthusiastic, "GOOD MORNING, Mrs. Fawcett . . . ," he greets his teacher, sheepishly grinning, as he unwittingly startles her.

"Dusty," Gay says as she quickly regains her composure, "You know how to wake up a person in the morning!" Dusty is apologetic, "Sorry, Mrs. Fawcett, but I wanted to tell you about the game on Saturday." Dusty plays in the Pee Wee Football league. Gay takes the time to listen to Dusty's recount of the game. She's genuinely pleased for him and wants to know more. They talk for a couple of minutes. Then Dusty goes to his desk and takes out a looseleaf notebook—his journal. "I'm going to write about it before school starts," he tells his teacher. "I want Mike to read it."

And so begins another week in Gay Fawcett's third-grade class. She teachers in a suburban school district in Northeastern Ohio. Most of the children in Gay's class, like Dusty, are bussed to the school. The morning scene in front of Gay's school, is fairly typical of most suburban schools. Her school is a one-story brick building, built in the 1950s, with a circular drive in front. About one-half hour before school starts, the ubiquitous yellow buses roll into the driveway, several at a time, staggered a few minutes apart according to schedule.

The children in Gay's class begin meandering into the room at about the time that Dusty arrived, thirty minutes or so before the morning announcements and the attendance check. During this time, they are free to socialize with other students or with the teacher, write in their journals, read books of choice, share writing with one another, or work on assignments in progress. After several minutes of socializing, most of the children settle into a literacy activity of one kind or another, naturally and without prodding. This is one of many "literacy rituals" that have become part of the culture of Gay's classroom.

Gay has been teaching for fourteen years, mostly in kindergarten and first grade. For the past several years, however, she has taught in third grade because she wanted the challenge of working with children at a different stage of development in their literacy learning.

Asked whether she would characterize herself as a whole language teacher, Gay nods affirmatively but is quick to note that she is in transition, "I know I'm not yet where I want to be." Her transformation to whole language teaching hasn't occurred overnight. She has witnessed gradual changes in the way she thinks about literacy learning and the way she puts her thinking into practice in the classroom. Each year she broadens her philosophical perspective. As Gay explains, "Whole language reflects my philosophy. Each year I gradually incorporate more and more of what I believe is right for children."

Gay has always had an intuitive feel for teaching in ways that have become associated with whole language. Yet what she believed intuitively often ran counter to what she had learned when she was studying to be a teacher as well as to the expectations of some of the school administrators for whom she has worked.

Her first teaching assignment was in a traditional, conservative community. According to Gay, the parents, the teachers with whom she worked, and her principal held narrow views of what it meant to teach reading and language skills. So she struggled through her first several years as a teacher using a basal reading program, "even though my first graders were bored and I was bored." After several years, Gay decided to use the basal program selectively, as an anthology of stories, not as a system of instruction for which it is intended.

She still does to some extent. The district in which Gay currently works mandates the use of basals in the elementary school as part of board of education policy. Yet she has learned to work within the context of the mandate in a manner consistent with her beliefs. Although obligated to use a basal reader, she strengthens and enriches children's participation in stories through the use of "real" books in three overlapping instructional contexts which will be described in greater detail later in the case: (1) sustained silent reading (SSR), (2) a literature-based program that Gay conducts as a reading workshop, and (3) the use of literature in content areas. In addition, she integrates reading and writing throughout the school day through a writing workshop, and the use of journals, poetry notebooks, and learning logs.

Gay credits her sense of inquiry as a factor in her growth as a whole language teacher. She never thought of herself as a researcher until recently, but that's just how she would describe herself today: "I like to explore what happens in my classroom. The more I understand, the more I want to know. The kids in my class are my teachers."

Gay does not view whole language as a series of methods and techniques. She stresses the importance of having a set of beliefs to guide her actions in the classroom. What worries her is when teachers talk about whole language as a method, without recognizing that it involves the way one thinks about children, learning, and education in general.

WHAT GAY THINKS ABOUT WHOLE LANGUAGE

Gay's philosophical stance has evolved over time. Today she is comfortable with the label "whole language teacher," although she has a personal bias against labels, whether applied to children, teachers, or people in general. She would rather think of herself as a teacher, nothing more or less. For Gay, being a teacher means that she plays a nurturing role in the lives of children. She serves children best when she brings out the best in them.

From a whole language perspective, Gay recognizes that language is a tool. Her job is to show children how to use language, as they would any tool, "to get things done; to accomplish goals." To this end, she wants them to recognize the meaningfulness of language and literacy in their lives.

As Gay reflects on her first years as a teacher, she realizes "I think there was a whole language teacher somewhere inside of me all along. I found ways to do things that I and the children enjoyed." One facet of Gay's philosophy that has emerged over the years is that literacy learning should be fun, not drudgery. As she puts it, the teaching that she enjoys always results in children's active participation and involvement.

When she first started teaching, Gay did things that she really believed in, but didn't know why: "I seemed to have an intuitive sense of what my students needed, but I also felt somewhat guilty because these fun activities might be taking time away from skills." With each year, however, her guilt pangs have subsided as she witnesses children reading and writing with confidence and competence.

Gay approaches teaching as a learner. Her curiosity over how children learn to read and write fuels a desire to know more about language and literacy processes. She recalls vividly the time in her professional development when she first began to read about emergent literacy and became fascinated with the work of New Zealand and Australian educators. At about the same time, she started attending workshops and conferences on the writing process and reading comprehension. Advances in the way educators were thinking about reading and writing left her thirsting for more knowledge. Today, she pursues doctoral studies in literacy at Kent State University.

Gay's philosophy of whole language is reflected in the way she interacts with her children during literacy lessons. They read and write for "lots" of reasons—to learn, to enjoy, to inform, to reflect, to laugh, to cry, to participate. But Gay also believes that children must become consciously aware of literacy processes. And this means building healthy concepts of reading, writing, speaking, and listening. Throughout the year, she and her students discuss what it means to be a reader, writer, listener, and speaker.

For example, Gay helps her children explore and refine their concepts of reading throughout the year. Several years ago, she was struck by the findings of a research study indicating that fewer than 10 percent of elementary students surveyed in the study gave a meaning-related response to the question, "What is reading?" Surprised by the finding, she searched the literature for additional studies on children's concepts of reading only to find similar results. At the beginning of the next school year, she decided to survey her own students only to find that their answers to the query were similar to those of their young counterparts in the research studies.

Gay realized then what is now a guiding principle in her work with students: *Children learn in the presence of the company they keep.* In other words, as a teacher she realizes that she exercises incredible influence over the way children think about and use literacy toward purposeful ends. Today, Gay weaves into her literacy lessons various kinds of interactions with children to ensure that they understand that reading *does not mean* sounding out words, doing worksheets, or spending forty-five minutes on a subject in school. From the very beginning of the school year, she involves her class in *process discussions,* often no more than ten minutes in length, to help students reflect on what it means to be literate. And in doing so, the class as a whole invariably wrestles with the questions, "What is reading? What is writing?" Through conversations about reading and writing, children grow in their understandings of reading and writing as meaning-making processes, the relationship of the reader to the writer, how reading and writing are alike and how they are different, and what reading and writing are for.

Soon the students in Gay's class believe they have a corner on some unique information that none of the other students in the school have. Gay once heard one of her students on the playground during recess ask a third grader from another class, "What do you think reading is?" Even the cafeteria supervisor, when handed lunch money, could not escape the question from Gay's students. The high point, however, came when the

president of a nearby university visited her class during a career awareness unit. After his presentation on the role of a university president, he
encouraged the students to ask questions. When one student asked what
job he would like to have if he were not a university president, his reply
surprised the class: "A first-grade teacher because the most important
thing one human being can do for others is teach them to read."

At that point, the hands went up. One girl asked, "Since you want to be
a teacher, then what is reading?" The president was caught by surprise
and responded to the question as best he could. The excited student listened to the president's response and then answered her own question:
"Let me tell you what I think. Reading is putting your own experience
with what the author tells you to get meaning." Needless to say, the president was impressed.

What Gay has come to believe with a passion is that children need to
develop knowledge and awareness of how to solve problems when they
are engaged in a literacy event. Later in the case, we will explore process
discussions as they relate to Gay's role as a model. These discussions
build knowledge and awareness of literacy strategies and help students to
monitor what they are reading and writing. They occur frequently in
Gay's class, because she believes that children learn not only by doing
but also from demonstrations and self-reflection.

INSIDE GAY'S CLASSROOM

The Environment

In many ways, the physical arrangement of Gay's room reflects her philosophy. Here's a room that's fun to enter. It's alive. Signs of literacy
learning are everywhere. Gay's desk is against the wall in a back corner:
"The only time I sit at it is when the students are out of the room attending a 'special' such as music or gym class." The students' desks are arranged in a U-shape, as indicated in Figure 5.1, with a large area in the
middle for informal class meetings, discussions, stories, and team work.
Key areas toward the back of the room are earmarked for learning centers
and a reading corner.

The room is print-rich. Displays of children's work are evident on bulletin board areas around the room. Students are responsible, for the most
part, for the content of the bulletin boards and for decorating them. One

Figure 5.1
Physical Arrangement in Gay's Classroom

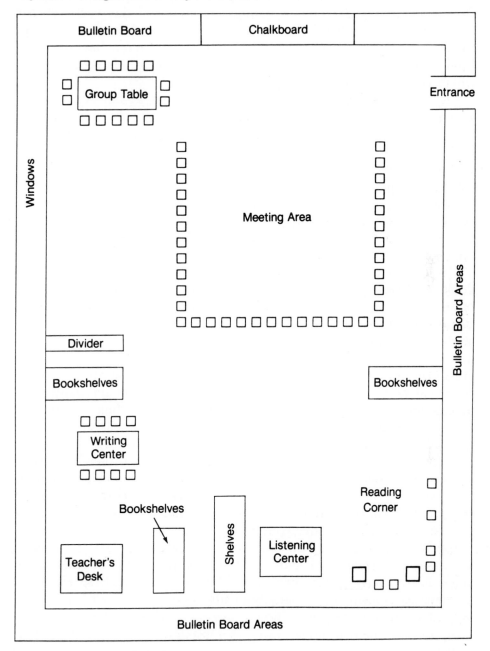

displays art work; another shows a collage of pictures and captions cut out of magazines and newspapers, depicting a particular theme that the class is studying; still another features an "author of the week," chosen from among the students. The walls often turn into "word walls." They are covered with words, stories, and poems. The room has a kind of lived-in look to it that proclaims to all who enter it: Here's a room in which I'd like to spend my time learning.

Each student gets a chance to be featured as the "author of the week." When selected for the honor, the student is responsible for arranging the board, which consists of the child's photograph, self-selected pieces of writing, and art work related to the pieces.

Poetry abounds in the room. Gay's love and enthusiasm for poetry rubs off on her students. She weaves poems into thematic units and literacy lessons whenever the opportunity arises. Poetry posters adorn the walls, and a chart stand holds poems printed on large paper. The students are free to read these poems throughout the day and often can be seen reading them chorally.

"Tons and tons" of books occupy every nook and cranny of the room. Books are everywhere—in the reading corner, on bookshelves throughout the room, on cabinet tops, and window ledges. The reading corner is furnished with beanbags, pillows, stuffed book characters made by the students, reading posters, and, of course, shelves teaming with books. In addition to several shelves of books that help to define the reading corner area, Gay has a shelf of books located near her desk that are part of her "personal favorites" collection. She uses the collection for daily read-alouds and to entice students to choose books for reading or rereading once they have been introduced in the read-alouds.

In addition to the reading corner, several learning centers are situated in the room including a listening center and a writing center. The listening center is stocked with audio cassettes for simultaneous listening/reading of stories. The writing center consists of tools for writing and for drawing, various kinds of paper, a computer for word processing, a publishing area, and student-published books.

Gay's room is neither still nor silent. The social context of the room is marked by a steady hub-bub of activity, punctuated with quiet, sometimes lively, conversation throughout the day. Nevertheless, a spirit of cooperation permeates the room. Students often work in pairs or in teams when they are involved in writing or reading workshop activity. A major component of the reading workshop, for example, involves team study of fictional and informational books. Based on their interest in a topic or a

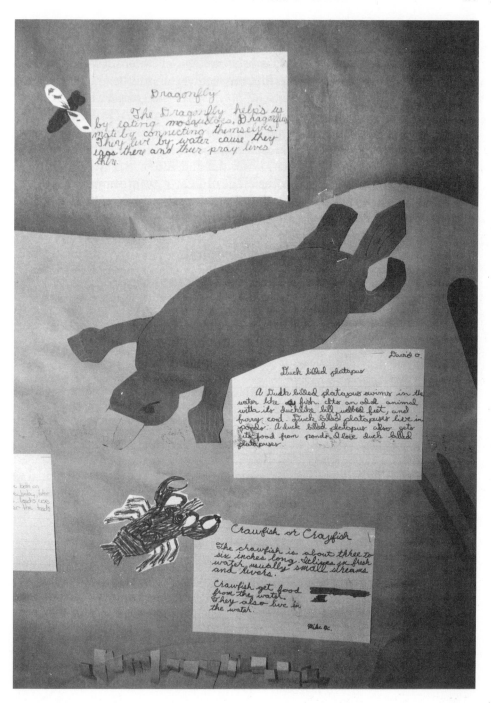

Dragonfly

The Dragonfly helps us by eating mosquitoes. Dragonflies mate by connecting themselves. They live by water cause they eggs there and their pray lives there.

Duck billed platapus

A Duck billed platapus swims in the water like a fish. It's an odd animal with its ducklike bill, webbed feet, and furry coat. Duck billed platapuses live in ponds. A duck billed platapus also gets its food from ponds. I love duck billed platapuses.

David O.

Crawfish or Crayfish

The crawfish is about three to six inches long. It lives in fresh water usually small streams and rivers.

Crawfish get food from the water. They also live in the water.

Mike Oc.

story, a team, usually ranging in size from three to six students, selects a book to read and then participates in a variety of composing and comprehending activities.

The activities vary from team to team, but throughout the collaborative environment that exists in the room, children can be observed in conversation that often involves debate and critical thought. To illustrate, study three brief verbal exchanges that occurred between Louis and Matthew, two members of a team studying an informational book on living things in the Earth's biosphere.

When a team selects a book for reading, the team members are expected to share what they already know about the topic before reading and then predict what they think the book will be about. Gay has demonstrated what good readers do before reading in mini-lessons that model the question-asking strategy, "What do I already know? What do I think the book will be about?"

Matthew: (*studying a text illustration*) Whales have smooth skin.

Louis: No, hair.

Matthew: They have smooth skin.

Louis: How do you know? You never petted one.

Matthew: I know that. But I saw Shamu at Sea World and his skin looked pretty smooth to me.

Louis: Whatever it is, we should find out because it says here (as he points to a heading in the text) "Characteristics of Whales."

(After reading a text passage, children are expected to engage in discussion or a comprehension activity. Louis and Matthew exchange thoughts related to how a clever monkey escapes the clutches of a tiger.)

Matthew: I would say he's lucky. Do you think he's lucky.

Louis: I think he's smart because he got out of all that danger.

Matthew: He's lucky because the tiger didn't bite him.

(Upon finishing the book . . .)

Matthew: This book's pretty much about nature, don't you think?

Louis: You just gave me an idea. We're living things and trees are living things, too.

When participating in cooperative teams, students demonstrate a high degree of on-task behavior and verbal interaction. Gay encourages a social environment based on the principles of cooperative learning, because she believes in the importance of shaping ideas through talk.

Beginning the School Year: The First Day, a Special Day

Gay introduces her students to literacy at the beginning of the school year in a highly personal and unique manner. Her first literacy lesson is one of the more memorable ones for the class. It revolves around a Christmas gift that she received from her mother several years ago. Much to Gay's delight, her mother surprised her with one of the best gifts that she has ever received, her "old red notebook" long forgotten from childhood. Gay hadn't seen the worn-out, overstuffed red notebook for more than twenty years. Between the covers of the notebook were those wonderful, creative, misspelled stories that Gay had written as a child. She was about eight years old when she wrote her first story, "Hankie and the Hawk." Story after story, now yellowed with time, filled the notebook. When her students returned from Christmas vacation, Gay couldn't wait to share her childhood stories with them.

Since then, Gay introduces her students to literacy the first half-hour of the first day of school with the "old red notebook." The notebook is the centerpiece of a strategy she uses to establish a sense of community in her class and to invite students to enter the world of reading and writing.

The literacy lesson is quite different from what the third graders in Gay's class typically expect to happen in the first half-hour of the first day of school. Upon completion of the morning announcements and the attendance report, Gay asks the class to gather in the meeting area. They sit on the carpeted floor around Gay, who occupies the "Author's Chair." As the children settle into a quiet, anticipatory mood, Gay opens the old red notebook and begins reading a story. At first, the children are confused. They're expecting Gay to pass out books, to recite the "rules of the classroom"—when to sharpen pencils, go to the lavatory, and the like.

Instead, Gay reads them a story that sounds like something they would write. They notice that the old red notebook is falling apart, the pages are yellow, and the teacher is grinning with satisfaction as she reads. Soon a few of the students' faces begin to light up with recognition as their teacher reads the author's name with each story: "Hankie and the Hawk" by Miss Gay Wilson, April 3, 1957; "How the Pig Got a Curly Tail" by

Miss Gay Wilson, December 10, 1959; "Sue's Birthday" by Miss Gay Wilson, February 21, 1958." The dates and the surname "Wilson" carry little meaning for the students, but a few recognize the name "Gay" and catch on to the teacher's gambit: "These must be stories the teacher wrote when she was a little girl!"

The students are amazed. Gay describes the scene this way, "I wish I could capture in words the looks on their faces as they realize that I'm reading my childhood stories to them. Sheer delight isn't descriptive enough!" After twenty minutes of reading from the old red notebook, Gay puts the book on one of the bookshelves in the reading corner, as the children beg for one more story to be read. Gay promises more another day. She tells the students that there are enough stories to read a new one each day.

Gay then springboards into a discussion of reading and writing in the class. She establishes a covenant with the students as she opens up the discussion: "Everyday this year each of you will get to write and read." She makes a distinction with the children between "getting to write" and "having to write." As Gay reflects, "I want them to feel the specialness of this promise."

What happens next? The class writes. According to Gay, no one declines the invitation to write. Gay models for the students what she is thinking about writing by telling them some of the topics that are on her mind right now. She then invites the students to share some of the topics they are thinking about, or have strong feelings about. On a sheet of paper, which eventually will be attached to the insides of their writing folders, she encourages students to make a list of possible topics: "Things To Write About." No one in the class says, "I don't know what to write." Of course, not all students write immediately. Some draw. Some "conference" with Gay individually to "brainstorm" ideas with her.

What happens after the writing period has elapsed? The class reads. Gay invites children to participate in a "group share" where children have an opportunity to read their drafts and to share what they have written with others. After the first child reads, Gay responds, and in doing so, she models the behavior of a good listener and responder. First, she "mirrors" the content of the piece by telling what it is about. She then tells the writer what she admired about the piece, focusing her praise on some aspect of the writing that she genuinely liked. Next, if she is confused by some aspect of the writing, Gay will ask a question to seek clarification from the writer about the piece. When Gay completes her response, she encourages children to follow suit. Most simply tell what they like about another writer's piece. Gay then encourages them to ask a question if there was something in the writing that they didn't understand.

The group share ends after fifteen minutes. To conclude the class's first literacy lesson, Gay and the students talk about the author inside each one of them and what it means to be a writer. She then proposes three simple "rules" for everyday writing in their class:

1. Each day there will be time for writing. A writer can begin a new piece or continue to work on a piece that has already been started.
2. When writing, a writer is not to be disturbed. There will be lots of time set aside for working together.
3. A writer saves all drafts of work, either in a journal or in a writing folder.

The class discusses each rule; Gay clarifies terminology that arises during discussion, for example, *journal, writing folder, a draft.* She then distributes writing folders and acquaints students with the "writer's cabinet" where folders are kept on file. Over the next several weeks, Gay reveals various facets of the "writing workshop" that will occur throughout the year. On the first day, however, she is concerned with creating strong expectations.

A Typical Day

From morning through afternoon the students in Gay's class use language and literacy toward purposeful ends. She plans lessons within two large blocks of time, as indicated in Figure 5.2. In the morning block, she enacts an integrated language/literacy curriculum around the following events: shared and guided learning experiences, sustained silent reading (SSR), and the writing workshop. In the afternoon block, the students use language to learn as they explore concepts and themes from content area textbooks as well as from narrative and informational books that support and extend learning.

A typical day begins with morning announcements, attendance check, and a lunch count. At 9:05 A.M., Gay usually begins the morning with a shared book experience. The students gather in the meeting area for a

Figure 5.2
Time Block

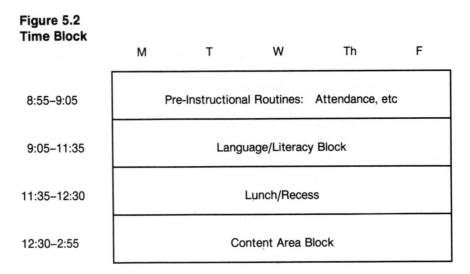

	M	T	W	Th	F
8:55–9:05	Pre-Instructional Routines: Attendance, etc				
9:05–11:35	Language/Literacy Block				
11:35–12:30	Lunch/Recess				
12:30–2:55	Content Area Block				

read-aloud. Gay calls this time "listening for fun (LFF) time. She does not make LFF too instructional. Often, she will ask no more than one or two prediction-type questions during the course of the reading. And she does so because the questions fit naturally within the flow of the story and sustain students' interest.

LFF creates an attitude—a frame of mind—for literacy. At other times during the day, Gay reads aloud from narrative and informational texts, but often within a larger context—a planned literacy lesson. LFF, however, says to students that at the onset of each school day they can enjoy a literacy experience on its own terms—as a source of pleasure, learning, wonder, and enchantment.

The shared book experience takes no more than fifteen minutes and is followed by group instruction. Gay calls the first of three groups for guided learning, which she describes as a time when children can think critically about "strategies" for reading and learning. She distinguishes between guided learning and independent learning. Both are important, Gay believes, in a whole language classroom. As part of guided learning instruction, she teaches strategically in small groups to build students' concepts of reading and writing, makes them aware of skills and strategies in the context of their use, and develops vocabulary in context. She directs learning by raising questions, explaining and demonstrating strategies, and facilitating discussions.

During independent learning situations, on the other hand, her role is more subtle. Informal teaching opportunities occur frequently when children participate in writing and reading workshop activities which encourage independent learning. In these situations, Gay serves as a coach and resource for students as they work on their own or in teams.

Gay will choose stories from books and the district-mandated basal for guided learning. She accepts the use of a basal as an anthology of stories, although she recognizes that the basal is anathema to some whole language advocates. However, she presents stories from a holistic, rather than an atomistic, perspective. If a story from a basal isn't worth reading because it is a nonstory, lacking a predictable structure and/or meaningful content, Gay skips it.

When using the basal as an anthology, she groups children flexibly by need and by the nature of the activity. Grouping practices often result in multi-ability level groups. When Gay is working with a group, she assigns seatwork for the remainder of the class. Seatwork consists of children reading books of choice and then writing about what they are reading in one of their learning logs—a "literature response log." The seatwork activities give children about 45 minutes a morning, not including SSR, to explore and respond to books they have selected. If children finish seatwork early, they are free to work at one of the learning centers in the room.

Sustained silent reading (SSR) follows guided learning. SSR is a regular feature of the literacy/language block. The strategy consists of 15 minutes of uninterrupted, sustained reading of self-selected texts and five to ten minutes of follow-up in which children share what they have been reading. SSR builds patience with print. It habituates children to reading—to sticking with print—and contributes to their development as silent readers.

When Gay announces SSR, some of the students make a mad dash to the reading corner to capture a beanbag or a pillow. Others sprawl out on the floor or find an inviting spot at one of the learning centers. The class settles into silent reading quickly. Gay settles into reading, also—an adult novel, introduced to her by the principal of the school.

Follow-up is an important component of the SSR program in Gay's class. Students share what they have been reading. This allows Gay to make some informal assessments as they retell their stories. Do the students have a sense of story? Do they relate what they are reading to their personal lives? She often encourages class members to predict what will happen next in a story that someone is telling about.

Occasionally during follow-up, Gay invites children to explore the process of silent reading and the strategies they use to stick with print:

Gay:	We've talked a lot about what makes a good reader. I want to tell you one more thing that good readers do, because it is something that I did today during SSR. Good readers know that you don't read everything the same way. They know when to read fast, when to slow down, when to read at a normal speed, and when to read something over again if it doesn't make sense. Did any of you notice yourselves changing your rate of reading?
Seth:	I was reading *The Boxcar Children* for the second time. I read it faster this time because I already know it.
Jeff:	I had to start reading faster because I saw that SSR was almost over, and I wanted to finish my chapter.
Gay:	Did anyone have to slow down?
Tia:	I came to some words I didn't know. I had to slow down to make sure I didn't miss anything.
Gay:	Last night in my college class, I was reading about "the symbolic interactionism paradigm in qualitative research." Do you think I read about that slowly or fast?
Several Children:	Slow!
Gay:	That's right! When material is hard, you have to read slowly. Can you think of materials that you sometimes need to read slowly?
Renee:	Social Studies.
Martha:	Science.
Josh:	Not me. I know lots of science from my dad so I can read it fast.
Gay:	Good point, Josh! Your background—what you know already—should help you decide whether to read fast, slow, or average. Now you know one more thing that good readers do.

On other occasions, Gay initiates follow-up conversations on what it means to concentrate during silent reading, why a reader may have found it easy to read a story one day and hard to follow it the next day, when to read for the "big ideas" and when to read for "details."

Upon completing SSR, the class moves into the writing workshop. Gay, as we described earlier, devotes the first morning of the school year to laying the groundwork for the writing workshop. Thereafter, the writing workshop follows SSR, and runs for about an hour every day of the week. The workshop invites students to engage in many kinds of writing experiences and allows Gay to integrate spelling and language skills development as children work through the writing process.

The workshop follows a predictable structure: a mini-lesson, writing time, and a group share. The mini-lesson serves many purposes. It may be as brief as two minutes or as long as ten minutes depending on the focus of the lesson. For example, Gay often uses the mini-lesson to have children tell about their plans for writing, the topics they are working on, or the problems they are having with a piece. On other occasions, she will use the lesson to brainstorm topics, or teach a skill in context.

For example, in one mini-lesson Gay spent several minutes explaining and demonstrating how contractions work in written language. The students were in the process of writing poems for their poetry notebook. The drafts of their poems indicated to Gay that the students might benefit from a discussion of the use of contractions. As a result, she used part of the mini-lesson to illustrate how and why a popular children's poet, Shel Silverstein, used contractions in his work. To accomplish this, she made overhead transparencies of several of Silverstein's poems. In unison, the students read a poem aloud and then talked about how the sound and rhythm of a poem might contribute to its meaning. They also discussed how contractions help to make written language informal and to sound like everyday talk. With a marking pen, Gay focused on the poet's use of contractions. What is a contraction? Why did the poet use contractions? How did the contractions help the poem? Then the students looked at their own drafts and were encouraged to find instances where they had used contractions or where a contraction might work for them just as effectively as it did for Silverstein. The contraction lesson helped many of the students polish their drafts, thereby facilitating an editing/revision of their poems.

During the writing workshop, the children and Gay write daily in journals. The journal is where first draft writing takes place. When the students are writing in their journals, so is Gay, at least for the first five to ten minutes of writing time. She will then circulate around the room or conduct conferences with individuals or groups. Sometimes the children respond to one another's journal entries in writing and orally. Other times Gay responds.

If writing in the journal goes beyond a first draft, children store their work in writing folders. Multi-draft pieces are for works to be published in one form or another: Individual and class books, the poetry notebook, letters to pen pals in Nebraska, pieces for the weekly newsletter to parents, writing for bulletin board displays, dialogue for skits, and research reports, are just a few of the forms published works take.

Toward the end of each writing workshop, Gay calls the class together for approximately ten to fifteen minutes of sharing. Children use this time to share a piece of writing or a draft in progress. A child sits in the "author's chair" to read the piece to the class for feedback and response.

After lunch and recess, the students engage in content area studies in which they use language and literacy to learn. Gay uses content area textbooks as a resource to provide a foundation for concept learning. She expects students to use textbooks as a tool for learning. Her lessons show them how to do so effectively.

What the class is studying in a content area textbook often becomes a springboard for reading and writing. Textbook study, for example, frequently provides a pathway into narrative and informational books to extend and broaden 'students' understanding of concepts introduced in a textbook. A unit on frogs in science leads children naturally to the *Toad and Frog* books and a wonderful collection of informational books on frogs that Gay has compiled from the public library and the school's library.

In addition, the students keep content area journals, which Gay calls *learning logs,* to explore and react to ideas they are studying. Unlike the journals that the students use during the writing workshop, where they are free to choose their own topics for writing, learning logs help students explore topics that are under study. More often than not, Gay poses a question or suggests the topic about which students will write.

Organization and Management

A typical day of language and literacy instruction mirrors Gay's organizational scheme. Figure 5.3 captures how she allocates time for the

Figure 5.3
Time Allocation in Language/Literacy Block

	M	T	W	Th	F
8:55–9:05	Pre-Instructional Routines				
9:05–10:35	Guided Learning	→→→→			Reading Workshop
10:35–11:00	Sustained Silent Reading	→→→→			
11:00–11:55	Writing Workshop	→→→→→			

recurring events in her language/literacy block. On Friday, as the chart in Figure 5.3 indicates, the underlying organizational plan changes to accommodate the reading workshop.

Gay replaces group instruction and SSR with the reading workshop, a literature-based program built upon the following principles: (1) self-selection, (2) multi-level grouping, (3) cooperative learning, (4) critical thinking, and (5) authentic texts representing quality children's literature. Students read their books prior to Friday, during the week's seatwork, SSR, and at home; then they meet on Friday in small groups for book discussions and meaning-centered activities.

The reading workshop works this way: Each Friday, Gay introduces several books to the class. If a book is fictional, she builds interest in the story by overviewing its plot, acquainting the students with characters, and reading parts of the story aloud. If the book is informational, she builds anticipation for ideas also by overviewing content, reading aloud, and showing the students several illustrations from the text. The students then select books, which are to be read by the following Friday. Teams form, not by ability level, but by the titles children select for the following week's workshop.

Teams usually vary in size from two to six students. During the week, each team member reads the book. Gay encourages the students to help one another with difficult words or if they experience any other problems while reading. On Friday, the teams meet in the workshop for one hour for book discussions that revolve around an activity guide, such as the one illustrated in the box. The activity guide involves students in oral

---

Activity Sheet for Reading Workshop

A Horse for Matthew Allen
by Virginia Kester Smiley

Cooperative Learning Activities

1. Find a page in the story that shows how a character feels. Each person in your group should read the page you have found, identify the feeling, and tell what clues the author gave you to describe the character's feelings.

2. Write 3 questions about the story. Each person in your group should have a turn to ask his/her questions.

3. Use the context to define these words:

   platform (p.10):

   C'mon (p.8):

   bolt (p.10):

   buggy (p.18):

4. Map the story.

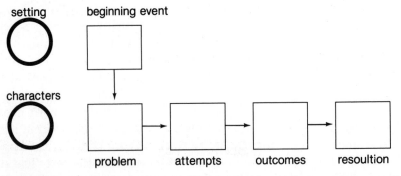

5. If you were the author, would you have written a different ending for the story? Write the ending that you would have had for the story.

reading with a purpose, response writing, semantic mapping, and other meaning-centered activities. As children participate in team activity, Gay circulates around the room. When teams complete their discussions, the whole class gets together for a debriefing session. Each team tells about their book and what they have learned from the experience. Gay also introduces several new titles for next week's workshop. The children then make new selections and form new teams based on their choices.

How does Gay manage her practice? First, she acknowledges that she must be organized: "A whole language classroom like mine needs to be well organized. I spend a great deal of time networking kids into various groups for guided reading and finding books and resources that will develop specific concepts and themes that I teach." Also, Gay feels it's important to teach the students to be organized. She spends time early in the year to "walk students through" the writing and reading workshops to make sure they understand their responsibilities and how to work together in teams.

One rule guides the management of Gay's classroom: Be kind to others. Her behavioral problems are minimal, she suggests, because of the meaningfulness of the activity in which children engage. As Gay suggests, "I respect my students as learners, and they respect me." She is direct in her interaction with children, letting them know how she feels or why something needs to be attended to.

Gay uses conversation as a management tool to solve problems. For example, during SSR children are bound to talk, and on occasion, interact with one another. According to Gay, "The second S in SSR, *Silent*, is a goal that she encourages but doesn't adhere to rigidly." The students sometimes slip into their own adaptation of SSR, which the class labeled SBR, "Sustained Buddy Reading." Two students, for example, may ask to take turns reading riddles to one another from a book of riddles. "It's only natural that "buddy readers" interact with one another as they are reading," Gay explains. Her comments to the class at the end of SSR early in the school year illustrates how conversation serves as a management tool.

Gay: Today, while we were doing SSR, it wasn't totally silent. I heard some giggling. I looked up and saw Chris reading a joke book. I couldn't ask Chris to be quiet. You're supposed to laugh when you read jokes. Reading is fun! If I see someone laughing over a good book, that's fine too. I won't ask you to be quiet because that wouldn't be "real" reading. I saw something else. Jason had a good book and he decided to share it with Bill. They were talking about the book. It's great to share a good book with a friend. Ms. Schofield (the principal) gave me the book that I was reading today because she thought I would enjoy it. Our goal is to try to keep SSR as silent as we can so that people can concentrate, but sometimes, it's just not possible to be totally silent.

Gay's comments, while focusing on a potential problem, set a positive tone, and demonstrated to the children her flexibility. The comments led to a brief process discussion that revolved around the importance of concentrating while reading silently.

Strategies

Gay's classroom practice mirrors her philosophical stance. In this section, we focus on strategies that support Gay's role as a model and a facilitator. Through discussion and demonstration, Gay models how literacy works for her, an adult who is an expert reader and writer. She invites students to become aware of and conversant with literacy processes within the context of exploring meaning through language use.

Strategies Related to Gay's Role as a Model.   Gay effectively uses discussion strategies to "strip away some of the mysteries of literacy" by helping students to develop insights into reading and writing strategies. These discussion strategies build and strengthen students' self-knowledge. As Gay puts it, "I want children to become aware of themselves as readers and writers. I want them to know that they can use a variety of strategies, depending on the nature of the literacy activity and the context in which it takes place."

In the process of helping students build knowledge of self, Gay also recognizes that "kids need to know how to use reading and writing strategies." As a result, many of her literacy lessons initiate *how to* discussions—for example, how to revise the opening of a piece of writing to make it more interesting to a reader; how to make predictions during reading. Not only do these discussions develop a sense of how to use strategies, but they also are designed to make students aware of *when* and *why* to use strategies to solve problems encountered in a literacy event. For example, why is it important to skip a difficult word and keep on reading or reread a passage if it doesn't make sense the first time?

Gay's use of process discussions, which we highlighted earlier in the case, revolve around *think-alouds* and *self-reflections*. When Gay uses think-alouds in a process discussion, she makes her thinking visible and explicit to students by verbalizing her thoughts during a literacy event. Gay's think-alouds provide explanations which helps students to understand how reading and writing work for her as an "expert" reader/writer. Self-reflections, as the name implies, allow students to ponder and verbalize their use of reading or writing strategies.

Process discussions progress from Gay's think-alouds (or from the questions she raises) to students' explanations of how they are making sense of text during a literacy event. Gay monitors what her students say and often provides additional explanations or questions to help them think about literacy processes. Think-alouds and self-reflections, as the two scenarios in the boxes illustrate, flow from Gay's interactions with students as they consider a strategy or reflect upon a point related to a literacy demonstration.

A Think-Aloud Scenario on Visual Imagery

Gay is working with a group of readers during a guided learning lesson. She provides a "think-aloud" on how she tries to visualize what she reads when she is reading.

> *Gay:* When I am reading I try to form pictures in my head. Sometimes I even close my eyes and try to see what I am reading. To do this, I always try to use what I know or have experienced in my own life. When I came to the word "cliff" in the story, I tried to picture in my mind what the cliff looked liked.

As the discussion continues, Gay, through her questions, invites the group to participate in a dialogue with her related to the visual imagery of the cliff in the story.

> *Gay:* In the story we read about a cliff. Who formed a mental picture of the cliff?
>
> *Joe:* I did. (Gay encourages Joe to describe his image and Joe responds by relating an incident in his life.) One day we were driving along and my mom yelled at her boyfriend to look out. He was about to drive right over a cliff!
>
> *Gay:* So when you saw the word "cliff" in the story, did a picture enter your mind?
>
> *Joe:* Yeah!
>
> *Gay:* What did it look like?

> Joe: It was like this hill and then it dropped off real fast. (Joe uses hand motions to explain what he means.)
>
> Gay: (provides an explanation) Joe has a picture in his mind. He reads well because he does what all good readers do. When they read things it reminds them of something that has happened to them or that they've seen on TV, or read about, or heard someone else talk about. A good reader forms pictures in their mind and that helps them to understand the story. Did anyone else get a picture in their head when you read about the cliff?
>
> Scott: One time me and my friend were riding our bikes and he skidded and went right over a cliff.
>
> Gay: So the picture you saw was different from Joe's, but both of your pictures helped you better understand the story.
>
> Several other children contribute their pictures of what a cliff looks like, based on their prior knowledge and experience. Gay then redirects the process discussion by asking another question.
>
> Gay: How was the cliff in the story different or the same from the ones all of you pictured in your heads?
>
> Meagan: They were all steep. A cliff is a cliff no matter what you did with it.
>
> Gay: (thinks-aloud and then asks the students to visualize other images from the story) It always helps me to make pictures in my mind while I am reading. Like I said earlier, I even close my eyes so I can see things that I am reading about. Now I would like all of us to close our eyes. I will also. Now let's try to picture some other things we saw in the story besides the cliff.

Strategies Related to Gay's Role as Facilitator.   Gay uses numerous strategies to facilitate literacy learning in her classroom. As a facilitator, Gay often assumes the roles of coach and guide. This is particularly the case in content area learning situations. When involved in content area study, the students in Gay's class participate in two types of learning experiences: (1) guided reading and writing lessons (which involve textbook study), and (2) thematic units (which involve interdisciplinary study) in which students have access to a wide array of tradebooks and informational texts.

Guided learning strategies in content areas span a range of concept-building, meaning-centered activities. Gay plans guided learning lessons to help students build concepts for topics under investigation. She often uses strategies to help them grasp and interpret relationships that exist

Self-Reflection Scenario on Difficult Words

Prior to reading a story, Gay initiates a discussion centered around a review of self-help strategies for difficult words in a text:

Gay: Before we begin reading our story today, I'm curious about something. How important are words when you're reading?

Natalie: Words help you make sense.

Gay: That's right! But how do we know when the words in the story make sense?

Natalie: They just do. When the words make sense I understand what I'm reading.

Dusty: You put what you know with what the author tells you and then you just "get it."

Gay: Yes. When you read for meaning, you're "getting it"; what you're reading is making sense. What are some of the things that good readers like you do when they come to hard words that they don't recognize?

Chris: We fix our mistakes.

Gay: Sure you do; that's because you know that reading has to make sense. If it doesn't, then you have to fix it. What else?

Tia: I make pictures in my head when I'm reading.

Natalie: We take risks.

Gay: And what do you mean by that, Natalie?

Natalie: I'm not afraid to try hard books.

Gay: What other kinds of risks do you take?

Jessica: We aren't afraid to try hard words. I try (to identify a word) before I ask for help.

Anna: If I don't know a word, I try to figure it out.

Gay: And how do you do that, Anna?

Anna: Lots of ways. I try to sound it out, or figure it out by using the clues in the story; or I just skip it if I can't still figure it out. Sometimes I just ask someone if it's (the word) really bothering me.

Gay: Anna, all of those ways are called "strategies." The important thing is that reading has to make sense. We'll learn even more strategies you can use as the year goes along.

among key concepts and ideas in a unit. Early in the school year, Gay shows students how they can connect ideas that they are studying through the use of *semantic mapping*. To illustrate, in one guided lesson, the students, with Gay's assistance, constructed a semantic map for the concept "polymers." Stow, Ohio, where Gay teaches, is adjacent to Akron, and is situated in a geographical area known as "Polymer Valley" because of the technological advances credited to the University of Akron, a pioneer institution in polymer research. The children in Gay's class bring a natural curiosity and awareness to the study of polymers. They want to know what polymers are and how they are used.

Gay uses a semantic map as a tool to help learners to depict the relationships among key words associated with a concept. Figure 5.4 illustrates the semantic map that one group of students constructed toward the end of their study. The map served as a culminating activity in which groups of students were given the opportunity to "show what they know" about polymers.

Gay began the lesson by having students *brainstorm* what they knew about polymers. The words were put on chart paper for everyone to view. She then wrote the target concept, polymers on the chalkboard, drew a circle around it, extended a line from the circled word and connected it to another word, characteristics, and then drew a circle around it. The students were invited to look at the list of words on the chart paper. Gay asked, "Which words are associated with the characteristics of polymers?" As students responded, Gay clustered their words around the term characteristics on the semantic map. Some discussion took place, with revisions made to the map, as students challenged some of the choices suggested.

Gay continued the construction of the semantic map by extending another line from the target concept and then wrote the word formation on the chalkboard and drew a circle around it. She asked, "What words on the chart are related to the formation of polymers? Which ones help us to understand how polymer are formed?" To facilitate the discussion, Gay suggested that the students do some more brainstorming to answer the question. She wrote additional words on the chart paper, which were then clustered around the formation circle on the semantic map.

Having walked students through part of the semantic map, Gay invited them to finish the map in groups on their own. She encouraged the groups to *sort* the remaining words on the chart paper. Word sorting is a strategy with which the students were familiar. As they sorted through the words, Gay circulated among the groups as a coach, encouraging them to "name" the categories they were forming. She explained that these names will become new circles on the map. The groups were also encouraged to generate new words that were not on the chart paper list, so that they could expand their clusters as they worked on the map.

Figure 5.4
Semantic Map for Polymers

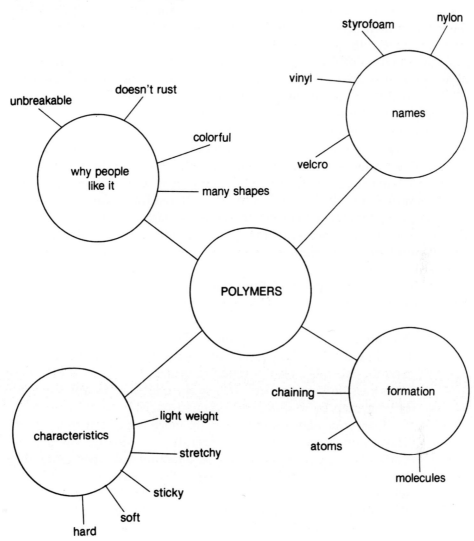

Throughout this process, Gay suggested that the groups might wish to use the books available on polymers to help them with their maps.

Gay likes to use map metaphors to help explain how reading works. As the instructional scenario that follows reveals, Gay occasionally uses a *reading road map* to guide students through the reading of textbook material. The purpose of the reading road map is to develop an awareness of how to adapt one's rate of reading for different purposes. By using the reading road map on potentially difficult text material, Gay is able to demonstrate to students how to read flexibly.

Consider the scenario: Gay is working with a group of students, about half of the class, whom she believes is ready to handle the tasks required of a flexible reader. The group is studying a chapter from their social studies textbook entitled, "Depending On Each Other." Gay initiates a process discussion dealing with strategies for flexible reading—for example, she introduces what it means to *skim* a text when a reader needs specific information. She also reminds students when a reader needs to *slow down* to study important ideas carefully, and when to *reread* if the text is confusing or doesn't make sense.

She then explains how to follow the reading road map (see box) as they study the chapter:

> *Gay:* You are going to take a trip today. This is your map for a tour of the first part of Chapter 14 in your social studies book. (Gay uses an overhead transparency to project the map on a screen.) Your mission is to find answers to the questions on the right side of your map by reading the assigned pages.
>
> When you read, some things are more important than others. Those things should be read carefully and slowly. The less important parts can be skimmed or sometimes skipped altogether. It takes practice to know which parts to read carefully and which parts to skim or skip. This road map will help you think this one through. We'll practice more with other books and in other ways throughout the year.
>
> The left side of your map tells you the location of the important ideas in the chapter. The road signs tell you at what speed to read so that you learn what you need to learn without wasting time.
>
> If you were to take a real trip you would look over the route on a map before you left. It's also important with reading to plan

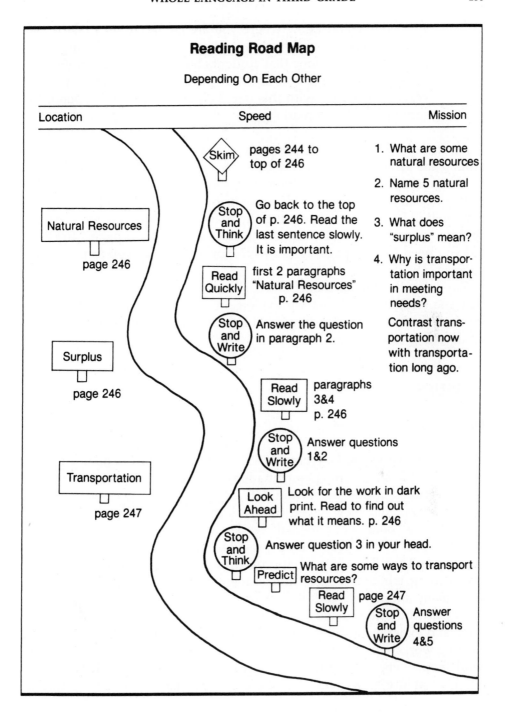

Reading Road Map

Depending On Each Other

Location	Speed	Mission

Skim — pages 244 to top of 246

1. What are some natural resources

2. Name 5 natural resources.

Natural Resources — page 246

Stop and Think — Go back to the top of p. 246. Read the last sentence slowly. It is important.

3. What does "surplus" mean?

4. Why is transportation important in meeting needs?

Read Quickly — first 2 paragraphs "Natural Resources" p. 246

Stop and Write — Answer the question in paragraph 2.

Contrast transportation now with transportation long ago.

Surplus — page 246

Read Slowly — paragraphs 3&4 p. 246

Stop and Write — Answer questions 1&2

Transportation — page 247

Look Ahead — Look for the work in dark print. Read to find out what it means. p. 246

Stop and Think — Answer question 3 in your head.

Predict — What are some ways to transport resources?

Read Slowly — page 247

Stop and Write — Answer questions 4&5

your course and know where you are going. So let's take a few
minutes to skim over the map and see where we are going. (Gay
responds to questions that students have and then continues):

As you see, you will start on page 244. Look at your map.
What will you do with this page? (Several students respond.) Be
sure to follow the road signs as you take your trip.

As students study the chapter using their road maps, Gay circulates
around the group to be sure that they are on target and to answer questions that they might have. When the group completes the map (on the
following day), Gay begins a discussion to build insight about the process: How did you feel about using the road map? Why did we skim the
first two pages? Why did you have to stop and think on page 246? Why
did you need to read page 247 slowly? How did it help you to predict on
page 247?

Gay takes her role as model and facilitator seriously. One of the issues
that she struggles with, as we explore in the next section of the case,
involves the balance between guided learning experiences and independent learning experiences.

ISSUES

Individual Differences

In the past five years, Gay has moved steadily away from ability grouping to multi-level grouping combinations. At one time in her career, Gay
met individual needs by forming "fixed groups of good, average, and
poor readers. And they stayed that way throughout the year. Today the
concept of a "poor" or "remedial" reader holds little meaning for her. "I
was trapped by the way basals provided for individual differences in
reading and the conventional approach to grouping I was exposed to in
my reading methods course and student teaching experience. I didn't
have many alternatives to fall back on."

Gay attributes her move away from fixed, ability groups to the knowledge and experience she gained from teaching writing. Implementing a
writing workshop in her class gave her a fresh perspective: "In a writing
workshop, every kid is different. They come into my class with different
levels of ability as writers." Yet she observes that the workshop format

values the differences that children bring to writing and accommodates their needs. If she could teach writing without grouping by ability, why couldn't she begin to do the same in reading? Gay recognizes that some readers (and writers) struggle with the process and some "take off." Others are somewhere in between. Regardless of where students are developmentally as readers and writers, they all have something to contribute to the literacy community in her classroom.

One of the terms that Gay likes to use when talking about individual differences is "networking." When she forms groups for guided learning during the literacy/language block or during the content area block, she sometimes networks children according to their strengths as well as their needs: "Depending on what we are working on, I form groups by mixing children who understand the strategy or the concept with ones needing help."

Gay offers an example to illustrate her point: Recently, as she was circulating around the room during a writing workshop, Gay observed Tia proofreading a final draft for spelling and having a difficult time using the dictionary to check words that might be misspelled. Tia has little concept of the use of guide words in a dictionary. Instead of using guide words as a locational aid, she flips through the pages of the dictionary, running her finger down the entry words page by page, until she gets frustrated with the task. Gay decided that she would network Tia with several other students during the next day's workshop by forming the following group: Ann (who, like Tia, lacks similar strategies for using the dictionary), Jason (who usually finds words quickly and correctly), Chris (who uses guide words but is slow and laborious), and Jessica (who will be a good model along with Jason). When the group meets, Gay will provide a brief mini-lesson on using guide words and then will ask the students to practice and help one another using drafts from which they are currently working.

Gay works on the principles of cooperation and collaboration. She encourages peer help. A student who does well on certain literacy tasks will be paired with a student who is having problems. The greatest success for Gay in the past year has been the way students work together and help one another during the reading workshop. Throughout the year, she videotaped her students working in teams as part of an action research project that she conducted with a colleague. When outside observers, not familiar with Gay's class, viewed the tapes, they could not determine proficient readers from less proficient readers from the team discussions.

During team discussions, Gay circulates around the room as a resource, but students are encouraged to help one another solve problems before asking her for assistance. For example, Matthew and Louis were working on a *semantic map*. As Matthew and Louis were constructing the semantic map together the following conversation took place:

Louis: I need Mrs. Fawcett.

Matthew: No, you don't. I'll show you how to do it.

Louis: Where should we write them [the supporting ideas and de-tails] down?

Matthew: Here, this is where the details go; that's what these lines are for. [Matthew points to the lines branching out from the center circle of the semantic map.]

Louis: What do you mean, details?

Matthew: Not the main idea, that goes here [pointing to the center circle of the semantic map], but the things that make you think about it [the main idea].

When asked to evaluate the reading workshop in their response logs, many of the students' comments reflected the cooperative nature of the program:

I like it (the workshop) because no one knows everything so we get ideas from other people.

If you don't no [sic] something you talk it over with the other kids and you all figure it out together.

You get to know what other kids know.

You may be with someone whose [sic] more smart then [sic] you and they help you out.

Evaluation

Gay believes that evaluation is her weakest area. She feels the pressure of state-wide competency tests at the third-grade level and district-wide ac-countability measures. Yet she has not succumbed to "teaching for the tests." She has seen the progress that her students have made as readers and writers within a holistic program: "They hold their own on competency tests."

Gay is the first to admit that she has to work harder at documenting the growth and progress that her children make during the school year. *Observation* is Gay's main evaluation tool. As some of the examples from previous sections of this case suggest, Gay assesses the needs of her students in the context of actual language use as they perform various kinds of literacy tasks. When asked how she records her observations, Gay responds: "I rely on mental notes. I am constantly watching what the kids do with literacy." Along with mental notes, Gay keeps a clip-board at hand to jot down observations about the students when they are involved in literacy work. These anecdotal notes are dated and put into a file for each student. Over the course of a grading period, the anecdotal information serves Gay well in making decisions about students' grades.

In addition to observation, Gay evaluates students' progress through *work samples*. Children's writing folders provide a rich source of information about their growth in writing over time. Gay studies the accumulated drafts in each student's writing folder to assess their progress and development as writers.

Gay's main focus of evaluation in reading is on students' comprehension. She assesses comprehension, in part, by the way children perform on various kinds of assigned tasks such as semantic mapping, the guide sheets used in conjunction with the reading workshop and content area activities, for example, the reading road map. When combined with anecdotal information, a picture of each child's development begins to emerge.

Gay aims for a close match between instruction and evaluation. However, she is required to administer reading skills tests which are associated with the basal reading program used in her school district. Her children "hold their own" on these tests, and Gay uses the results to "lobby" her principal whenever possible. According to Gay, her students' performance on basal skill tests demonstrate that they can be involved in holistic literacy events and still learn skills in context.

Home Connections

At the beginning of each school year, Gay sends a letter to parents highlighting her philosophy toward literacy. She explains in the communique that children learn to read and write by reading and writing. Very few worksheets practicing skills in isolation will be sent home. However, children will learn the skills of reading and writing in the context of actual reading and writing. In the letter, Gay also encourages parents to read to children. By third grade, some, if not many, parents have discontinued the practice of reading aloud. When they attend their first conference at open house, Gay underscores the parents' role as model and the benefits of a good read-aloud.

The letter is the first of periodic written communications to parents to keep them abreast of what's happening in language and literacy throughout the year. In Figure 5.5, one of Gay's communiques explains what parents may expect to encounter as they review their child's writing folder when they attend the first open house of the school year. In the letter, she introduces parents to the importance of invented spellings in a child's development as a writer and speller.

Gay informs parents in one of her letters that the students will be writing weekly letters to the parents describing what they are reading and writing about, the activities they have engaged in, and how they feel about the week's work. Space is provided in the letter for the parents to respond, if they wish to do so. The letters are sent home, signed, and returned with parents' reactions and comments. Figure 5.6 illustrates one such letter.

Parents have numerous opportunities throughout the school year to respond to their children's work. When the students in Gay's class compose books, a section in the back is always reserved for parents' responses. Parents are pleased to respond to class books, especially poetry anthologies that the students compile; and children are proud to read the range of responses from all of the parents.

Gay encourages openness. She invites parents to visit her classroom anytime or, better yet, actively get involved in the language/literacy program. Parents respond well to Gay's invitation to be a volunteer. On most days throughout the year, a parent or two is working with Gay. Most of the parent volunteers conduct read-alouds with small groups of children, while Gay is working with a group on a guided learning lesson. Other volunteers get involved in the publishing of children's writing. When a draft is ready for publication, a parent types the manuscript in consultation with its author. Together, the child and the parent discuss lay-out issues such as the amount of print to be typed on a page, and where illustrations are to be placed. Such student/parent discussions serve to maintain the child's ownership of the writing.

Figure 5.5
Letter to Parents Explaining Invented Spellings

Dear Parents,

When you attend Open House on September 17 you will see a folder of your child's writings. There will be many spelling errors—you may not even be able to read some of it, but your child should be able to tell you what it says. The children are using "Inventive Spelling" because they have not learned to spell all the words they need for expressing themselves in writing. "Inventive Spelling" is based on the philosophy that writing is a developmental process that follows much the same course as learning to talk. In learning to talk, children make many mistakes but gradually correct errors as they practice and become proficient language users. Children learning to write make many errors in letter formation, spelling, and punctuation. As children gain greater knowledge of concepts (through reading, writing, and sharing) their writing becomes closer to correct form.

Extensive research has shown that children go through the following stages in learning to spell. See if you can identify where your child's writing fits into this scheme:

Stage 1: Drawing/Scribbling

Stage 2: The child knows how letters are formed but not how they work.

Stage 3: The child writes beginning letters only or beginning and ending letters of words.

     Example: Book might be B or BK
                 Table might be TBL

Stage 4: The child sounds out spellings that produce readable words.

     Example: Back might be BAK
                 Sink might be SEK

Stage 5: The child recognizes that vowels are not always written as they sound.

     Example: Feet might be FEAT
                 Bike might be BICKE

Stage 6: Conventional or correct spelling

We write everyday. Encourage your child to write at home and praise the effort. The more they write, the better they will become.

                                         G. Fawcett

Figure 5.6
BJ's Letter to His Parents

Stow, Ohio 44224
March 5, 1990

Dear Mom & Mark,
We had two plays

And I read a poem on the announcement speaker. We had an english test.

B.J.
Which proper noun did you forget to capitalize? Sounds like you had a pretty interesting week.
Love
Mom

love,
BJ

Lynn Bibble

School Connections

When Gay began to innovate with whole language teaching, some of the more traditional teachers in her school were outwardly critical. Grounded in a skills perspective, the teachers believed that whole language would result in the reinforcement of bad habits. Children's handwriting and spelling skills, they predicted, would deteriorate. Moreover, they believed that whole language would lead to severe gaps in students' skills because the emphasis in whole language, *as they perceived it,* was not on correcting errors, but allowing them to go unchecked. Fortunately, the principal supported Gay's efforts and encouraged her to continue innovating and experimenting with whole language practices. The principal's only stipulation was that Gay stay within the district's policy, which included, but was not limited to, using the basal.

Today, the principal is Gay's closest colleague and cohort in the change process. They exchange articles and books on whole language and attend workshops and conferences together. Often the principal shares informally with other teachers the kinds of changes Gay has made. She visits Gay's class frequently to read with the students during SSR, to respond to their writing, and to lead read-alouds. Throughout Gay's own development as a teacher, the principal has been a catalyst for change. As a result of her instructional leadership, teachers in Gay's school have begun to seek her advice and suggestions.

The reading workshop that Gay initiated has been a pivotal factor in creating change. Since beginning the reading workshop, Gay's classroom has become an informal demonstration center for other teachers in the school and in the district. The word has spread. In the past year, fifteen teachers from within the district have visited Gay's classroom to observe the program in action. They are asking to begin similar programs in their schools and want to meet informally as a "support group."

Keeping Current

Gay is a learner. She currently is engaged in advanced studies in literacy education. She is an active member of the International Reading Association and the National Council of Teachers of English at local, state, and national levels. She attends local and state conferences regularly, and recently, she has enjoyed success as a presenter at professional meetings.

Such activities satisfy a need on Gay's part to explore new ideas related to literacy and to seek answers to questions that she raises.

In this respect, Gay is a self-professed action researcher. She satisfies her curiosity about literacy development by trying to understand why and how children learn in her classroom. She recently inquired into the literature-based reading workshop that she initiated. Working in collaboration with a doctoral student from Kent State University, Gay's inquiry sought answers to the following questions: How and under what conditions is critical thinking encouraged within a literature-based workshop context? How do children interact with one another, as well as with various kinds of texts, in a mixed-ability group situation? How do children make choices when permitted to self-select books for reading? How do children respond to literature in a reading workshop context? Efforts such as this keep Gay in touch with what's happening in her class and allows her to reflect on learning/teaching dynamics in her classroom.

Challenges

As you study Gay's story, it is evident that she has made major moves toward whole language. While she recognizes that she is "not yet where she wants to be," Gay's major challenge is to keep growing professionally in a school district that has placed implicit constraints on her growth as a whole language teacher. She continually questions the required use of a basal. On one hand, she has outgrown the basal as a viable instructional tool. Yet she is obligated to use it. As supportive and encouraging as her principal is, she "has her hands tied": Gay must use the basal within the context of the holistic literacy program that has evolved in her classroom.

Gay grapples continually with the question: Is the basal an authentic text? To the extent that it serves as an anthology, it may be. But she realizes that many of the stories have been condensed from their original texts and "watered down" stylistically. Sometimes she will have students contrast a basal adaptation of a story with the genuine, original version, as she did with "Little Red Riding Hood." It's an eye-opening experience for students. Some express strong feelings when they realize that the basal version is simplified: "Do they (the basal publishers) think we're stupid or something."

Gay recognizes the limitations of working with the basal as an anthology. But, in her mind she has to be realistic and work within "the system" as she tries to change it. There are tradeoffs. Working closely and collaboratively with her principal, Gay received board of education permission to begin a literature-based reading workshop to augment, but not replace, the basal one day a week. She also weaves real books into her program through SSR and content area studies. Permission to initiate a literature-based program, albeit on a limited and supplemental basis has resulted in a unique set of challenges.

Although Gay received district approval to implement the reading workshop, there were no monies budgeted by the board to purchase books for the program. Lack of funding, however, was a temporary problem. Gay overcame this obstacle by obtaining books from bonus points through a book order club, donations from a sales representative for a publishing company, and a grant, based on a proposal she submitted, from the Ohio Department of Education. With these sources of funding, Gay was able to purchase six multiple copies for each book title selected for the program. Criteria for book selection included relevant and interesting content, age appropriateness, and quality illustrations.

Without district support for literature-based instruction, the real challenge that lies ahead for Gay and other teachers moving toward whole language is political in nature. How much of an advocate and activist will Gay be in influencing changes in board policy? Working within the system is a sensible course of action. As she and other teachers support one another for change, their collective voice undoubtedly will be heard.

SUMMING UP

Gay's story profiles a teacher in transition. She is in the process of becoming—and recognizes that change is a slow, gradual process. Gay's journey into whole language has not been an easy one. Her teacher preparation courses as an undergraduate socialized her into a profession that prized a skills-based perspective on learning to read and write. Gay's entire professional career has been spent in traditional, conservative school districts where a competency-based curriculum has been more the rule than the exception. Yet a lack of satisfaction with the status quo, a strong desire to learn, to inquire, and to grow has resulted in where Gay is today as a teacher of literacy. She's come a long way. Where does she want to be? Gay really doesn't have an answer to the question, but she knows that the process of trying to get there is what her professional development is all about.

Chapter 6

WHOLE LANGUAGE IN A FOURTH-GRADE CLASSROOM

"Ten years ago, if I skipped reading, the kids were thrilled. Today, I try to make the classroom the type of place where students would like to spend the day—reading!"

The last day of school in Ann Burns' fourth-grade class is a time for celebration and reflection. The class has much to celebrate. As a community of readers, each student has read, on average, 26 books. Two of the children have read more than 60 books during the year. The fewest number of books read is 13, and the student who accomplished that feat is quick to put the number in perspective, "Some of the books were real thick ones."

The students are sitting at their desks, arranged in a semi-circle, ready to engage in their final book talk of the year. Ann asks them to think about what they have accomplished as readers. She divides the chalkboard into three columns, identifying each with the headings, "Must-Read," "Almost Must-Read," and "Read-Alouds." She then invites the students to talk about what they have read: "Let's talk about your reading this year. Take out your journals and look at the list of books you have read. What is the *one* book you would recommend to next year's class? Let's come up with a top-ten list."

Before Ann completes the directions, the students are peppering her with titles. Each child has a personal favorite. Their hands shoot upward, waving wildly to attract her attention. Ann writes several of the spontaneous responses on board. "Let's talk about these." She calls on Reggie, a slightly overweight boy with a cherubic face and thick eyeglasses. He can't sit still in his desk. So he stands on one leg, kneels the other on the desk chair, and offers his opinion: "*Hatchet* is the best book I ever read, without a doubt."

Gary Paulsen's *Hatchet* is a winner with Ann's class. Nine students support Reggie's choice as she writes the title in the "Must-Read" column. Mildred Taylor's *Let the Circle Be Unbroken* joins the list. So does Theodore Taylor's *The Cay* and Robert O'Brien's *Mrs. Frisby and the Rats of NIMH*. Spontaneous talk breaks out about the books as the students share reasons and rationales for their personal favorites. In addition to the top ten books, the students identify the second ten best and classify those in the "Almost Must-Read" column. Some friendly disagreements break out, but the children recognize that all of the books are terrific in their own right. They also reach consensus on the Read-Aloud books: Roald Dahl's *Witches*, Mildred Taylor's *Roll of Thunder, Hear My Cry*, and Natalie Babbitt's *Tuck Everlasting*. These are the books they think should be read to next year's class because they are "great stories," but may be a little difficult for some of next year's fourth graders to read on their own. Some of the students talk freely and openly about why these books were hard for them.

Afterwards, Ann reflects on the book talk, "What a difference a decade makes." Ten years ago she was a different teacher, with a different set of assumptions. She taught from a basal and assumed that if children knew how to read, they would want to read. But she started noticing that many of her students were not reading the books that they had checked out of the school library each week. Some even kept the books in their lockers and never took them home, so that they would be sure to have them to return on "library day."

Library day was a weekly event in Ann's class. It gave the students an opportunity to visit the library to choose books for independent reading. Unfortunately the event turned into a game between the students and the librarian. They checked the books out and she checked them back in a week later. But nothing happened in-between. "Books just weren't being read," Ann recalls. "They sat in the kids' lockers collecting dust."

The library day phenomenon was a symptom of a much larger problem, *aliteracy,* a term used to describe reluctant readers: Children who can read but choose not to. The students' apparent aliteracy troubled Ann. She conducted an informal attitude survey on their favorite and least favorite school subjects. She randomly wrote on the chalkboard the five major subjects in her classroom. She then had the students write each subject on a note card and asked them to rank order the subjects from most to least favorite. The students invariably ranked reading and writing *at or near* the least favorite end of the scale.

The students' negative attitude toward literacy, combined with their aliterate behavior, forced Ann to do some professional soul searching. What was she about as a literacy educator? After eight years as an elementary teacher, she found herself at a crossroads: "I had the courage to admit to myself, 'Well, let's try something else.' I decided that whatever I would do, it couldn't be any worse than what I had been doing. The way I've been doing things wasn't working. These kids may know how to read, but they're not reading."

Ann describes her first eight years of teaching as "the good old basal days." Looking back on those years, she views herself as having been more a technician than a teacher. As a technician, she was the "expert" that ensured the "system" (the basal reading program) ran smoothly according to predetermined lessons specified in the teacher's manual. She did her best to make the stories in the basal meaningful for her students, but no matter how hard she tried to make reading exciting, she found that "the grade-level basal was too difficult for some, too easy for others, and too bland for most." Something had to change.

So Ann began to study alternatives to the basal. She read the professional literature on literacy learning, and then read some more. The work of Nancie Atwell, Don Graves, Frank Smith, Don Holdaway, and Yetta and Ken Goodman had an immediate and lasting impact on her thinking about language, literacy, and learning. She entered a masters program, attended numerous conferences, workshops, and professional development meetings, all of which have led Ann to where she is today.

WHAT ANN THINKS ABOUT WHOLE LANGUAGE

A passage from Alfred Whitehead's, *The Aims of Education*, written in 1929, reflects the way Ann thinks about teaching and learning: "I don't recall the exact quote, but Whitehead said something to the effect, 'No matter at what age you start learning, you should begin to learn playfully, almost romantically, with wonderful teachers who make it exciting and interesting'." These words have served as an organizing principle for Ann's work in the classroom.

She believes, quite simply and fundamentally, that the role of the whole language teacher is to broker a love affair between children and books. Her job, in a nutshell, is to create the kind of environment in her classroom where students will "fall in love with reading, writing, literature, language, authors, characters, and illustrations." She wants them to be fluent readers who talk about authors and books with their friends.

Ann downplays her beliefs and attitudes about teaching and learning as nothing new: "I mean, I'm not the first to believe that children should love reading. A lot of what I embrace comes from ideas that I've read about and thought about. I really believe that children learn to read and write by reading and writing."

The crux of her teaching rests with the relationships that students form with authors. She doesn't encumber those relationships with "gimmicks" or worksheets which may prevent students from getting to know authors well: "What takes place between the student and the author is more important than having to diagram a story for each book, or do a report, or even write a personal response in a reading journal." This is not to say that Ann doesn't use teaching strategies. However, the bond between reader and author is such that "learning and enjoyment come from the book itself—actually reading it—not necessarily from giving the students something to do along with the book experience."

In articulating her philosophy, Ann turns the situation around from a child to an adult perspective: "If a friend said, 'Here, I would like you to read this book,' and when I was finished, turned around and said, 'Here, I would like you to do this worksheet,' I wouldn't be too thrilled about that . . . and I certainly would be reluctant to read another book, if I knew a worksheet was in the offing." One of the tragic things a teacher can do with literature, according to Ann, is to "basalize it. Children need to experience books and explore meaning in personal ways. They do not need a worksheet or a set of study questions to go along with each book they read.

Instead, Ann's students do what readers in the real world do. They talk to one another about books. She invites them to share a good read: "If kids want to talk to me about books, if they want to talk to their friends about those books, they have the opportunity to do so. They can talk individually with one another on the playground or on the bus, or in small groups in class. We also have a large group share once in a while, which turns into commercials for books, as students try to sell one another on their favorites."

In addition, the students "talk to one another" through correspondences in their reading journals, an idea Ann adapted from Nancie Atwell's *In The Middle: Writing, Reading, and Learning with Adolescents* (Heinemann, Boynton/Cook, 1987). The reading journal is a place where the students can respond and react to literature. They write informal notes or letters to one another or Ann about books they're reading; and, they receive correspondence back from the individuals to whom they wrote. Ann qualifies the use of the reading journal by noting that students aren't required to write each day about what they are reading: "My expectation is that the students will write to one another or me in their journals, but I don't box them into a corner where they have to write every day. Most of them would like to use the reading workshop time just reading." As a result, the students write in their journals at least once a week. "Often the kids write more frequently," observes Ann. "They like to correspond with one another in writing."

Ann confronts the whole idea of what a teacher is and what a teacher does. "Many of us," she believes, "get caught up in the trappings of teaching." A teacher is suppose to instruct, is suppose to inform, is suppose to correct errors, is suppose to intervene when a child comes across a word he doesn't recognize." Over the years, however, Ann's suppositions have changed. "I think sometimes we interfere with the whole learning process by the things we do. An author can teach a child more about reading than I can." Rather than instructing, Ann creates an environment for literacy learning. Rather than informing, she demonstrates her passion and enthusiasm for books. Rather than correcting errors, she supports learning by encouraging risk-taking.

When Ann thinks about the role that books play in her classroom, she underscores two whole language principles: choice and self-selection. "Kids like to choose what they read for a variety of reasons." Her literacy program is based on total self-selection. She estimates that she has more than a 1000 books in her classroom from which children can choose.

When Ann first began to use real books instead of a basal, she found it difficult to give up total control of what students read. As a result, she had them reading class sets of a novel. She also experimented with literature study in small groups, using multiple copies of four or five different books for instructional purposes. But she didn't have much success with either approach. She found that a whole class literature study held students back and "lockstepped" them into reading at the same rate and in the same piecemeal fashion. They enjoyed the stories, but Ann recognized that she was aping the basal lesson format. In addition, small group studies were too distracting. While she worked with one group of readers, the rest of the students spent time at their seats reading books. Invariably, however, they listened to what was going on in the group discussion, out of curiosity, rather than concentrating on what they were reading. Ann realized, "As a reader, I can't read in an area where there's a lot of conversation going on. I need quiet concentration. Kids, especially, need a quiet atmosphere to concentrate on what they're reading."

The progression from whole class and small group studies of literature to total self-selection was gradual. With total self-selection, however, Ann has come to believe that silent reading isn't a component of the reading program, but rather *it is the program:* "When we're reading, that's all that's going on. That's the time, and it's at least 45 minutes each day, where you don't even get up for a drink of water unless you're gasping." The sanctity of silent reading is rarely betrayed in Ann's class: "We close the door and that's our time. We've even had one principal who used to like to come into our room at the start of silent reading, especially if he had some reading to do—some serious reading—because he knew he wasn't going to be distracted by anything."

By springtime, the students are well into the groove as readers. On the first warm day, they ask to read outside. "We read outside a lot when the weather gets nice," Ann notes. "My students have asked to read for an entire day outside. And I honor their request. They think that reading a book on the grass or under a tree is a wonderful way to spend a day. So that's what we'll do. We'll talk about books we've loved and enjoyed, but the atmosphere is very informal."

Another principle that guides Ann's actions in the classroom involves integrated learning through thematic, interdisciplinary studies. She and two other fourth-grade teachers team in the afternoon to use reading, writing, talking, and listening to learn across the curriculum. Last summer, she and her two colleagues attended a summer workshop on interdisciplinary, thematic studies. Inspired by the workshop leaders, thematic units have added a new dimension to Ann's work as a whole language teacher.

Ann's thinking about learning, curriculum, and teaching has changed dramatically in the eighteen years that she has been a teacher. Even more dramatic is the contrast between her instructional practices now and what she did instructionally during "the good old basal days."

INSIDE ANN'S CLASSROOM

The Environment

Stepping into Ann's room is like stepping into a friend's den. The room has couches and chairs and comfortable places to curl up with a good book. She emphasizes the importance of a pleasant, homelike setting: "The comfort level of the students is very important—the environment is important. I like to have plants because they help to create a soothing, relaxed atmosphere. This is their home for a good part of the day, so I try to get away from an institutional look as much as possible, especially in the reading area."

As you enter the room, you are greeted by a tank full of colorful fish that sits on a book shelf to your right; the reading area is to your left. The diagram in Figure 6.1 hardly does justice to the intimate environment for literacy that permeates the room. Bookcases, overflowing with books, line the perimeter of the room. Books are on display wherever space allows.

Informational books, on loan from the community and school libraries, are propped on the top of the window sill along the window side of the room; these reflect the themes and disciplines that students are currently studying as part of a nature unit on plants and animals. One cluster of books include Joseph Brown's *Wonders of a Kelp Forest,* James Newton's *A Forest Reborn,* and Millicent Selsam and Jerome Wexler's *Mimosa, the Sensitive Plant,* as well as ten or more additional titles. A huge display of animal books, wonderfully illustrated, occupy an area next to the plant

Figure 6.1
Physical Arrangement in Ann's Classroom

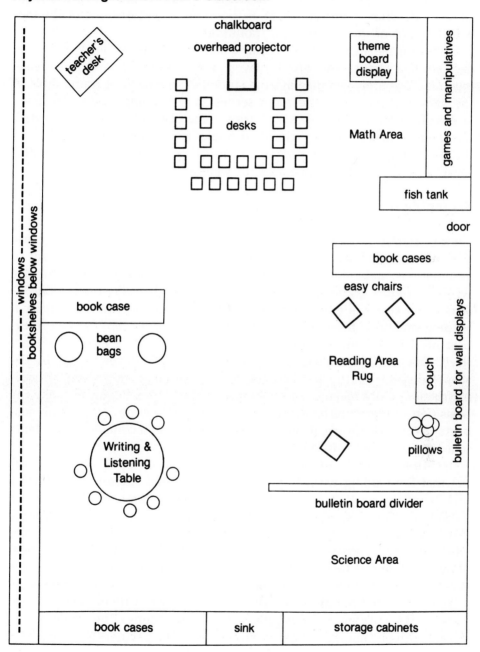

books. Posters of animals, and rain forests, and the earth as viewed from space also highlight the nature theme. A bulletin board on rollers is located in the front, right quadrant of the room; it features one of the thematic strands of the nature unit, "pollution."

Student-constructed posters from a math project—scale drawings of each student's bedroom—are displayed on the bulletin board in the reading area. This area also displays the students' writing. The round table in the back, left corner of the room serves as a listening post. Ann has a large collection of audiotapes of stories, some of which she has recorded. If students choose to, they can read books and listen simultaneously to the recordings during reading workshop time. The listening post also serves as a group conference area for writing.

Beginning the School Year: A Basket of Books

Getting started in a whole language classroom can be difficult because the students must adjust to a different set of values, a different set of assumptions, and a different set of practices. Ann finds this to be the case with her fourth graders. The students feed into her classroom from instructional contexts that have relied, for the most part, on conventional reading practices. Interestingly, she finds that the students are more experienced in writing workshop practices than reading workshop practices. One of the emphases in professional staff development in the school district for the past several years has been on writing process instruction. Only recently have the primary teachers begun to make the transition to literature-based, reading workshop environments. Ann suspects that in the future, it will be easier for her to acclimate the students to a reading workshop format.

The first six weeks of the school year are crucial, especially for ensuring that the reading workshop gets off the ground smoothly. Ann actually begins by writing a letter to each student in August. She welcomes them to the fourth grade and explains that they will have many opportunities to read books of their choice. She closes with an invitation to bring "their all-time favorite book" to school on the first day. She tells them about some of her favorites and encourages them to bring any kind of a book, "a picture book or whatever" to share with the rest of the class.

When the children arrive on the first day, most of them have brought their books. The morning begins with introductions. The students are paired with one another as partners. She gives the partners a few minutes to chat with one another, to find out how they have spent their summer, what are their favorite hobbies and sports, and the like. Then one partner introduces the other to the class.

Upon completion of the introductions, Ann invites the students to share the books they brought from home with the rest of the class: "We arrange our desks in a large circle and go from kid to kid; it's sort of like round-robin sharing. It doesn't take long for the kids to notice that some kids have brought the same book and, of course, they start chatting about the books. Pretty soon the kids are saying, 'Oh yeah, I've read that,' and 'I love that.' And that's what gets them off and running."

Now it's Ann's turn to share. She walks to the front of the room and brings out a basket full of books from behind her desk. She tells the kids that in the basket are the books that were voted "the very best and most exciting" by last year's class. Borrowing a technique from Bill Halloran, the noted children's literature consultant, she shares each book with the students, intriguing them with elements of plot, introducing them to wonderful characters, and hinting at the problems and challenges faced by each of the main characters.

Ann doesn't insist that students should read any of the books in the basket, but she does everything she can "to try and spur them on. I would like all of my students to read *View from a Cherry Tree*. So when I introduce it, I give it a hard sell and get very excited about it. In fact, I single it out as my first read-aloud book to the class." In the process of "selling" all of the books in the basket, Ann demonstrates her passion and enthusiasm for reading.

A few minutes are spent explaining the reading workshop, introducing the reading journal, and reviewing the rules for silent reading. Ann gives them each a handout (displayed in Figure 6.2) that walks the students through their responsibilities in relation to the reading journal. Ann has them tape the handout to the inside cover of a spiral notebook, which becomes the reading journal.

Next, the students are given the opportunity to rummage through the basket and to search the bookshelves for other great books. They take several minutes to browse and to select books for reading. And then the first reading workshop begins.

Ann announces that they are going to have their first reading workshop period, 20 minutes of sustained silent reading. She begins with 20 minutes, because many of the students haven't developed "patience with

Figure 6.2
Letter to Readers Explaining the Reading

Dear Students,

   Welcome back from your summer vacations! As part of your reading class this year, we're going to try something different which you may not have done in previous grades. Each of us is going to keep a Reading Journal.

   What is the Reading Journal all about? The Journal is a place where you will be able to write about the books that you will be reading throughout the year in my class. In the Journal, you will write letters to me or to other students in the class.

   What will the letters be about? You can write anything you want about the book you are reading. You can express your thoughts, your feelings, or your reactions. How do you feel about the book? What does the book make you think about? What do you like or dislike about it? What's the story about? Who are the characters? Can you relate to their problems? Will the person you are writing to like the book? What does the story mean to you?

   When you finish writing your new entry, place your journal on my desk or the desk of the student you are writing to. When I or a classmate receive your letter, we will be able to write back to you in your Journal.

   Here are some simple guidelines to follow to make sure that the Reading Journal is a success:

   1. You may write as many letters as you wish, but at least one letter each week.

   2. If you receive a letter from a classmate, respond to it by the next day.

   3. Make sure you date each letter and mention the name of the book you are reading.

   I will explain other details about the Reading Journal in class. You will have plenty of class time to write your letters. I hope that you are as excited as I am by the prospects of sharing what you are reading. The Reading Journal will be a great way to help us explore what we are feeling and thinking about the books that we are reading.

   Happy reading! Happy writing!

                                                              Sincerely,

                                                              Mrs. Burns

This memo is based on ideas from a letter published in a book by Nancie Atwell *In The Middle: Writing, Reading and Learning with Adolescents* (Heinemann, Boynton/Cook, 1987).

print over a sustained period of time." By the sixth week of school, however, Ann increases silent reading time to 45 minutes.

The students' reactions are predictable on the first day of silent reading. Ann describes the scenario that unfolds this way: "I usually have a little group of boys who will sit together in close proximity on the rug in the reading area, and their eyes keep looking up and looking over, and I can tell by the expressions on their faces that they're wondering, 'What are we doing? What's going on?' They just can't get a handle on what's going on. And, of course, they look over at me and see me reading, deep in thought, and nothing else is going on in the room, except kids' reading. Pretty soon, they start to read because everybody else is reading by now."

By hearing what other children are reading or seeing what their friends are reading, the students want to read the same books. Eventually, they are asking one another, "Can I have that book when you're finished with it?" As Ann puts it, "By the sixth week of school, what's happening in the workshop is contagious. We're rolling. And I can afford to get sick and not worry about a substitute coming in. Up to that point, however, I wouldn't want to miss school. It's the modeling and the attitude building that make a difference in the first few weeks of school."

In the first month of the school year, Ann gets the reading workshop off to a good start, introduces the students to the writing workshop, initiates book talks, whole class group shares, and read-alouds. She also introduces students to thematic studies.

A Typical Day

The morning begins at 8:15 A.M. with a "coming together time." Ann likes to focus on a literacy event. Usually it involves sharing a poem or two, discussing a news item relating to a theme the students are studying, or leading a group share of what the students currently are reading.

For example, as part of the unit on plants and animals, the class comes together to share two "great poems about nature." The first, "Nature Is . . ." is a short, quiet poem that Ann found in a teachers' magazine several years ago. Just before she begins reading it to the class, she asks the students to close their eyes and to listen to the language of the poem. She reads the poem aloud so that students "can hear the language and form images in their heads."

Ann has the poem on an overhead transparency and projects it on the screen in the front of the room. As she reads it again, she invites the students to follow along. She asks, "What do you like about the poem? How does it make you feel?" Several students respond. They like the tone of the poem. One student says, "It makes me want to relax and not think about anything but the woods we play in."

Ann asks the class to join her in a choral reading of the poem. Then she invites four volunteers to each read a stanza aloud. As a class, they discuss some of the images in the poem as well as the sounds: "A poem is meant to be heard as well as to be read. What sounds do you hear that make the poem feel so quiet and peaceful to you?"

"Earth, What Will You Give Me" by Beverly McLoughland, first published in *Humpty, Dumpty* in 1977, is the subject of the next group share. The poem has a predictable pattern. The stanzas alternate in the form of questions and answers. Whereas the first poem is quiet and peaceful, this one is robust and majestic throughout. Ann begins with the same presentational pattern, first reading it aloud and then reading it in unison with the class.

They play with the poem. Ann invites the class to try a variation on choral reading. The girls read the question stanzas and the boys read the answer stanzas. As a class, they tie the two poems into the theme they have been studying in the unit. The coming together session takes eighteen minutes to complete. Ann then cues the group for the reading workshop simply by saying, "It's time to read."

The students bolt from their desks and make a dash for the back of the room to get their favorite seats. Some head for the reading area. Two lay claim to the beanbag chairs. Six students sit at the listening table, adjusting headphones. Others prop themselves up against one of the walls or lie on the rug. Within two minutes, everyone is reading with minimal distraction. The reading workshop has started.

During the reading workshop, which runs from 45 to 60 minutes, and sometimes longer, the students either will be reading, searching for a new book, writing in their journals about their reading, engaging in book talks, or participating in mini-lessons.

Since students self-select the books they will read, and hardly any two students read the same book at the same time, the reading journals are an important part of Ann's reading workshop. She finds that students need practice in talking and writing about their books. Most students, for example, begin by writing things like, "This is a good book. You should try it." Some simply retell the story. As a result, Ann helps her students articulate their reactions and feelings about books by creating an environment that invites literary talk.

She begins with a mini-lesson to make students aware of themselves as readers. She has them complete the reading survey shown in the box. The questions on the survey prompt a thoughtful discussion. As Ann notes, "In the beginning of a reading workshop it's easier to talk about yourself than about a book. The kids become aware that they are as different from one another as readers as they are alike." As the workshop progresses, Ann plans additional mini-lessons to have students writing and talking thoughtfully about books.

The students decide, for the most part, how they will spend the time during the workshop, except in cases where Ann has planned a mini-lesson or book talk discussions. Some of the children will read for the entire time. Others, at varying points in the workshop, will locate their journals to write a letter to one of their classmates or to Ann; or they might exchange journals to write their responses to the letters that they have received.

In one exchange of correspondences, Amy writes to her teacher. (See Figure 6.3.) In her letter, she tells Ann that even though *The Yearling* is "really long," it's a wonderful book, "the best book I ever read. It should be a Newberry [sic] Award Winner, or at least an honer [sic] book." *The Yearling* originally was intended by the author to be for adults, but has since been claimed by children. Amy retells aspects of the plot in the

---

Reading Survey

Name _____   Date _____

    1. If you had to guess . . .

       How many books would you say you owned? _____

       How many books would you say there are in your house? _____

       How many novels would you say you've read in the last year? _____

    2. How did you learn to read? _____

       _____

       _____

3. Why do people read? _____

_____

_____

4. What does someone have to do in order to be a good reader? _____

_____

_____

5. How does a teacher decide which students are good readers? _____

_____

_____

6. What kinds of books do you like to read? _____

_____

_____

7. How do you decide which books you'll read? _____

_____

_____

8. Have you ever re-read a book? ____ If so, can you name it/them here? ____

_____

_____

_____

_____

9. Do you ever read books at home for pleasure? ____ If so, how often do you read at home? _____

10. Who are your favorite authors?

_____

_____

_____

11. Do you like to have your teacher read to you? ____ If so, is there anything special you'd like to hear? _____

12. In general, how do you feel about reading? _____

_____

_____

Figure 6.3
Amy's Letter and Ann's Reply

Dear Mrs. Burns,

I'm reading <u>The Yearling</u>. It is wonderful. It's really long but it's worth it! The author is a wonderful writer. The book seems so life-like. I feel sorry for Penny and Ma Baxter-they would have had about fifteen children if they hadn't all died but Jody.

Jody, I feel sorry for the most though. His best friend just died. But I think the fawn will help sooth the pain.

His father, Penny, is much better. He's doing the chores a little now! When I read about Penny being bitten by a snake a practically cried. Luckily, Penny got better.

Unfortunately Fodder-Wing wasn't as lucky. I did cry when Fodder-Wing died. It all seemed so sad even though it's a story. The Foresters wouldn't have cared as much if another person had died, but they couldn't bare the loss of Fodder-Wing, even though he was

Figure 6.3 *(Continued)*

so crippled and unlike them.
The *Yearling* is the best book I've
ever read, It should be a Newberry
Award Winner, or atleast an honer
book.

    As I said before its long but
it sure is worth it!

                Sincerely,
                Amy
P.S. Read anything good lately?

                      3/1/89

Dear Amy,
    Yes, I am reading something good,
Fourth Grade Celebrity. I wanted to
read something by Giff before her visit.
You and Casey, the main character
have something in common; you both
have older sisters to torment and be
tormented by. Also to love. Its fairly
easy reading but you might enjoy it
for a break after the challenging text
of *The Yearling*. I'm so proud of you
for tackling it. Your letter makes me
want to read it to see what I've missed.

               Enjoy,
               Mrs. Burns

letter to Ann but also shares her reactions and strong feelings toward the events in the story.

In her return correspondence to Amy, Ann responds directly to the postscript: "P.S. Read anything good lately?" The postscript is an invitation to "talk up" another engaging and worthwhile book that Amy might want to try, such as, *Fourth Grade Celebrity.* Ann praises Amy for tackling "the challenging text of *The Yearling* . . . . Your letter makes me want to read it to see what I've missed."

Book talks occur at least once a week in the reading workshop. Ann explains, "The kids have strong feelings about the books they have read. They entice one another to consider reading books they may otherwise not consider." In one book talk, the students form groups of four and read some of the letters they have written in their journal. In another, they relate how the authors they are reading begin their stories. They read the beginnings to one another.

For approximately 35 minutes each day, immediately following the reading workshop, the children engage in process writing. Many types of writing activity occur during this time. Some students may elect to continue letters they are writing in the reading journals. Others might be in the middle of a research report they are composing as part of the thematic unit. In addition, all of the students have writing folders. The folders contain current "work in progress" on topics that are generated by the students. Stapled to the inside of their writing folders is a "topics" list containing ideas to write about. These topics are generated by the students in mini-lessons. The students consult the lists for ideas and, from time to time, monitor the list by updating and revising topics.

Like the reading workshop, the children make decisions as to how to use their time during writing. At any given time, students may be working on various stages of the writing process: brainstorming, planning, drafting, revising, editing, or preparing a final draft for publication.

During the writing workshop, Ann either writes with the children, circulates around the room to confer with individuals, or holds a conference at the listening table. When the occasion calls for it, she will begin a workshop with a mini-lesson. These mini-lessons vary in content. Some are designed to help students brainstorm ideas; others might model a revising or editing strategy; still others might teach a skill, such as using quotation marks to write dialogue in a story.

Ann spends the first six weeks of the year acclimating students to the writing process. She uses the mini-lesson extensively at the beginning of the school year to demonstrate the various stages of process writing, the routines the students will be involved in, and their responsibilities as writers and responders.

With the conclusion of the writing workshop, the students attend a "special," either music, art, or gym. When they return, Ann teaches math as a separate subject for approximately one hour. She teaches math as problem solving, using games and manipulatives, and incorporating writing-to-learn strategies into her lesson. Lunch and recess follow.

When the children return from recess, the afternoon begins with a half-hour story time. The students listen to a read-aloud. Often, Ann will choose a book that introduces a series of books by the same author. Mildred Taylor's *Roll of Thunder, Hear My Cry*, a powerful story about a black family's encounter with poverty and discrimination, is a prime example. The students cheer for the book's heroine, Cassie Logan, as the story ends. Ann coincides her reading of Taylor's Newbery Medal book with Black Awareness Month in February.

The read-aloud is a stepping stone for other books by Taylor, including *Gold Cadillac* and *Let the Circle Be Unbroken*. Ann uses her basket of books strategy to introduce the children to other authors and books about the black experience, including Virginia Hamilton's *Zeely*, Theodore Taylor's *The Cay*, Paula Fox's *Slave Dancer*, Enid LaMonte's *By Secret Railway*, William Armstrong's *Sounder*, Walter Dean Myers' *Scorpions*, Dorothy Sterling's *Freedom Train, The Story of Harriet Tubman*, Julius Lester's *To Be a Slave*, and Emma Sterne's *Slave Ship*.

After story time concludes, the students have the remainder of the afternoon, about an hour and one-half, to participate in thematic studies. These studies are co-taught by Ann and her two fourth-grade colleagues. Each teacher is responsible for planning interdisciplinary activities on a different aspect of the theme. The students from the three classes choose which aspect of the theme they would like to study and report to that teacher's room. Themes for the year have explored the following topics: self-esteem, geology, weather, Indians and pioneers, economics, light, the human body, Ireland, world civilizations, United States government, and plants and animals.

Organization and Management

Ann uses two organizational tools to help her keep track of what's happening during the reading workshop. First, she maintains a class record

Figure 6.4
Class Record

	Monday	Tuesday	Wednesday	Thursday	Friday
Cigler, James	Matilda p. 56	→ 96	135	(184)	Georges Marv. Md beg.
Clevenger, Elizabeth	Anne of Green Gables p.33	→ p. 58	92	126	→ p. 150
Conn, Brooks	Boy p. 113	→ p. 131	(148)	A Wrinkle In Time p. 12	→ p. 35
Depetro, Wyndsor	Boxcar Children p.81	→ Boxcar p. 91	103	→ (p. 133)	B.C. Surprise Island p. 25
Grugle, Charles	Mrs. Frisby p. 104	119	133	→ 159	→ 195
Harbage, Louisa	(Stage Fright p. 61)	(Class Clown p. 49)	TAG	Sarah, Plain & Tall p. 18	P.V. Bk.
Hlavin, Kimberly	Dollhouse Murders beg. p. 2	→ p. 16	37	→ 62	→ 100
Podor, Jacque	Half Magic p. 10	→ p. 42	93	(162)	Calico Captive p. 39
Kruse, Trina	(Sign of the Beaver p. 88)	Boy beg.	30	64	→ p. 88
Laidman, Michael	The Witches p. 118	133	137	149	LD
Macey, Katie	Matilda p. 86	→ 90	107	124	SR
Male, Christopher	AB	View from Cherry Tree p. 81	91	107	P.V. Bk.
Morrison, Peter	Bummer Summer beg.	→ 15	Trapped In Death Cave beg.	Operation Dump p. 9	69
Padavick, Bradley	Trapped In Death Cave p. 38	→ (p. 145)	Sideways Stories	40	P.V. Bk.
Rutkowski, Daniel	Westing Game p. 97	→ 112	131	(170)	Boy p. 44
Sandmann, Julie	View from Cherry Tree p. 64	AB	AB	→ p. 91	→ 115
Santoro, Alan	The Witches p. 30	→ 43	52	p. 69	SR
Seaman, Angie	(Prince Caspian p.179)	Slave Dancer beg.	25	40	→ p. 63
Simmons, Jonathan	Racso & Rats of Nimh p. 134	→ p. 157	170	193	218
Wyszynski, Alexis	Young Ru 144	→ (224)	BFG 43	92	→ 159
Yuratovac, Amy	Matilda p. 114	→ 136	158	183	→ 219

for each day's workshop (Figure 6.4). The class record helps her to monitor what the students are reading and how much they have accomplished during each day of the week. It helps her to decide which students are having difficulty choosing or sticking with a book and who may need to confer with her.

During the first five minutes of silent reading, Ann surveys each student and records the book's title and page number where they begin reading. The students are used to her quick survey and it causes minimal distraction. When Ann is finished, she begins reading with the class.

A second organizational feature of the reading workshop is the reading journal. At the end of the journal, students divide a page into three columns and keep a running tally of the books that they have completed. They record the title, author, and date of completion. Figure 6.5 illustrates a tally sheet from one student's journal, reflecting the first three months of the school year. By the end of the year, Amy had read 69 books.

Ann's students are well-behaved and she has few problems with discipline. The students respond well to the environment that she creates. However, she does establish rules, especially for the reading and writing workshops. She makes the rules explicit during the first day of school and maintains high expectations for their adherence. The rules for the reading workshop are displayed in Figure 6.6.

Strategies

Many of the instructional strategies that Ann uses with the reading and writing workshops involve the ways in which she creates environments for reading, organizes for instruction, and interacts with students. These already have been described in preceding sections of the case.

Ann's use of the mini-lesson is an opportunity for her to teach strategically. The mini-lessons allow her to make students aware of what readers and writers need to do to be successful. In addition to mini-lessons, Ann is strategic in her approach to thematic learning. She creates many occasions and opportunities to learn through active involvement as students read and write across the curriculum.

Mini-Lessons.   As alluded to earlier, Ann uses the mini-lesson for a variety of purposes. One is to introduce students to the whole idea of "writing about reading." In addition to the reading survey described in the box on page 183, Ann plans a mini-lesson around another survey,

Figure 6.5
Tally of Books Completed in Amy's Reading Journal

Title	Author	Date Completed
1. Nine Witch Tales	Abby Kedabray	9-3-88
2. Andersons Fairy Tales	Frig Littledale	9-3-88
3. Where the Sidewalk Ends	Shel Silverstein	9-2-88
4. Flat On My Face	Julia First	9-1-88
5. The Against Taffy's Club	Betsy Haynes	9-1-88
6. Lauren's Big Mix Up	Susan Saunders	9-6-88
7. The Shy One	Dorothy Nathan	9-8-88
8. Don't cross your Bridge Before You Pay the Toll	Judith First Stork	9-7-88
9. Baby Island	Carol Ryrie Brink	9-20-88
10. Starring Stephanie	Susan Saunders	9-15-88
11. The Borrowers		9-19-88
12. I'd like to Hear A Flower Grow		9-13-88
13. Blubber		9-28-88
14 Say cheese	Patricia Reilly Giff	9-25-88
15. Pickle Puss	Pat Giff	9-25-88
16. Valentine Star	Pat Giff	10-1-88
17. Fish Face	Pat Giff	10-1-88
18. Lilac		10-6-88
19. A Day No Pigs Would Die	Ronald Dahl	10-19-88
20. Veronica the Showoff		10-22-88
21. Samantha Slade Monster Sitter	Susan Smith	10-26-88
22. Miss Hickory	Carolyn Bailey	10-14-88
23. With You and Without You		11-4-88
24 Sadako and the Thousand paper Cranes	Eleanor Corre	10-28-88
25. Sara Crewe	Frances Burnett	11-9-88
26. Mr. Poppers Penguins		11-28-88
27. Dollhouse Murderers	Betty Wright	11-30-88
28. Behind The Attic Wall	Sylvia Cassate	11-21-88

Figure 6.5 (Continued)

Title	Author	Date Completed
29. Dinah and the Green Fat Kingdom		12-2-88
30. Sixth Grade Sleepover	Eve Bunting	12-7-88
31. The Enormous Alligator	Roald Dahl	12-9-88
32. Fantastic Mr. Fox	Roald Dahl	12-13-88
33. Baby Sitting is a Dangerous Job	Willo Davis Roberts	12-23-88
34. Be a Perfect Person in Just Three Days	Stephen Manes	1-3-89
35. A Wrinkle in Time	Madeleine L'Engle	1-6-89
36. Ferret in the Bedroom, Lizard in the Fridge		1-1-89
37. In Real Life Im Just Kate	Barbara Morginroth	1-3-89
38. That Was Then This is Now	S. E. Hinton	1-10-89
39. Cross Your Fingers Spit In Your Hat		1-18-89
40. Stranger With My Face		1-20-89
41. Roll of Thunder Hear My Cry	Mildred Taylor	1-25-89
42. View From the Cherry Tree	Willo Davis Roberts	
43. The Witch Craft of Salem Village	Shirley Jackson	2-1-89
44. But We Are Not Of Earth	Jean E. Karl	2-7-89
45. Bummer Summer	Ann M. Martin	2-7-89

Figure 6.6
Roles for Using Reading Workshop Time

1. Students must read for the entire period.

2. Students cannot do homework or read textbooks during this time.

3. Students must read a book, preferably one that tells a story such as novels, histories and biographies rather than books of lists or facts where readers can't sustain attention, build up speed and fluency, or grow to love good stories.

4. Students must have a book in their possession when class begins. Students who need help finding a book or who finish a book during the workshop may search for a book.

5. Students may not talk to or disturb others.

6. Students may sit wherever they'd like as long as feet do not go up on furniture.

7. There are no lavatory or water fountain breaks to disturb me or other readers except in an emergency. Before class begins is the time to use the restroom facilities.

8. A student who is absent can make up time and receive points by reading at home.

which is highlighted in the box. This survey allows students to "gauge" how well they are reading a book on a particular day. The mini-lesson follows the silent reading period of the workshop. Ann invites the student to complete the survey and then engages them in a discussion. She does not ask the students to talk about every question on the survey. Instead, she asks, "Which questions really helped you to think about yourself as a reader? What did you learn from the survey?"

In talking about reading from an individual perspective, the students build an awareness of their reading processes, recognizing that many factors affect the quality of their interactions with text on any given day.

Other mini-lessons develop a literary perspective and help the students to write about their reading. These include: how authors begin stories (the students share the beginnings of their current book); how to be descriptive (the students describe the main character and the setting of their current book); and how to determine realistic fiction (the students are asked to make connections between the books they are reading and their lives).

A culminating mini-lesson revolves around a list of prompts which Ann distributes to the class (See box). The prompts serve to remind the students that they have a variety of possibilities for writing letters in their journals.

Personal Reading Survey

1. Did you have a good reading period today? _____

   Did you read well? _____

   Did you get a lot done? _____

2. Did you read better today than yesterday? _____

3. Were you able to concentrate today on your silent reading? _____

4. Did the ideas in the book hold your attention? _____

   Did you have the feeling of moving right along with them?_____

5. Did you have the feeling of wanting to go ahead faster to find out what
   happened? _____

   Were you constantly moving ahead to get to the next good part? _____

6. Was it hard for you to keep your mind on what you were reading today?

   _____

7. Were you bothered by others or by outside noises? _____

8. Could you keep the ideas in your book straight in your mind? _____

9. Did you get mixed up in any place? _____

   Did you have to go back and straighten yourself out? _____

10. Were there words you did not know? _____

    How did you figure them out? _____

11. What did you do when you got to the good parts? _____

    _____

    Did you read faster or slower? _____

12. Were you always counting to see how many pages you had to go? _____

    Were you wondering how long it would take you to finish? _____

    _____

13. Were you kind of hoping that the book would go on and on—that it would
    not really end? _____

WRITING ABOUT READING

What did you like?

What, if anything, didn't you like?

What did you think or wonder about while you were reading?

Connect the experiences of the characters with your own life.

Predict while you are reading what will happen next.

Comment on the beginning, the ending, the length.

Comment on the author's style of writing.

Write about a good part in the book.

Give recommendations.

Tell about your future reading plans.

Early in the reading workshop, the students come together in a mini-lesson to discuss how to choose a book. Through discussion and brainstorming, the class generates a list of suggestions for self-selection. These suggestions include the following: Stick with a good series, ask a friend about favorites, read more books by the same author, look for award winning books, read at least two or three chapters before deciding to abandon a book, pick a subject you like to read about, read the title and cover information, and read books similar to the books you have enjoyed.

Reading and Writing Across the Curriculum.   Ann recognizes, that given their choice, many of the children would prefer to read narrative rather than expository text. In conjunction with units, she will often put on display informational books, but as Ann observes, "I have a real hard time getting kids to look at these books; if I bring in, for example, a display on plant books, those aren't the types of reading material they naturally go for."

As a result, Ann uses strategies to pique their interest and to get them involved in raising questions. One such strategy is a variation on a procedure called *active comprehension.* This strategy begins with the teacher sharing a portion of text from a selection and then asking, "Who would like to know more about _____? She completes the question, either by focusing on a character, plot, setting, or a concept. The important part of the strategy is that the teacher asks the question in such a way that it *begets* more questions from the students. They then read to find out the answers to their questions.

Here's how Ann describes her use of the active comprehension strategy in the plant and animal unit: "In our room we have a large ant farm surrounded by books, charts, and poems about ants. One of the books is Chris Van Allsburg's *Two Bad Ants.* After sharing a poem and discussing the pros and cons of ants, I pick up Van Allsburg's book and discuss the jacket illustration and the implications of the title. I invite predictions.

Then I read the first four pages, sharing with the children the wondrous, bigger than life, illustrations. At this point, I close the book and ask the kids, "What would you like to know about ants?" They ask a lot of questions, and I record them on chart paper. I then ask them to find answers to their questions, using Van Allsburg's book and the other informational texts."

The Biosphere Adventure

Find, draw and label the following. Describe its physical features, habitat, food, movement, other features.

1. Something that lives under a rock.

2. Something that lives in a log.

3. Something that flies.

4. Something that crawls on leaves.

5. A green plant.

Ann tries to encourage a wide range of reading and writing in science. One third of the science curriculum in the fourth grade revolves around the plants and animals unit. In addition to stimulating reading, she provides many occasions to write. For example, the students participated in a "biosphere adventure" in the woods behind the school. They spent one hour in the woods observing and writing about their discoveries during the trip to the woods. They used the "observation guide" in the box to record their findings.

When they returned to their classroom, the students were asked to write about the biosphere adventure from their own personal perspectives. But first, as a class, Ann led the students in an idea-generating activity: the students reviewed the observations they recorded and reported on what they had seen, heard, smelled, touched, and perhaps, even tasted. As they talked about their observations, Ann recorded them on the board. The students then wrote their drafts and shared them with the class. Figure 6.7 illustrates one of the personal perspectives written by Jean, a fourth grader in Ann's class.

The next day, the students were invited to think about what the biosphere adventure might have been like from the perspective of the plants and animals living in the woods. After a brief period of speculation, the students were eager to explore the topic in writing from a different point of view. Jean's piece is illustrated in Figure 6.8. As Ann commented on the sharing session, "We all shared a lot of laughs over these pieces."

Figure 6.7

My Biosphere Adventure
By Jean Ziegler

Yesterday was beautiful; the sun was shining and the air was cool. Mrs. Burns, our teacher, said, "Class, for science we'll go on a nature walk."

In the woods we saw a variety of leafless or bud-filled trees. In some trees there were some birds' nests. We also saw some birds such as a robin and a woodpecker. Our class saw some smooth or rough rocks. Some kids lifted them up and found worms and even a red backed salamander. We also saw some wild flowers. They smelled fresh and sweet. We smelled pine needles, too. We heard and felt cool crisp wind moving the branches on the trees. Our class saw a little creek. Its trickling water made us feel refreshed.

Figure 6.8

The Invasion

By Jean Ziegler

Dear Journal,

Today we got invaded by humans. It was terrifying! The humans came in and started going on a walk of theirs. Their voices were like thunder. I was at a party when this happened. When Sam the spider came out, there were these two girls standing there. They screamed. It sure scared Sam. He fainted. I followed them. They almost stepped on me 20 times, but I kept on going.

They wrecked our peaceful day. Fred and Sally were getting married and Fred dropped the ring and the humans smashed it to pieces and didn't even say they were sorry. They looked at everything in the woods. Tom, the tree, tried to hit a boy with one of his branches, but the boy moved away in time. When they picked up Ronald the rock, Ronald tasted their awful sweat. One good thing is that they were interested in our habitats. Maybe they just didn't know how to behave or what they were doing yet.

At least the rest of the day was peaceful. I guess it was an interesting day in our woods. I hope Fred buys a new ring.

Love,

Bob the Bug

Ann uses a learning log strategy in math to help students interact personally with information and concepts, explore ideas, and record their thinking. The learning log provides a permanent record of the learning that takes place in math during the year. Ann introduces the learning log in a letter to students. (See Figure 6.9.) She explains the purpose and goals of the log and has students staple the letter to the log's front cover.

In the learning logs, the students write for various audiences and in various discourse forms, depending on the activity. Audiences consist of the following: self, other students, real or fictional characters, parents, teachers. The writing may take these forms: interviews, directions, guide, survival manual, dictionary entry, mini report, debate, poem, cartoon, letter, request, summary, song, observations, and fact book.

Some of the topics and activities that students have responded to in their math learning logs are shown in the box.

Figure 6.9
Letter to Students Explaining Learning Logs

Dear Mathematicians,

   This math learning log will serve as a record of the learning you will do in math
this year. It will be your personal textbook containing ideas, examples, and problem
solutions. It is a place to learn and to practice thinking, problem solving, and writing.
In your log please include practice work, assigned problems, personal observations
and commentaries.

   I will be assigning topics to be addressed and explored in this journal so please be
sure to have it with you daily during math class. Number the pages as you go along and
date each entry. Good ideas, solutions, questions and your experiences at math stations
should all be recorded.

   Your journal will reflect one fourth of your grade in math, the other fourths being
class participation, homework, and tests. I will be collecting and commenting on the
books periodically. You will also be given the opportunity to share your writing in class.
Share your writing and experiences with family and friends too.

                                                           Enjoy!

Learning Log Activities for Math

- After tallying, collecting data, and graphing the results of probability experiments ask students to write to tell another fourth grader about probability.

- After much practice with "mental math" in addition, subtraction, and regrouping, ask students to explain the advantages and shortcuts they use in solving
  problems in their head. Students should be able to skip count to 100 and back
  down again by numbers 2 through 9 before this assignment.

- Have students find and write about newspaper stories which include large
  numbers. Then encourage them to write problems using the situation and the
  numbers in the problem.

- Write a story problem having more than two addends. Write the answer upside
  down in equation form.

- Ask each student to make up an addition or subtraction equation and write a
  story to go with it. As students read their stories see if the class can write the
  equation that would go with it.

- Given a grocery ad, ask students to prepare a shopping list for a dinner party, look up the prices, round to the nearest dollar, and add to find an estimate of the bill.
- Have students choose 4 single digit numbers. Ask them to use the digits to see how many different numbers they can create. Next have them list the numbers from largest to smallest.
- Have the students write several questions that are to be answered with Roman numerals. They may want to use their best in a class book with answers on the back of each page.
- Tell the students that they have just been awarded 5,000 free miles of air travel. Have them plan the trip they would take. Maps and mileage charts must be available.
- Ask students to tell what an estimate is and when one would be appropriate.
- Ask students to write about their average daily schedule, the times they do certain things, and the amount of time spent at each activity. In groups, have students compare the amount of time spent doing various activities.
- Go on an imaginary shopping spree. Tell what you would buy, cut out pictures of items from the newspaper and find the total cost of the items.
- Ask students to write what is meant by an even number and how they can tell if a number is even. Write a dialog about an even and an odd number meeting for the first time.
- Tell what you know about factors and multiples to a second grader.
- Find a chart in a newspaper or magazine, cut it out and paste it in your log. What information is given?
- Complete the following: Graphs are used for . . . Graphs are used to . . . Graphs are helpful when . . . Graphs make life easier by . . . The most important things about graphs are . . .
- Write what you would say to another fourth grader to describe a fraction. Can you think of a way to demonstrate fractions?
- What does it mean when we say that a fraction is in its lowest terms?
- Describe how you would add fractions that have unlike denominators.
- After studying the unit of measurement, have the children measure and graph their bedrooms and furnishings. Cut and paste these in the log and have the students then write about and describe their rooms.
- Have the students bring in sports clippings about games, players, teams, scores etc. Ask the students to write a math question using the information. Would any of the information be suitable or better shown on a graph?

ISSUES

Individual Differences

The abilities in Ann's class range widely from children who are strug-gling with reading, writing, and learning to children who are gifted. Yet, when she "outgrew" the basal system a decade ago, she essentially de-parted from ability grouping. According to Ann, "I tried to have those three-ring circuses going in my room, but there was just too much com-motion. I had one group that I was working with, two groups that were doing something else (seatwork, which was really busy work to keep the students occupied until I could work with them), and individual students at different learning stations in the room working on the skills they sup-posedly needed. There was just too much going on and very little time on task for actual reading and writing."

Ann believes that the reading workshop takes care of individual differ-ences because the students self-select their books and work at their own pace. "I try to provide the kids with as many books on their level as I possibly can." Sometimes, some of the students who are struggling try to choose books that are too challenging because of the peer pressure. Ann counsels these students and tries, in her words, "to create a comfort level, where they recognize that it's okay to read a picture book or a less com-plicated novel rather than some of the more sophisticated, adolescent novels that some of the other children choose."

Ann's main goal is to try to have students, especially those who strug-gle, develop a patience with silent reading: "These kids just don't have the ability to concentrate, because they have never been in a school situa-tion where it is quiet, and they really have to think and work through something for a long period of time. What I'm trying to do is to provide that atmosphere of quiet concentration and give them that encouragement they need to build self-confidence in themselves as readers."

Gifted readers, Ann claims, also like to self-select. She is amazed how some of these children can be reading several different books at the same time: "When I was a kid, I'd pick up one book, read it through, and when I finished, I'd start another. But these kids, they'll hear about a book from another student, and they have to read it, while they're read-ing something else. They'll jump back and forth on my daily class record chart. (See Figure 6.4.) At first I though they were abandoning books, and then I realized—now wait a minute—they are always reading. They have one book going at home, and one at school, and one on the bus! These kids love self-selection and choice because they can read what they want to read."

Evaluation

Ann uses multiple assessment sources to evaluate students' reading and writing. Most of her ongoing assessment involves observation and informal interviews or conferences with students. However, she also collects a variety of pertinent information, "I keep what is now being called a portfolio on each student to measure their progress."

First, Ann relies heavily on students' reading journals, the writing that they do to one another, the books that they have read, her class records, and their writing folders. She doesn't count pages or the number of books read, but she does assess what they are reading and how they are reacting to what they read.

Second, Ann holds individual conferences with the students just prior to a grading period. She confers with the children on the importance of variety. She talks with them about mixing challenging texts with easier ones. Also, she has students chart the types of book they are reading on the "Variety in Reading Chart" in the box. Ann doesn't insist that the students read different types of books, but she does try to make them aware of possibilities.

To prepare for the conference, each student completes the self-evaluation form in the box. Ann uses this form to determine from the student's perspective what was accomplished during the grading period. She also talks with students about their reading plans and their goals for improvement.

In addition to these informal measures, Ann also administers the fourth grade basal unit test. "I use this test because it does provide an indicator. If students are reading a lot, usually they do real well on the test. The school district also administers in the fall the *California Test of Achievement*, so that's another indicator. So far I haven't had any of the fifth-grade teachers come to me and say they are disappointed in my students' reading scores. However, one of the comments that a fifth-grade teacher made just made my day: 'I can always tell the students that come from your room, because if there's any lull in the day, they pull out a book to read.'"

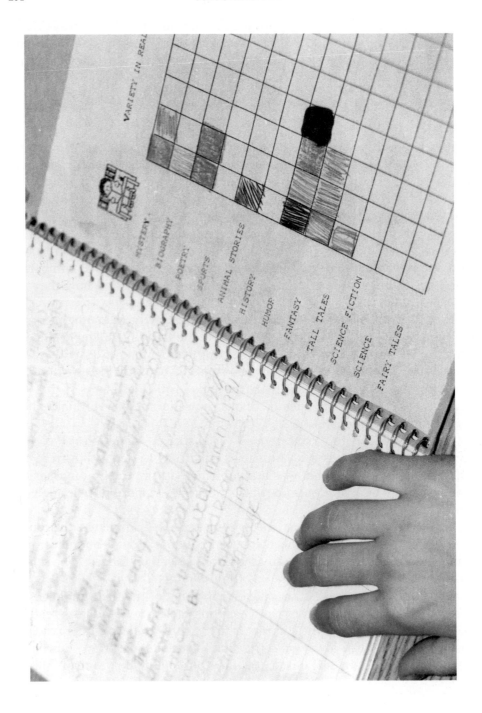

Self-Evaluation Form

1. What does someone have to do in order to be a good reader? _____

   _____

   _____

   _____

2. What is the best book you read this quarter and what makes it the best?

   _____

   _____

   _____

3. What do you want to do as a reader during the next nine weeks? _____

   _____

   _____

   _____

4. My goals for improvement are: _____

   _____

   _____

   _____

   _____

                                                [Signed]

Home Connections

The comment of the fifth-grade teacher, Ann says, "ranks right up there with one that a parent made when she said, 'It's the first time I had ever driven boys anyplace and heard them talking about authors and the books they were reading.'" Ann works closely with parents. In fact, some of the parents of the third-grade students have heard about Ann's work with readers and writers and make special requests to have their children placed in her classroom.

Ann keeps parents informed of their children's progress through the conventional routes: open house, parent's night, and letters to the home. She explains her program's goals and encourages parents to maintain an environment for reading at home. She also invites them to visit the reading workshop and read with the students.

School Connections

The school administration encourages professional decision-making among the faculty. Ann had little trouble transforming from a basal to the reading workshop format. Over the years, her principals have been supportive and have made provisions in their budgets to purchase books.

Her colleagues "sometimes wonder what's going on in my room, but generally they have been accepting of the way I teach literacy." Since eschewing the basal a decade ago, two colleagues have also converted to a reading workshop format. This has encouraged Ann and has given her a support group within the school.

Keeping Current

Ann keeps current by reading professional textbooks on whole language, writing, and children's literature. She follows the writing of certain authors who have had an impact on her philosophy and practice, particularly Nancie Atwell and Don Graves. She also reads professional journals, especially *Language Arts*, published by The National Council of Teachers of English (NCTE) and *The Reading Teacher*, published by the International Reading Association (IRA).

Ann is a professional student. She attends workshops in the summer and during the school year. Several years ago, she enrolled in a doctoral program in literacy studies and continues to take courses regularly.

Challenges

The time commitment it takes to plan a whole language classroom is Ann's greatest challenge. She finds it difficult to do everything she wants to do in a single day. When she started using thematic units, she found that students did less personal writing on self-generated topics. Although students write regularly in her classroom, process writing occurs within the context of interdisciplinary learning. Ann's students have

Figure 6.10
Letters from Amy, Charles, and Michael Evaluating Ann's Reading Program

Dear Mrs Burns,

I really like our reading program! I have had all of them free-read, basil, grouping, everything. This one is my favorite! I also had free-read when I had Miss Roads. Last year I had basil and grouping. The basil was o.k. but I really didn't like the stories. I also had grouping. The books we read were great, but I am sort of a slow reader and when we came back the next day people were farther than me and giving the story away.

Writing is one of my favorite subjects! I loved writing this year (only I wish we would've done more)! I think it is fun every once in a while to be given a subject to write about. I really enjoyed making up my own things to write about!

Sincerely,
Your student
Amy Y.

Figure 6.10 *(Continued)*

Dear Mrs. Burns

This has been my favoret year in Elementary School, mostly because of the reading program.

I think I like it because we are not told "You have to read this." We get to go at our own rate or level. Its fun saying "I read The Slugs and things like that in the begining. But now I have read for Zacharia wich is a very hard book, but a good one."

We haven't writen that much, but what we did was fun!

Sincerely,
Charles A.
Grugle

Figure 6.10 *(Continued)*

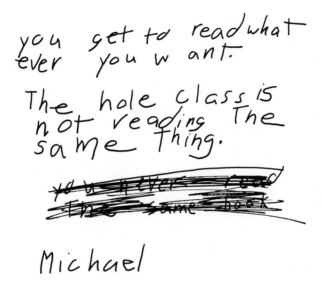

noticed that they are doing less personal writing and more academic-related, topic driven writing and have lobbied for more time exploring topics of personal relevance.

As Ann puts it, "To keep a classroom an interesting and exciting place is a difficult and time-consuming task." She currently wrestles "with how to do it all."

SUMMING UP

Ann is one of those remarkable teachers who has followed a path less traveled by most of her colleagues. Her priorities for literacy learning are supported by the belief that children should get to know authors as friends and confidantes. Pleasure, appreciation, involvement, fluency, and personal satisfaction are the hallmarks of her work as a whole language teacher.

Ann's students have formed their own conclusions about her work. In an end-of-the year letter to her, they wrote about the reading workshop. Here's what Amy, Charles, and Michael—children of varying ability—have to say. (See Figure 6.10.)

Chapter 7

WHOLE LANGUAGE IN A FIFTH-GRADE CLASSROOM

. . . I'm learning from them, and they're learning from me. And we sort of just find our way together. . . .

Chapter 7

WHOLE LANGUAGE IN A FIFTH-GRADE CLASSROOM

. . . I'm learning from them, and they're learning from me. And we sort of just find our way together. . . .

When Brenda Church begins talking about her fifth-grade students, it's hard to get her to stop. She's proud of them, and justifiably so. Yet to the outside world, Brenda's students easily and summarily might be written off as losers, children without dreams, tomorrow's dropouts.

Brenda teaches in inner-city Akron where 70 percent of the children in her school are black, 10 percent are Hispanic or Oriental, and 20 percent, Caucasian. All are poor. The free lunch program serves more than 95 percent of the school's student body. The majority of children in Brenda's class are black (20); three are Laotian, and 5 are white. Of these, 23 of the 28 children are from homes without fathers. This year, one boy's father was murdered; a girl's mother returned home from drug rehabilitation for the second time; and another girl was just removed from her home, along with her brothers and sisters, by Children's Services.

At one point in the year, Brenda missed three weeks of school, during which time 8 of her students were suspended by the principal for misconduct. The hard realities of teaching in an inner-city school do not discourage her. Quite the contrary. Brenda's response to the students' suspensions exemplifies her commitment to learning and teaching: "While I was gone, two gangs formed in the class and some of the kids got into trouble. When I got back, I asked the children to write to me about what happened while I was away. We used their writings to talk about things and work things out like a family would."

Family. Much of Brenda's philosophy of whole language, her educational stance in general, revolves around the concept of family. As she and her children enter into relationship as extended family members in a community might, the classroom is home, a place where the students can develop independence in and control of their learning as well as their behavior. The presence of high expectations, demonstrations, engagements in learning, sensitivity, and the use of literacy to solve problems contributes to student empowerment in Brenda's class.

WHAT BRENDA THINKS ABOUT WHOLE LANGUAGE

When Brenda hears teachers in her school district "talking whole language," they often do so in terms of materials and strategies. Yet she prefers to talk about attitudes and beliefs. Whole language, for Brenda, is an attitude, a "state of mind." She expresses a whole language philosophy with these words as she talks about her work with the children in her classroom: "I'm learning from them, and they're learning from me. And we sort of find our way together.

Brenda is of the strong disposition that "every child who enters my room is a learner, no matter what." Whether children come from broken homes, abject poverty, or a culture and language that differs from her's, Brenda believes that children are natural learners. Her job is to support them as learners.

Gaddis is a case in point. A lean and gangling eleven-year-old whose body impatiently waits for manhood, Gaddis spent the first couple of weeks in Brenda's class stomping around the room. Angry. Defiant. Unwilling. He railed against most activities involving literacy, especially writing. His outward demeanor masked an inner fear that conveyed the message: "If I don't try, then I can't fail."

The class was engaged in "book clubs," a term Brenda uses to describe literature study in small groups. Gaddis's group was reading Jean Georges's, *My Side of the Mountain.* With the first parent's night of the year approaching, the students in the book club had decided to illustrate and then write thumbnail sketches of the main characters in the novel. These were to be put on display for the parents. Although Gaddis worked painstakingly on his character's picture, he could not bring a written description to completion. He would start to write only to crumple the paper, stomp across the room, and slam dunk it into the waste paper basket. According to Brenda, "He proceeded to crumple his drafts, stomp across the room, and dispose of them in the waste paper basket, maybe eight or nine times."

Brenda could easily have been intimidated by Gaddis's behavior, given up on him, accepted his drawing as the best he could do, and not have him follow-through on the character description. But she knew that he had something to say. A crumpled draft, which she retrieved from the waste paper basket, indicated the same, although it was riddled with spelling and other mechanical errors. So they talked. Gaddis, it turns out, had not written anything of any length or substance in previous grades, other than to fill-in-blanks on worksheets or write one or sentence responses to story starters. Putting ideas on a blank sheet of paper frightened him.

Brenda worked with Gaddis, supporting him in the writing process. He stuck with it and completed a two-paragraph description. (See Figure 7.1.) His mother, who worked nights, had never been to a parent's night,

Figure 7.1
Gaddis's Character Sketch

Sam Gribley is the wildboy. He weighs 109 pounds and is thirteen years old. He lives in the Catskill mountains and is missing from home for about one year. Sam has dreamed about living in the wilderness. Now it has come true. He wanted to prove to his father that he could live out there in the mountains.

He made a tree for his home. He was proud of himself. This boy even found his self a falcon so he could have company through the winter days. He named his bird Frightful. Frightful helped him find his food. He was a great help to Sam.

and she didn't attend on this occasion either. But it didn't matter. His contribution was proudly displayed with the work of his classmates. Gaddis, the writer, visited the display every so often over the course of the next several days, reading his piece and other character descriptions. Something unexpected then happened. Brenda invited his mother to visit the class during the school day to see Gaddis's work and discuss his progress. She did. As the year progressed, Gaddis maintained his familiar stomp, but continued to make significant strides as well in his literacy development.

The notion that every child is a learner has been part of Brenda's educational stance since becoming a teacher. She attributes this belief to her student teaching experience in the late 1960s. She apprenticed in a first-grade classroom and was fortunate to have as a mentor, Leona, her cooperating teacher: "Leona was a very creative teacher in a school that was quite traditional. She was different from the other teachers in that school. As I reflect on the experience, Leona was child-centered; she believed in creating very stimulating environments for learning."

Children in Leona's class explored meaningful language use through the expressive arts. Art and music were an integral part of children's language learning experiences: Drawing, painting, singing, acting out stories, and displaying children's work at every opportunity were integrated smoothly and naturally into the language arts program. Reading aloud to children, engaging in story discussions, and using language-experience stories to initiate reading lessons were stepping stones into literacy. "She taught a lot of phonics, too," Brenda recalls, "but she believed in using more than phonics."

Looking back on her student teaching experience, Brenda recognizes that her first mentor provided a powerful role model. Leona believed that children learned in a variety of ways, "There was not just one way to learn to read: We would explore how children were learning to read and watch them carefully. And then we would sit and talk and make plans on how we might approach the next reading lesson."

Helping children to make decisions about their own learning underlies Brenda's thinking about teaching and curriculum. She recalls how student teaching again provided a vivid and powerful experience which contributes richly to her present philosophical base as a whole language teacher. The children in Leona's class were "the products" of two kindergarten rooms in the building. In one, the children were taught to do everything the "correct" way. Brenda remembers that the art work of the children in this kindergarten class was always characterized by its sameness: "The pictures were always neat and tidy looking. All the birds in the children's drawings were made the same as were all the houses, because the teacher showed the children how to make a house and how to make a bird the 'right' way. There was no room for error."

In the second kindergarten class, however, the teacher was quite similar to Leona in terms of philosophy and approach. As a student teacher, Brenda quickly noticed the contrast between the children from the two different kindergartens: "The kids from the creative kindergarten could make their own decisions and weren't always asking for your attention or seeking approval when an activity was initiated. What a world of difference from the children in the other kindergarten. They were a little frustrated for the first several weeks because neither Leona nor I would tell them what to do or how to do it. Instead, we would say things like, 'How do you think you should do it?' and 'How do you want to do it?'"

The children, however, wanted Brenda or Leona to sit with them and show them, step-by-step, how to complete a task. It was a real transition for these children to make some of their own decisions and to learn that it was okay to make mistakes in the process of learning. In retrospect, to see the two groups of children come together and to watch the purposefulness and self-confidence of the children that had been taught to make decisions impacted Brenda's thinking about what it means to teach and learn.

Brenda sums up her thinking about whole language this way: "I believe that school must be a place where children engage, individually and collectively, in making sense. . . . All learning is connected and interrelated. I see my role as setting the conditions to help students make the connections and experience the interrelatedness of what they are learning." In Brenda's class, learning is active; it's participatory; it's exploratory.

INSIDE BRENDA'S CLASSROOM

The Environment

Brenda claims not to be the one who creates a literate environment in her classroom. The children do. Her job is to set the conditions for literacy to occur. Setting these conditions means, in part, that children have access to a wide variety of authentic texts and materials for reading and writing.

The writing center in the room is a focal point for student activity. As the room diagram in Figure 7.2 shows, the writing center is located in the

Figure 7.2
Physical Arrangement in Brenda's Room

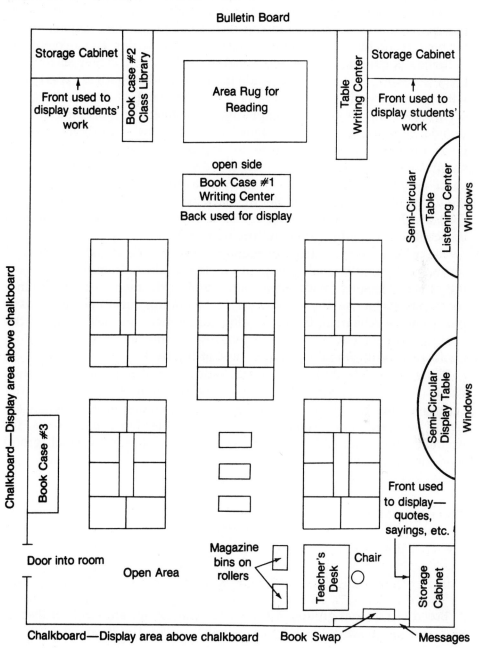

center of the back part of the room, directly in front of an area rug for reading. To the right of the reading area is a long rectangular table for writing. Within the writing center is a wealth of different kinds of paper, pencils, pens, markers, crayons, water colors, stamps, inkpads, rings for binders, braids, a paper punch, scissors, a typewriter, and a computer.

Brenda is quite conscious about making the writing center an inviting place to work. Most of her students have had negative experiences with writing in other classrooms. Like Gaddis, much of their writing has occurred in the context of completing worksheets or story starters. As Brenda explains, displaying students' writing, along with their art work, is an open invitation to engage in a process of communicating and sharing with others. Consequently, she displays student work wherever space permits, but particularly in those areas that are eye-level or accessible to the children, for example, the back side of bookcase 1 (See Figure 7.1.) which borders the writing center, the fronts of the storage cabinets adjacent to the reading area and the writing table.

The open area in the front of Brenda's room by the chalkboard is used for instruction with small groups. Here she conducts mini-lessons, reading strategy lessons, math intervention and enrichment sessions. Sometimes, students use the open area for planning meetings, perhaps a puppet show rehearsal. Group writing conferences are held either at the writing table in the back of the room or in the open area. Individual conferences with Brenda are often held at her desk.

The students sit at flat-top, movable desks with movable, unattached chairs. The arrangement displayed in the diagram is what Brenda describes as the "formal" room arrangement. Depending on the literacy activity, however, many combinations are possible. On a daily basis, for example, the desks and chairs are arranged into triads for small group work or discussion:

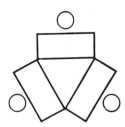

Brenda finds that groups of three are ideal for certain kinds of discussion and group work. Each group member, given the triad arrangement above, is able to establish eye contact with the other members of the group. The group is small enough for each child to participate in discussion, diminishing the possibility of nonparticipation. Each triad group has a specified area of the room in which to locate. The movement into triads, according to Brenda, "is a very structured and controlled activity." That is to say, she teaches her students the rules for "slow motion movement": She says, "Let's move to our groups now" and the students slowly slide their desks to the appropriate places in the room, in slow motion, as in a video replay of a sporting event. The class rehearses slow motion movement and discuses its importance many times in the beginning of the school year, until the students learn to proceed in a relatively quiet and orderly manner.

Other desk arrangements occur throughout the day depending on the literacy event. Brenda uses an open rectangle format for whole class meetings and presentations:

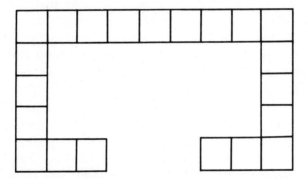

Also, bookcase 1 serves as a puppet stage for story re-enactments, using a variation on the rectangular format:

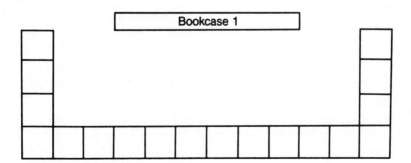

In certain instances, desks are pushed together to form large squares for art activities, book clubs, and cooperative learning experiences:

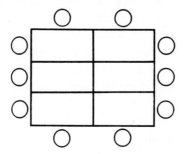

At times, desks are moved back along the perimeter of the room, close to the walls, to make room for dancing, plays, and demonstrations.

Throughout the room, there is an abundance of books and other types of authentic reading texts, including catalogs, junk mail, advertisements, encyclopedias, dictionaries, and magazines for children. Each of the bookcases serve special functions: bookcase 1 houses the writing materials, dictionaries, and thesauruses); bookcase 2 contains the classroom library that includes novels and student-authored books; bookcase 3 holds reference books, including the encyclopedias, atlases, and miscellaneous reference materials. Also in the room are magazine bins on rollers, containing back issues of *Ranger Rick, Highlights for Children, Cricket,* comic books, and science and social studies-related magazines for children. Brenda's classroom provides an environment that encourages students to take risks. To create a risk-taking environment, she finds it extremely valuable to work on the development of personal relationships with the children. The more she gets to know them on a personal basis, the greater their level of trust and willingness to take risks as language learners: "I spend time talking with my kids before school, after school, during playground duty. Much of the time is spent listening to them, encouraging them when they're down on themselves, and making time for them when they come to me with a problem or concern. You never know when your support will make a difference with students, but if you don't try to give the extra attention and care that they need, you'll never make any difference at all."

Celebrations, big and small, occur daily in Brenda's classroom. One of her favorite books, Byrd Baylor's *I'm in Charge of Celebrations,* is a perfect read-aloud to help students to reflect upon the importance of celebrating.

And there is much to celebrate in room 205, whether the celebration involves publishing a class book, concluding a thematic unit, or walking away from a fight on the playground.

Beginning the School Year: Making the Transition from Traditional Classrooms

Every school year begins a bit differently for Brenda, but her underlying goal remains the same: to help her students to make the transition from traditional classrooms. As Brenda explains, "I've never been fortunate enough to receive kids directly from another whole language classroom. I've had some kids who have had holistic experiences in first or second grade, if they've been lucky, but usually not in the third or fourth grade." As a result, Brenda's students have been used to sitting in straight rows, having little choice or decision-making power, and completing tons of worksheets.

How does she help students make the transition into whole language? The first minutes of the first day of school begin with a literacy event. Brenda reads a poem to the children by Shel Silverstein called "Nobody's Perfect." "Nobody's Perfect" is about a teacher who wants everything to be perfect in her class. Yet when she goes up to Heaven, she finds that she is not accepted because she's not perfect. The poem is quite humorous and the children enjoy it immensely.

Brenda uses the occasion to share with the students that she's not going to be perfect either. And she doesn't expect them to be. She explains that there are many different ways to learn. "Things are going to be quite different in this room from other years," Brenda forewarns the class and then adds, "I will help you to learn in many different ways."

That is Brenda's pledge to the students. She follows through on her words by introducing the class to their first new learning experience—a whole class study of a novel. Most of the students have never read a novel as a class. Brenda begins with one of her favorites, *Julie of the Wolves*, by Jean George. She reads the opening chapters aloud and engages the class in discussion over the next several days.

Over the years, Brenda has accumulated class sets and multiple copies of "great and exciting" books. She makes copies of *Julie of the Wolves* available for all of the students and invites them to continue reading the story in class. As an aside, Brenda notes that, in addition to her book collection, she works collaboratively with the librarians at the Akron Public Library.

As a service to teachers, the Akron Public Library will provide class sets of 30 books for instructional purposes for some of the more popular children's titles.

Brenda shares responsibility with the students for reading *Julie of the Wolves*. Sometimes she will read the story aloud; other times, the students will read silently. Class discussions follow on each occasion, but at this beginning point of the year, Brenda does not introduce the students to literature response logs. Not yet, at least. Getting comfortable with a novel is a big enough chore for the students.

Class discussions of *Julie of the Wolves*, with Brenda as the instructional leader, revolve around directed reading-thinking activity (DR-TA) questions. At one point in the story, Brenda pauses from several minutes of reading aloud to ask: "What do you think Miyax will do next?" Several children offer predictions. Brenda then responds by asking a follow-up question, "Do you think Miyax can depend on the wolves? Won't daylight only last for one more month? What will she do?" Jacobie, one of the students, shoots his arm skyward and responds, ". . . make some kind of weapon." Darnell adds, "Go back home if she smart."

DR-TA type questions invite readers to predict, to verify, to reconsider, and to evaluate. Questions such as, "What do you think this story's about? What will happen next? Why do you think so? Help me to understand— Can you show me . . .?", as Brenda demonstrates to the students, trigger the kinds of "thinking with text" common to thoughtful readers. Toward the end of the questioning cycle initiated above, the students are fully and thoughtfully into the flow of the story. Natisha predicts that Miyax will follow the North Star to the ocean and to San Francisco. Souchavanh suggests that the birds will guide her. When Brenda asks, "What would you do to survive 30 days in the wilderness?", several of the children respond quickly without raising hands, "Pray." "Ask God to help." Others hypothesize, "Get some food." Brenda picks up on both lines of thought: "Why do you think she should pray? How will that help? And for those who think she should get food, what would you do to get food?" The class then reads silently to find out how their predictions will turn out.

Within the first few weeks of the school year, there is a gradual release of responsibility that shifts from Brenda's shoulders to the students': "I try to introduce the kids to some new ways of learning. I talk to them about reading, what it means to be a good reader, and my own philosophy of teaching and learning. I like to move slowly, and I mean slowly. Weaning kids from several years of basal reading isn't easy. So I begin first with a class study of a novel, then with book clubs and eventually with total self-selection."

Brenda is the first to admit, however, that things don't always run as smoothly as she would like: "One year, I started with a class study of a novel, and the students were visibly upset because they did not have a basal reader. The kids wanted to know if they were going to be in the fifth-grade basal or the sixth-grade basal the next year. And one student even asked me if the principal knew that I was using 'these other books'." Predictably, many of Brenda's children, when they first arrive in her class, are unfamiliar with and unsure of a learning context that emphasizes real books rather than short narrative selections in a basal reader. Some even insist on worksheets from basal workbooks rather than writing in a literature response journal because, as Brenda puts it, "That's all they know."

For the class that balked so strenuously to "these other books," Brenda decided that she would have to take a step or two backward in order to move forward. She honored the students' concerns and went back to the basal reader. She picked out some of what she thought was the best of the series in the basal and used those for class instruction, but not in conventional ways. She continued to use DR-TA lessons to demonstrate thoughtful reading. And while she was using basal stories, Brenda extended the literacy lessons with literature read-alouds. Eventually she eased the students into a class study of a novel and then into book clubs, when they started feeling more secure: "By February, the class was into total self-selection, book discussions, and literature response journals. They were having fun, and enjoying books, despite their initial anxiety at the beginning of the year."

A Typical Day

"If teaching is a journey on a river, then my class likes to shoot the rapids," Brenda chuckles in response to the question, "What is a typical day like in your whole language classroom?" No two days ever turn out exactly the way she anticipates they will, but she is quick to acknowledge that there is a "well-thought out" structure underlying literacy learning. Sometimes the class veers off into unexpected directions, depending on the students' questions and interests. Most times, however, Brenda sticks to a general game plan that provides ample opportunities for choice, student decision making, and unanticipated but valuable invitations to learn, "teachable moments," that emerge as events in the classroom unfold.

The game plan for literacy calls for book-shares and read-alouds, interdisciplinary studies through thematic units, many occasions to write including journal writing, sustained silent reading, inquiry learning, and reading strategy lessons. These literacy events blend together in different combinations from day to day. Although Brenda claims that it's difficult to describe a typical day of whole language teaching, the way she organizes for instruction, manages the class, and employs strategies for literacy learning provides a strong indication of what a whole language day might look like in her classroom.

Organization and Management

The students arrive at school at around 9:00 A.M. and are in their rooms by 9:15. They have about 20 minutes to informally mix with one another, swap books, read, write in journals, or work on assignments and projects in progress. During this time, Brenda also plans informal lessons for those students who need additional help with math or science concepts.

After the morning announcements, Brenda begins the day by sharing a book with the children. The read-aloud introduces them to her favorite children's books. Some are picture books. Some are poetry anthologies. Some are informational books. Besides the sheer fun of starting the day off with a book-share, the occasion serves at least two other purposes.

Brenda's class is involved in a paired reading program with the kindergarten. Once a week they prepare a story to read to a "buddy" in the kindergarten classroom. The morning read-aloud introduces the students to possible book choices. During the week, the students select their books, practice for fluency, and decide how they will interact with their buddies. Many of the students use DR-TA questions, which have been demonstrated extensively by Brenda. Together buddy pairs also have made puppets of story characters and performed puppet shows. In addition, buddies have written and published their own books for sharing with one another. On these occasions, the kindergarteners dictate stories to Brenda's students who serve as scribes.

A second purpose for book-shares is more therapeutic in nature. Brenda finds that children's books are excellent springboards for discussion of issues and problems that the students face in their own lives. She believes it's important to discuss these issues from the children's perspectives. The stories, which often include themes related to issues such as sibling rivalry, friendships, divorce, fear, and relationships, allow children to relate their personal experiences, identify with characters, and understand their feelings. Through discussion, the students recognize that what they are feeling are often common to others.

The remainder of the morning revolves around the exploration of themes, interdisciplinary study, and journal writing. In the afternoon, Brenda initiates sustained silent reading (SSR), mathematics (which she teaches as a separate subject), reading strategy lessons, and an afternoon book-share to end the day.

Themes allow Brenda to integrate literature, writing, social studies, science, health, art, music, drama, and occasionally math. The theme revolves around literature, usually a class study of a novel and/or book clubs and/or self-selection. In the beginning of the school year, Brenda selects the theme. As the class progresses through the year, she invites the students to contribute their ideas about what they would like to learn: "I try to get the kids to help me in a share of the planning. Most of the time I need to give more direction than I would like to give. I'm real careful not to give more guidance than is needed, although sometimes the kids flounder and too much time is wasted. So I'll suggest some possible themes. We brainstorm ideas. We make some decisions and narrow choices. And the unit begins to evolve."

One of Brenda's favorite themes is "survival," one that she initiates at the beginning of the year. She often selects *Julie of the Wolves* as a class study to launch the survival unit. As the unit evolves, the students also read novels in groups (the book clubs). They select a novel from the choices that Brenda gives them from the Survival Tales Book List. (See box.)

Brenda provides a commercial for each book on the list and the students select the book club of their choice. Book club members have time to read their books in the morning and during SSR in the afternoon, if they choose to. Each day they write whatever reactions they have to the story in a response log. Brenda monitors the logs and responds to the entries, either in writing or informally through casual conversation with the students. When the tales are read, the book clubs meet to discuss their stories and to engage in projects.

Brenda has compiled a list of questions to help focus discussion in the book clubs. These questions are adapted from Joy Moss's *Focus Units in Literature: A Handbook for Elementary School Teachers,* published by The National Council of Teachers of English, 1984. In addition to these questions, a book club member can raise any question that comes to mind about the story. Brenda plans at least one mini-lesson to model the type of questions that helps a reader relate the story to personal experience. The discussion questions that cut across the books for Survival Tales theme are shown in the box on page 228.

Projects related to the Survival Tales unit are outlined in the box on pages 229–230. Most of these require the students to engage in the writing process. Brenda incorporates a writing workshop format around the projects. She does not conduct a separate writing workshop during the day, where children develop self-selected topics from personal

Survival Tales: Book List

1. Holman, Felice. *Slake's Limbo.* New York: Charles Scribner's Sons, 1974.
2. Sperry, Arnstron. *Call It Courage.* New York: Macmillan, 1940.
3. Aurembou, Renee. *Snowbound.* New York: Abelard-Schuman, 1965.
4. Byars, Betsy. *Trouble River.* New York: Viking Press, 1969.
5. Christopher, John. *The White Mountains.* New York: Macmillan, 1967.
6. Collier, James and Christopher Collier. *Jump Ship to Freedom.* New York: Delacorte Press, 1981.
7. Farley, Walter. *The Black Stallion Legend.* New York: Random House, 1983.
8. George, Jean. *Julie of the Wolves.* New York: Harper & Row, 1959.
9. George, Jean. *My Side of the Mountain.* New York: E. P. Dutton, 1959.
10. Hamilton, Virginia. *The Planet of Junior Brown.* New York: Macmillan, 1971.
11. Konigsburg, E. L. *From the Mixed-up Files of Mrs. Basil E. Frankweiler.* New York: Atheneum, 1967.
12. O'Dell, Scott. *Island of the Blue Dolphins.* Boston: Houghton Mifflin, 1960.
13. O'Dell, Scott. *Sarah Bishop.* Boston: Houghton Mifflin, 1980.
14. O'Dell, Scott. *Sing Down the Moon.* Boston: Houghton Mifflin, 1970.
15. Spears, Elizabeth. *The Sign of the Beaver.* Boston: Houghton Mifflin, 1983.
16. Taylor, Mildred. *Roll of Thunder, Hear My Cry.* New York: Dial Press, 1976.

experience. Instead, various facets of writing process instruction are integrated into thematic study.

The children also explore the theme from an interdisciplinary perspective, engaging in expository text learning from textbooks, informational trade books, encyclopedias, and magazine articles. As a part of the survival theme in science, for example, they might study the survival of animals by engaging in group projects. One group worked on developing a "teaching poster" on rabbits and the means by which they survive.

In the social studies, survival is explored from the perspective of the American Revolution and life in Colonial America. The students, for example, become involved in studying how our forefathers established the Committee of Correspondences and created an elaborate system of letter writing to communicate—an important survival tool in times of war and revolution. The box on page 231 shows how Brenda engaged students in

Survival Tales: Discussion Questions for Book Clubs

1. How would you catagorize this tale (Historical fiction, science fiction, contemporary realism, fantasy, wilderness, and natural disaster)? Explain why.

2. What do you notice about how this story is told? Map the basic plot pattern of the story.

3. What did you learn about the main character(s)? What method or way did the author use to portray the character(s)? What signs of growth or change in the character did you notice?

4. How does the setting affect the development of the plot and characters?

5. What qualities of the main character(s) are very important for helping them survive the things that happen to them?

6. What is the theme?

7. Compare this story with other survival tales?

Survival Tales: Theme Projects

1. Compare and contrast the main character(s) in the book you are reading with the character(s) in our class read aloud book.

2. Step inside the shoes of the main character. Imagine how you might feel if you were this character.

    a. As you read your book, keep a diary and make entries as if you were the main character.

    b. Select another character in the story with whom you could communicate through telephone conversations and/or letters. Write letters to each other which will be shared and/or be ready to enact several telephone conversations between the characters.

3. A sequel is a continuation of a story. Sequels are made of books and movies. Write a sequel to your book. The only requirement is that you use the main character and it connects or "flows" from the book you read.

4. Make a map of the setting(s) in the story in which your main character(s) lived. Be ready to explain how the setting(s) either helped or hindered the characters survival.

5. Select several important scenes throughout your story which show how your main character grows and changes. Prepare to act out these scenes. Make sure they show how the character changes!!

6. Make an object which is significant to the story. Tell why it is significant. Also, share with the group the descriptions from the book which helped you know what the object looked like.

7. Write a description of the main character. Make sure you refer frequently to your book so that your description is accurate. Make a picture of the main character(s) of your story. Use appropriate media so that you "capture" the character's physical features and personality.

8. Select some picture books (at least three) which are also related to the survival theme. Be able to tell how these books relate to the survival theme and why you chose them. Prepare to read them aloud to our class and/or a group of younger children.

9. Compare and contrast the plot of your story with our class read aloud. Tell how they are similar and different. Be sure to relate them to the various plot structures we have studied.

10. Write a personal account (first person) of a time in your life that you experienced a situation which was scary, dangerous, and/or frightening.

Option: Create your own project and conference with teacher *before* starting it.

writing letters to one another by "stepping into the shoes" of different revolutionary leaders.

The beginning of the year Brenda lays the groundwork for various kinds of classroom interactions: "The class and I sit down together and make up the rules for the classroom. These rules are reached by group consensus. Often they do not stay the same throughout the year because we process how we're doing, and we decide if the rules are still viable or need to be changed."

Letter Writing Project for Colonial America Study

As part of our theme of survival, we have been studying the Revolutionary period in American history. We have learned about events and the people and circumstances surrounding those events.

You will now "step into the shoes" of one of the famous Revolutionary leaders that you have read about. Maybe you will pretend to be Paul Revere, Samuel Adams, George Washington, Thomas Jefferson, Ben Franklin, or someone else we have studied.

Write a letter to someone of your choice telling them about something that you want them to know about, something that happened to you, or something that concerns you.

Be sure to include references to the events of this period.

Brenda works assiduously to have the students take ownership of their behavior. She explains that many of them come to school with poor social behavior. They lack role models: "We have parents in the neighborhood who fight in the street and shoot at one another. There are even confrontations that take place at school." Fighting is a way of life for many of the students, yet Brenda's strong expectation persists: the children have to learn to take responsibility for their behavior and their learning. This process is slow, sometimes very frustrating, but necessary if the classroom is to become a community of learners.

Periodically, the class meets to evaluate and reflect upon how "things are going in our classroom." What do the students like about it? What needs to be changed? And how are they going to go about making the changes? Also, Brenda institutes a "time-out zone" in the back of the room in a secluded area. If a student is having difficulty interacting with other students, is angry and upset, or just wants to be alone, he or she may take a time-out and voluntarily re-enter the group at a later time. At times, particularly in the beginning of the year, if a student is disruptive, Brenda will ask the child to take a time-out and think about his or her behavior. After several minutes, she will confer with the child, and they'll often come to some resolution concerning the behavior in question.

Brenda concentrates on how to work in groups since much of what the class will do as a community involves group work: "I spend a large amount of time setting up how we will interact in groups. Much of what we do in class involves collaboration and cooperative learning. One of my favorite quotations—I share it with the students and then tape it to the front of my desk—is a line from Peter Elbow's book (*Writing with Power*, New York: Oxford University Press, 1981): 'We can learn to do alone what at first we could only do with others.'"

Brenda's commitment to cooperative learning demands that she models and demonstrates how to work in groups. This takes time, patience, and repetition. Her students are not used to working with one another in an instructional context. Ironically, they have been taught in previous grades not to interact. According to Brenda, noise in an inner-city school, even "good noise," where students are engaging in meaningful talk with one another, is anathema to some teachers and principals. In such cases, an orderly environment for learning (which she works hard to foster and maintain) is narrowly interpreted to mean a quiet environment (which often is not the case in her room when students are working in groups).

Talking and listening to one another go hand-in-hand in Brenda's class. She explains: "When discussing a story in a group, the students and I process what it means to be a good group participant and a good listener." In one lesson, Brenda asks, "What makes a good listener?" The students generate a list of behaviors which she records on chart paper. The students reflect on the list; some behaviors are discussed and clarified; several more are added to the list. Brenda then follows up with another question, "What makes you feel that someone values your opinion when you say something in a group?" She follows the process of recording student responses and engaging in discussion and clarification.

These types of questions culminate with the formation of guidelines for being good members of a group. The class comes to consensus on the rules, several students volunteer to make a poster, which is displayed in Figure 7.3, and then begins the process of learning how to apply them as they work on a group activity.

Brenda also helps the students to monitor their participation in groups. She raises three questions that the students must consider as they engage in group work: (1) What does your group have to accomplish today? (Brenda wants students to be aware of the goal and the task ahead of them.) (2) What are the rules for good group work? (She calls their attention to their roles as participants and listeners.) And (3) What does your group need to do next? (Toward the conclusion of group work, Brenda wants the students to decide on what will be their responsibilities when they convene in order to finish the task.)

Underlying Brenda's approach to classroom management is the recognition that the children in her class need affirmation and validation. Within

Figure 7.3
Student-Generated Poster Outlining the Rules for Good Group Work

What Does Good
Group Work Look Like

1. No arguing or fighting.
2. Watch your language.
3. Share your ideas.
4. Stay on task.
5. Talk things over.
6. Listen to what people say.

the framework of high expectations, she praises them often and provides them with consistent feedback when their behavior runs counter to the rules established by the class.

Strategies

The environment in Brenda's room unmistakably conveys the message that children are immersed in learning literacy and using literacy to learn. She relies on a host of strategies to invite students to explore meaning through oral and written language. Many of the strategies already have been described or hinted at in other sections of the case. In this section, several are highlighted to underscore the application of Brenda's philosophical stance as a whole language teacher.

Book Involvement. One of Brenda's goals is to keep children continually involved with and immersed in authentic texts. Real books are the vehicles for learning and enjoying throughout the year within the context of book-shares, paired reading, thematic units, and SSR. Brenda employs two additional strategies to get books into the hands of her students.

The Book Swap. One of these is a functional activity that students organize and monitor throughout the school year. Brenda enacts a book recycling strategy called "the book swap" early in the school year. The book swap underscores ownership and permits a continual flow of books to circulate among the children. Here's how it works: Students often receive books free from various programs like RIF (Reading Is Fundamental). In time, many of the students choose to swap these books for different ones. For each book they bring to class to swap, they are given a paper coupon. The amount of the coupon depends on the condition of a book. A coupon ranges in value from 1 to 3 points. The students conduct the book swaps twice a week in the morning before school starts. Part of the fun of the book swap is watching children create interest in books by "selling" them to one another, spontaneously sharing story lines, describing favorite characters, and what they liked most about the books.

Book Displays. Another functional activity that generates interest, arouses curiosity, and fosters inquiry is the "book display" strategy that Brenda uses. Periodically, she will "bring a bunch of books to school, centered around a theme or a topic." As part of the book display, she sets up artifacts to dramatize the theme or topic. One of her favorite book displays features these huge hawk wings that a friend, who is a farmer, found in his field. Brenda displays the hawk wings, which span almost seven feet in length, putting them on a table with a collection of books about birds. As the children examine the hawk wings, they begin to ask questions: How did the hawk lose its wings? How big are hawks? Why are their wings so long, yet light? Why do wings have feathers? Why do birds fly? Are hawks bigger than eagles? Do hawks attack humans? She encourages the students to write their questions on slips of paper which are then tacked to one of the bulletin boards near the display. As the students raise questions, they begin to explore the various books to seek answers.

Whoever finds an answer to a question, writes it down and tacks it to the bulletin board, and then celebrates by orally sharing the answer with the class.

As interest mounts in the book display, Brenda brings in additional books—about flight and aerodynamics—and the children expand their explorations into the relationships between birds, flight, and aerodynamics. As she explains, "Through these displays, I often move kids into asking questions, exploring texts, answering questions, and generating more questions."

Occasions to Write.   There are numerous occasions to write throughout the day. Writing is integrated into thematic study through literature response logs and unit projects. Also, a half-hour a day is spent on journal writing just prior to lunch hour; the journals allow the students to write on topics that they have strong feelings about. In addition to these occasions, Brenda initiates class book strategies throughout the year, including the three described below.

The Book of Excuses. Brenda introduces the "Book of Excuses" early in the year and explains that it will be an ongoing activity. Whenever a child's behavior warrants an excuse, it is written in the book, which occupies a prominent spot in the writing center. Students write down their excuses for being late for school, incomplete homework, forgetting to have a note signed by a parent, forgetting to bring a book from home, and the like. The children enjoy reading the excuses, which often are accompanied by humorous anecdotes.

The Book of Best Writing. Brenda employs "The Book of Best Writing" to showcase student-selected pieces of what they feel represent their "best" work. To publish in the "Book of Best Writing," a child must engage in the writing process. Any piece of writing, whether it originates from a journal entry, a response log, or a unit project, is eligible for inclusion in the book. Brenda uses a photograph album with magnetic pages to showcase the writing. The "Book of Best Writing" is one of the most widely read books in the room. Brenda notes that the strategy helps the students to self-evaluate their work. The book is updated every other month with new pieces. "Old pieces" are then placed in students' writing portfolio, which Brenda uses for assessment and grading purposes.

Poetry Books. Poetry is one of the students' favorite forms of writing. Brenda reads many poems to the children and invites them to compose their own. Brenda also arranges to have "a real poet" from the Akron community spend several weeks in her class working with the students. She is part of an "author in-residence" program sponsored by the Akron Public Library. Under the poet's tutelage, the children create class poetry anthologies around the themes: Halloween, Families, and Friendship.

Discourse Forms. One of Brenda's "writing to learn" strategies is to wean students from writing as an academic exercise. Instead of assigning students to "write a paragraph on . . .", she invites them to use real forms of discourse. They write, for example, letters, dialogues, teaching posters, advertisements, speeches, wanted posters, and thumbnail sketches of characters. Often such writing is connected to a thematic units project. The box depicts a wanted poster written and illustrated by one of Brenda's students for "Wildboy," one of the main characters in the novel, *My Side of the Mountain.*

Reading Strategy Lessons.   On most afternoons, after SSR, Brenda holds a reading strategy lesson with groups of students in the open area of the room. The purpose of the strategy lessons is to demonstrate pivotal strategies that may be used by the students to solve problems that they encounter when comprehending and learning from text. Brenda ties "strategy instruction" to the texts that students are reading in their thematic units.

Brenda uses the strategy lesson in the box to make students aware of the importance of previewing a textbook chapter and becoming "text smart." As a result, she "walks students through" the strategy of previewing by showing them how to take advantage of the organizational features of the text to predict what the material will be about. Notice how Brenda combines direct explanation of previewing procedures with explicit demonstrations from the text chapter.

Becoming Text Smart

PURPOSE: The purpose of this lesson is to teach the content of Chapter 6, which focuses on *why, how,* and *when* our Nation came to be the United States of America and to familiarize students with the process of learning how to preview a chapter before reading it.

CONTENT: The strategy lesson involves introducing Chapter 6, "Birth of a Nation," in the Social Studies textbook, *The United States and Its Neighbors*, Silver Burdett Co., 1984, (Grade 5).

Brenda (Begins the lesson): What do you think this chapter, "Birth of a Nation" is about?

[Brenda writes students' predictions on chart paper. She then reviews the importance of using predictions during reading.]

Brenda: When we look over the material before we read it, it's called "previewing." Previewing gives you an idea about what you can expect to read, about what you're going to learn. You get a "feel" for the material. Previewing will help you read and understand the material better. It's a strategy you can use to help you learn from a textbook."

[Brenda uses transparencies of the text pages 106–109 to model and demonstrate the previewing procedure. Students refer to these pages in their textbooks.]

Brenda: Let's look at the chapter title again. We have already made some predictions about it. Now we're going to turn the title into some questions. A step in previewing is to ask questions about what we're going to read. Who can turn the title into a question?

[Brenda records the students' questions on chart paper for later use.]

Brenda: When you change the title into questions, it not only helps you to focus on what you are going to read but it also helps you to remember what you read because you will be looking for answers to your questions.

Brenda: The next step in previewing the chapter also involves making questions. Let's look at the first heading in this section. It's in dark print like the title, but it's a little smaller. It's the heading for this section of the chapter. Who can read the heading for us? [Student reads the heading.] Now let's turn this heading into some questions we have about the bad feelings that grew between Britain and the colonies. [Students orally respond with questions and Brenda writes it on the chart paper for use during actual reading and discussion of the chapter content.] Who remembers how this will help you in your reading?" [Students respond orally.]

Brenda: The words in bold-face print are important, too. Let's make a list of all the words in bold-face print in this section. [Brenda lists the words that the students find on chart paper for later use. Through questioning and discussion, Brenda helps the students understand that these words are important because they represent ideas and concepts which are important to the topic about which they are going to read.]

Brenda: Pictures also help us understand what we're reading. They are very concrete and help us visualize the written material. As you encounter pictures, be aware of how they help you understand the material. Let's look at the picture on page 109. What do you know by looking at the picture? [Students interpret the picture orally.]

Brenda: There's one more part we can use in this section to help us know about this section. What kind of information does the time line give us? [Through questioning and discussion, the students identify the contents of the time line and why information is put on a time line.]

Brenda: Now that we've previewed this section, let's predict what we're going to learn just in this section of the chapter. I want you to work in your groups to either make a list or write a paragraph about what you will learn about in this section. [The students write their predictions.]

Reward of 2,000,000 dollars in cash.

WILD BOY

On November 12,1987 a wild boy was spotted. He was taking the hunters game that they could not find. Mrs. Fielder also says she has seen him. She had asked him to help her pick strawberries. She has been a resident of the Catskill Moutains for ninty-seven years. When ever she sees something we beleive it because she has been right about everything else she has seen.

If you know him or if you have seen him, please contact me at 253-358. Please contact Stephanie Becker. There is an award of 2,00,000 dollars in cash!

By
Stephanie
Becker

Room 205

ISSUES

Individual Differences

On the *California Achievement Test,* Brenda's students, as a group, scored below the 25th percentile on reading comprehension and below the 17th percentile on vocabulary based on national norms. Yet in her class, they do what literate people do: The students read authentic texts for real reasons. Language is a tool for communicating, solving problems, enjoying, and learning. In Brenda's class, they learn to make decisions about the uses of literacy in their lives. The students exercise ownership in their learning, not overnight but gradually, as they begin to believe in themselves and view themselves as readers and writers.

Brenda explains the apparent contrast between their performance on standardized tests and actual demonstrations of their literate behavior in her classroom this way: "You can argue that standardized tests aren't very good indicators of what urban, inner-city children can do. Much has been written on that. But there is another way to argue the differences in the way they perform on tests and what they do in my class. I was a special education teacher for eight years, working with learning disability students, and I have been an elementary teacher in inner-city schools for almost a decade. And I have found this truth to hold: *Good teaching is good teaching and it doesn't matter what kind of kid you're working with.*

According to Brenda, societal conditions and socioeconomic class differences place the urban poor child at risk of school failure, but schools and curriculums and teachers do not have to compound the problem: "By trying to make learning easy for children who are experiencing difficulties in life and in school, educators can actually make it harder for them."

Brenda deals with individual differences in her classroom "by celebrating the differences in children, rather than trying to fix-up what's wrong with them. My kids need affirmation, not negative feedback or remedial help." Her role as a teacher, no matter how cliche it sounds to her, "is to meet kids where they're at." For Brenda, this means teaching from the concrete to the abstract, from what the students know already to what they need to learn.

Evaluation

Brenda views evaluation as a broad concept and defines it from a practical perspective: as *grading,* something she can't ignore, and as *assessment,* an ongoing process of recording and monitoring the progress that the students are making as literacy learners.

Report cards demand that grades be assigned to students. In Brenda's school, the report card requires two grades for reading. The first grade is based on whether the students are performing *at grade level, below grade level,* or *above grade level.* On the report card, Brenda must indicate which level each students is at and then assign a letter grade. Such determinations fly in the face of whole language teaching. If a child is below grade level, school policy prevents Brenda from assigning an A grade for reading.

Along with the letter grade, however, Brenda can assign a number grade for effort in reading. She laments, "I would love to grade my students against their own progress, but I can't do that. But I can give them an effort grade of 1, which is the top grade for effort in reading."

When Brenda sends report cards home, she always attaches a note for parents, explaining that the effort grades are the most important in her class. In addition, she holds an evaluation conference with each student at the end of the grading period. The conference includes the student's self-evaluation of the progress he or she has made in reading and writing. As part of the self-evaluation, the students are asked to assign themselves letter and number grades. Brenda is surprised by how close the match is between the students' perceptions of their grades and her's.

Far more important to Brenda than assigning grades is the ongoing assessment she conducts of each students' progress as readers and writers. She keeps *portfolios* of students' work. Portfolio assessment, as the name implies, represents a collection of many indicators of student progress. She maintains a portfolio folder for each child: "I keep oral reading samples, writing pieces, samples of work from the thematic units, lists of books that they have read, and observation notes on 3 × 5 index cards." These cards describe how the students are doing, the interest they are showing in reading, and the kinds of reading they are doing.

Brenda uses portfolios to assess students' progress for instructional purposes. She examines the portfolios periodically to determine where each child is as a reader and writer. She asks herself, "What is the child doing well? What does the child need help in?" When she holds the evaluation conferences at the end of the grading period, Brenda uses the work samples in the portfolio as the basis for her comments. She makes sure that the children know what they are doing well and what they may need to work on to continue growing as readers and writers.

Home Connections

Home visits are an integral part of what Brenda does as a teacher. She affirms the importance of home visits: "One way that helps me to establish an environment for learning and risk-taking in my classroom is to visit all of my students' homes by the middle of October. Visiting with students and parents in the home gives me another context to use in working with the students in school. After visiting a home I always have a better understanding of the student." Brenda never leaves a home without feeling that she has gained valuable insights and information. The students frequently remind her to come visit them again.

Brenda finds that the parents never have any difficulty accepting whole language teaching. She works at keeping them informed of what she and the students are doing: "I send notes home explaining the reading and writing program and what I am trying to accomplish. I talk to the kids about what they need to tell their parents when they take an assignment home." When Brenda does home visits, she always brings work samples from the children's portfolios. These provide an opportunity to talk about the children's work and to explain to the parents how learning in her classroom may be different from learning in previous classrooms that their children have attended.

School Connections

For the past two years, Brenda's school has served as a "demonstration center," targeted by the school district as an experimental school for student empowerment and teacher reform. The school is small; there is one teacher for each grade level, in addition to support personnel. The school was chosen as the demonstration site because of its demographics. As Brenda puts it, "If reform practices can work here, then they can work anywhere."

Teachers from across the district applied to work at Brenda's school. As a result, the teachers selected have brought an openness toward change and strong credentials as instructional leaders. They vary in their knowledge of and experience with whole language theory and practice. Some maintain traditional perspectives; others, like Brenda, are deeply committed to whole language as a vehicle for educational reform.

By group consensus of the teachers, whole language has been targeted as one of the priority areas for curriculum reform at the school. Brenda plays a lead role in working with her colleagues. They have participated in informal "lunch groups" where they discuss whole language as well as in more formal professional development activities such as workshops and conferences. Brenda conducts many workshops and holds demonstrations. Next year, she will serve as a "support teacher." In this role, she is available to work with her colleagues in their classrooms to create whole language environments.

Keeping Current

Professional development is a way of life for Brenda. In the school district, she attends a whole language support group on a regular basis. Here, teachers engage in dialogue about whole language, sharing perspectives as well as problems. They support one another by exploring ideas, issues, and new possibilities related to whole language teaching and learning.

By her own admission, Brenda is "a conference junkie." She attends professional meetings regularly and is active in the International Reading Association and the National Council of Teachers of English. She is a member of a local TAWL (Teachers Applying Whole Language) group and has attended the annual national conference of the Whole Language Umbrella. She also is sought after as a speaker at local reading and language arts meetings. In the summer months, Brenda teaches graduate level workshops on whole language at Kent State University.

Brenda keeps current by reading journals and monographs on literacy and language learning. She subscribes to *The Reading Teacher, Language Arts,* and *The Phi Delta Kappan.* She owns an extensive collection of books and monographs on whole language.

Challenges

Brenda identifies two curricular challenges as a whole language teacher. The first involves the transition that students in her classroom must make from traditional reading and writing practices. By fifth grade, the students are ingrained in a conventional way of thinking about reading and writing instruction. Their self-concepts related to literacy learning are often negative, and they are hesitant about trying new ways of learning.

In the beginning of the year, the challenge is to help the students overcome their fear of failure and their lack of self-worth. They do not view themselves as readers and writers. Breaking through the barriers that the students have imposed is one of Brenda's persistent struggles as a whole language teacher: "It takes a lot of patience and commitment on my part to move kids in a new direction. At times it's very frustrating. But I have the satisfaction of knowing that when that year is over no one can ever take away what they have learned."

A second challenge involves easy access to books and other authentic texts. Brenda spends large sums of money buying books and collecting class sets. She expends even a greater amount of energy gathering resources and networking with others to get real books into the hands of her students: "It seems at times, at least to my husband and two sons, that I spend more time in the public library than I do at home. It would be nice if books were readily accessible to me and the students at school." One of the battles that Brenda is waging with school officials is the purchasing of short shelf-life materials: "There's a reluctance on the part of administrators to purchase materials that have a short shelf-life. Paperbacks, for example, are worn thin by the students very quickly whereas textbooks can be used for years before they need to be replaced."

SUMMING UP

Brenda is the type of teacher who recognizes that children need to feel good about themselves and about their ability to learn. She affirms their talents, validates their feelings, and supports them in their use of literacy for learning. Her classroom provides an environment that encourages students to take risks. To create a risk-taking environment, she finds it extremely valuable to work on the development of personal relationships with the children. The more she gets to know them on a personal basis, the greater their level of trust and willingness to take risks as language learners.

Whatever conclusions that can be made from Brenda's case are best drawn from her own words: "I spend time talking with my kids before school, after school, during playground duty. Much of the time is spent listening to them, encouraging them when they're down on themselves, and making time for them when they come to me with a problem or concern. You never know when your support will make a difference with students, but if you don't try to give the extra attention and care that they need, you'll never make any difference at all."

QUESTIONS FOR REFLECTION AND DISCUSSION

Third-Grade Classroom

1. Gay believes in the powerful role of demonstration and modeling as a teacher of literacy. Yet she does not view herself as a whole language teacher. Where would you rank Gay in her transition from skills-based teaching to whole language teaching on the continuum below. Why?

Skills   Whole Language

2. How do your values and beliefs about teaching coincide or differ from Gay's?
3. How does Gay explore, nurture, and promote literacy learning with her students?

Fourth-Grade Classroom

4. To what extent does Ann Burns' thinking about whole language match her instructional practices? Where would you rank Ann's transition to whole language on the continuum below. Why?

Skills   Whole Language

5. Do your values or beliefs about teaching coincide or differ from Ann's? Explain.
6. Is Ann "complete" as a whole language teacher? Where is there room for professional growth and development?

Fifth-Grade Classroom

7. Brenda Church works in an inner-city school. Does an inner-city school place constraints on what she can or can't do as a whole language teacher? Where would you rank Brenda in her transition to whole language? Why?

Skills   Whole Language

8. Do your values and beliefs about teaching coincide or differ from Brenda's? Why?

9. What do you like about Brenda's classroom? Is Brenda "complete" as a whole language teacher? Where is there room for continued change and growth in her teaching?

COMPARISONS ACROSS THE THIRD, FOURTH, AND FIFTH GRADES

1. Compare and contrast the instruction practices of Gay, Ann, and Brenda. How are they alike? How do they differ? And, as a group, how do these practices differ from teachers who operate from a traditional context for literacy instruction? In your opinion, which of the three teachers is closest to the ideal of a whole language teacher? Why?

2. Teachers come to whole language in different ways. Describe how Gay, Ann, and Brenda were drawn to whole language. What have been the powerful forces and models in your life as a teacher thus far? Have these forces and models helped or hindered your transition into whole language teaching?

3. Critically analyze the teaching strategies of Gay, Ann, and Brenda. For each, list potential areas of instructional strength and concern. How might each teacher modify or change their strategies within a whole language framework to overcome the perceived concerns?

4. Compare and contrast the philosophies held by each teacher. On what does each focus? How do the philosophies compare with some of the principles of whole language outlined in Chapter 1?

5. Each teacher works with parents in different ways. What principles guide Gay, Ann, and Brenda in their home-school literacy efforts? Childhood/ primary section of this book?

IV
BECOMING . . .

Teachers never stay the same. They are always changing or becoming something different from what they currently are. In some cases, change happens unintentionally. In other cases, teachers make a conscious decision to change. The focus of this section is on teachers who wish to change toward a more holistic orientation to literacy instruction. How does one become a whole language teacher? We recognize that many teachers who move toward whole language follow similar paths. In this chapter, we consider issues related to becoming a whole language teacher. We point out some milestones that may help guide one's movement toward whole language, we suggest ways in which teachers in this process received support and assistance from like-minded colleagues, and we consider what it means to be a *whole language scholar.*

Chapter 8

MOVING TOWARD WHOLE LANGUAGE

"Becoming a whole language teacher not only changed the way I taught, but also the way I viewed myself as a professional educator."

"Whole language means more than teaching children how to read and write."

How does one become a whole language teacher? This one question may be the most perplexing concern facing teachers who feel attracted to a more holistic orientation, yet do not know where or how to begin to change. Teachers are often intuitively drawn to the notions of using real books, functional applications of literacy, and giving teachers (and students) control over their own curriculum. But these ideas are so different from traditional ways of teaching reading and writing that teachers can easily feel overwhelmed by the change that must occur to get from "here to there." One reason that this type of change is such a difficult issue to address is that there is no one way to become a whole language teacher. There is no formula. There are no specific set of university courses or staff development workshops that one must take to become whole language. Each teacher who has embraced whole language as a philosophy of schooling and as a way of teaching has taken his or her own path to achieving it. In the case studies presented here, some teachers seemed to have a personal inclination toward whole language while others were drawn to it after taking courses or listening to a speaker on whole language. Indeed, inasmuch as there are numerous manifestations of whole language curricula, there are equally varied ways for becoming a whole language teacher.

Whole language should be viewed more as a continuous process of professional change rather than some distant goal or endpoint. In this sense, all whole language teachers are still on their way to becoming whole language teachers. This suggests that whole language teachers are continually open and responsive to change and innovation. It also implies that whole language teachers are not so dogmatic as to assume that there can be only one manifestation of the whole language approach. A key principle underlying whole language is an openness to consider new ideas as well as a knowledge base and scholarly attitude to evaluate those ideas.

Although we believe there is no single way to become a whole language teacher, most whole language teachers make a conscious decision to pursue whole language teaching to literacy education. They may have taken a college course in which whole language was introduced or attended an in-service presentation on whole language. While these opportunities may have planted the idea, individual teachers need to commit themselves to move toward a holistic orientation before real, substantive change will occur.

It is difficult to legislate or demand that teachers assume a whole language stance. When change is administratively imposed on teachers it is usually doomed and the mandate may result in resistance or morale problems. Teachers who are not knowledgeable nor comfortable with the whole language instructional philosophy or the implications for teaching that are based on the philosophy may resist a change imposed on them or may lack the commitment and dedication required to make such a change work. Half-hearted implementation of whole language is a recipe for failure and, if teachers feel that change to whole language is arbitrarily imposed on them with little or no consultation, then half-hearted implementation is very likely. The move from a skills to a holistic orientation involves such a fundamental shift in one's personal pedagogical philosophy that attempts to mandate such a shift lead to superficial changes in the curriculum that will fade once the administrative enthusiasm for whole language fades (as it surely will when the superficial changes fail to achieve the desired results). Based upon her personal experience as a change facilitator, Ridley (1990) argues that for whole language change to take root, schools need to establish a tolerant environment in which teacher variation is acknowledged and in which teachers are free to accept or reject whole language principles.

Shanklin and Rhodes (1989) note that university-school collaborations are one way for schools and teachers to move toward more holistic approaches to instruction. The role of university personnel, however, cannot be directive. University "experts" cannot impose their own notions of curricular change on teachers. Rather, they must try to create conditions and opportunities that allow teachers to reflect on their own teaching, discover alternative approaches to current methods, and implement those alternatives with the support and encouragement of colleagues and administrators, and university partners.

In her own school district's movement to whole language, Robbins (1990) observed that teachers cannot be expected to implement a whole language curriculum on the basis of a few workshops on the subject. Consultants need to be readily available to provide support and training, and model whole language instruction for teachers. According to Shanklin and Rhodes (1989) university consultants help create these conditions by providing professional materials and materials for students to replace workbooks, basal readers, skill kits, and so on. Teacher self-reflection is fostered through discussions of current specific teaching practices and viewing videotapes of their own teaching. Sharing ideas about reading and writing instruction and collaboratively developing solutions to specific problems in the classroom helps teachers to reconsider their pedagogical beliefs and to develop a sense of control over their own teaching.

Although it is difficult to impose change administratively that is lasting, Shanklin and Rhodes (1989) note that it is important that administrators become knowledgeable about whole language and support movement toward whole language initiated by teachers. Administrators need to rethink their notions about effective instruction, evaluation, and, indeed, the ultimate goals of education. The use and interpretation of standardized test scores as well as the employment of alternative, more comprehensive and in-depth approaches to instruction and evaluation needs to be considered. Administrators may wish to identify and empower groups of their best and most open-minded teachers to facilitate continued growth in whole language once a formal inservice program on the subject concludes.

In the final analysis, whole language change requires a personal decision. However, it can be facilitated and influenced by others. In this chapter, we will explore how change can occur for teachers who wish to become whole language practitioners. We will suggest some guideposts that many whole language teachers have described in their own professional transitions.

DISSATISFACTION WITH THE STATUS QUO

The first milestone that most teachers encounter in moving toward a whole language orientation is a dissatisfaction with the traditional ways reading is taught. Weaver (1990) describes traditional approaches to literacy instruction as based upon a transmission model of education. The transmission model can be characterized as textbook- and teacher-directed, objective, and analytic (See Figure 8.1).

After teaching in a traditional skills-based program, many whole language teachers come to the realization that such a curriculum doesn't work. Many students fail to achieve appropriate levels of literacy. Other students learn to view reading as a set of skills and competency tests to master rather than a way of learning about the world. And, perhaps most distressing, many students fail to develop any enjoyment of or satisfaction in reading. The emphasis on skills and drills has drained them of any love for reading. First-grade teacher, Betsy Pryor, specifically identified

Figure 8.1
Contrasting Models of Education: Transmission Versus
Transactional Transmission ModelTransactional Model
(Weaver, 1990)

Emphasis is on direct teaching, which is controlled first by the program and second by the teacher.	Emphasis is on learning, which is facilitated but not directly controlled by the teacher.
Basis is the behaviorist model of learning (for example, Skinner).	Basis is the cognitive/social model of learning (for example, Vygotsky, Halliday).
Learning is viewed as a matter of building from simple to complex, from smaller to larger skills.	Smaller "parts" of a task are seen as more readily learned within the context of a meaningful whole.
Learning is viewed as habit formation; thus verbalizing/writing correct responses and avoiding incorrect responses are seen as crucial.	Learning is seen as the result of complex cognitive process that can be facilitated by teachers and enhanced by peer interaction.
Since correctness is valued, risk-taking is discouraged and/or penalized.	Risk-taking, and hence "errors" are seen as absolutely essential for learning.
All learners are expected to master what is taught when it is taught; thus, most children experience varying degrees of failure.	Learners are expected to be at different stages and to develop at their own pace and in their own ways; thus, there is no concept of "failure."
Ability to reproduce or verbalize a predetermined correct response is taken as evidence of learning.	Ability to apply knowledge and to think in novel ways is considered evidence of learning, as is the ability to use general strategies across a wide range of tasks and contexts.

such dissatisfaction as a major reason for her considering alternative approaches to teaching reading and writing. Although students learn to read in traditional approaches, they also learn to dislike and avoid reading. Indeed, reading instruction reaches a point where it is neither enjoyable nor exciting for teachers or students. When teachers observe this occurring in their classrooms, they begin to ask if there aren't other ways to teach reading.

LEARNING ABOUT NEW WAYS TO TEACH LITERACY

Dissatisfaction with the way things are *does not* guarantee teachers will change. They must develop a vision of what literacy education can be like. Those that don't develop such a vision may become dissatisfied with teaching altogether and become victims of teacher burnout.

In contrast to the transmission model of education, Weaver (1990) suggests a *transactional* model that she suggests is the basis for whole language. In the transactional model, emphasis is placed on the interactions between learner, teacher, and text, between cognitive, social, and affective dimensions of schooling, and between componential learning within meaningful and functional contexts (see Figure 8.1 for more detailed contrasts of transmission and transactional models of education). The focus in transactional models is more contextual or global, hence the notion of holistic education or whole language.

How a teacher first learns about whole language as an alternative approach to reading can be quite varied. Some teachers learn about whole language through a colleague in the school who is beginning to implement a whole language curriculum. Others may have taken a graduate level course in reading in which the professor and other students have described whole language. Still others may have learned about whole language through a school-based inservice meeting, a presentation made during a teachers' convention, by reading articles about whole language in professional journals (see Figure 8.2), or through meetings of a professional group such as a local council of the International Reading Association of Phi Delta Kappa. For example, Betsy's initiation to whole language (Chapter 2) began with a presentation she attended on invented spelling and journal writing. Regardless of the source, teachers learn enough about whole language to realize that it has potential, to want to learn more about it, and to try out some aspects of it.

To be truly sympathetic to whole language, a teacher needs to understand and accept at least some of its principles. As we suggested in Chapter 1, these include focusing on children and their language as appropriate starting points for literacy instruction (as opposed to a reliance on a set of skills as the focus of instructional attention), a realization that children bring to school their own interests and needs and that reading instruction should be aimed at satisfying those interests and needs, an understanding that literacy can be used for a variety of personal and social purposes, that reading can be taught using a variety of authentic

Figure 8.2
Sources of Articles on Whole Language

Journal	Publisher
Educational Leadership	Association of Supervision & Curriculum Development
Elementary School Journal	University of Chicago
Journal of Reading	International Reading Association
Language Arts	National Council Teachers of English
Learning	Springhouse Corporation
The New Advocate	Christopher Gordon
Phi Delta Kappan	Phi Delta Kappa
Reading Horizons	Western Michigan University
The Reading Teacher	International Reading Association
Teaching and Learning	University of North Dakota
Teaching, PreK-8	Early Years, Inc.
Teachers Networking	Richard C. Owen Publishers
The WEB	Ohio State University
The Whole Idea	The Wright Group Company

texts, an acknowledgment that reading is best taught within the context of all the language arts, including writing, and that it is best taught when functional, purposeful, and interesting reading activities are integrated into all areas of the school curriculum.

Unless teachers are willing to accept initially at least some of these principles, it is highly unlikely that they can remain dedicated to whole language.

OPENING MOVES

Once teachers become aware of whole language in action and begin to understand and accept the principles that underlie it, the way they think about learning and teaching will change. Rather than seeing teaching and learning as a series of gradual and sequential steps involving the transmission of component skills or segments of content, teachers will see effective teaching and learning as done in authentic and functional contexts in which real purposes and uses of literacy replace the contrived practice routines of the traditional approach. Teachers will want to begin implementing whole language instruction in their own classrooms. The problem, at this point, however, is that because whole language is so different from traditional approaches and more demanding of the teacher, it may be difficult at first to implement a full whole language curriculum. As the teachers we observed suggest in terms of their own transitions to whole language teaching, the best approach may be to implement a whole language curriculum gradually. (See Figure 8.3.)

For many teachers, the first move toward a whole language orientation may involve nothing more than reading a wide variety of books to the class on a daily basis. This one activity exposes children and teacher to the enjoyment, language, and structure of stories and poetry. Students learn that the teacher values reading and view the teacher as a model of fluent reading. Other activities fit nicely into initiating a whole language approach. Having a regular period for self-selected recreational reading (sustained silent reading) gives students an opportunity to develop recreational reading habits in school. Current research suggests that most elementary students read very little for enjoyment outside of school. Sustained silent reading encourages students to experience the enjoyment and satisfaction that comes from recreational reading. Having students keep and share journals on a regular basis initiates writing regularly and for real purposes. Students write about their own experiences and their own feelings rather than on topics imposed by the teacher or textbook. Developing a literate classroom environment by creating an extensive classroom library and putting together comfortable areas for students to read, write, and share what they are reading and writing provides students easy access to materials for reading and writing. Most readers prefer reading in comfortable and relaxed atmospheres. Classrooms can

Figure 8.3
Some Initial Instructional Activities in Whole Language

Daily periods of read-aloud.

Daily periods of sustained silent recreational reading.

Keep and share student journals regularly.

Develop a classroom environment conducive to functional, meaningful, and enjoyable uses of literacy.

Begin to develop a varied classroom library.

easily be modified, often with some rugs, pillows, bookcases, and rear-rangement of furniture, so as to be conducive for reading. These initiating ideas are easy to implement, yet are a decisive move toward literacy instruction that is based on functional uses of literacy, authentic texts, and curricular integration of literacy.

SHIFTING INTO HIGH GEAR

From such beginnings, teachers continue to add to their curriculum as they become more comfortable and satisfied with the changes they have already made, more knowledgeable of whole language, and more willing to take risks with curriculum and instruction. Integrated thematic units on topics negotiated with students, writing process workshops integrated with reading and other subject areas, in-depth literature study and discussion groups, and reading and writing (in various forms) on important current issues in the community, country, and world are a few of the next steps teachers may consider in developing their whole language curriculum.

Thematic and integrated units of study are often seen as the most imposing obstacle to full implementation of whole language (Since whole language implementation is more philosophy than prescribed method, thematic units do not necessarily have to be a part of a whole language classroom. Nevertheless, most experienced whole language teachers do use thematic units to some extent). Thematic units allow whole language classrooms to study in the various subject areas through one common theme or topic. Lukasevich (1991) describes the steps a teacher might go through in developing a unit of study (Figure 8.4). In thematic units, the major themes become the context around which the various subject areas are taught and explored.

A subtle alternative to thematic units is the thematic cycle (Edelsky, Altwerger, & Flores, 1991). In thematic cycles, the subject areas are used to investigate the topic. The cycle begins with a question such as Sylvia's, "How can we stop pollution in our city?" The question and not the subject areas becomes the central focus of study. The content areas are brought to bear on the topic as needed to answer the question or one of the questions that might spin-off from the original.

Both thematic units and thematic cycles work to tie the curriculum together into a more coherent whole. In thematic units, the central topic

Figure 8.4
Steps in Developing a Thematic Unit (Lukasevich, 1991)

1. Selection of an interesting theme around which to study other subject areas.

2. Brainstorm/web directions to take the theme. Consider how the theme can impact on the various subject areas through learning activities.

3. Set goals and objectives for the unit.

4. Collect relevant resources and materials.

5. Plan an introduction to the unit. Focus on developing student interests and questions about the topic.

6. Plan learning activities and experiences. Include activities for whole class, small groups, and individual students. Organize activities by subject areas or teaching strategies.

7. Plant a culmination experience. The experience should help pull together or summarize the unit of study for students.

is extended into the subject areas. Teachers think of ways in which the theme can be brought into the subject areas. This may result in only superficial integrations of the theme and connections between subject areas. In thematic cycles, by contrast, the art, music, literature, social studies, and sciences are used for exploring, expanding, and answering the question that defines the central topic. Here teachers and students consider ways in which subject areas can be used to explore the theme. In thematic cycles, subject areas are more closely connected as they are used to investigate the thematic question.

Heibert and Fisher (1990) distinguish the types of explorations with two examples. A thematic unit of study on spiders might include the reading of *Charlotte's Web*. Although this kind of unit may begin to connect the subject areas, the connection lacks depth and maintains the separation of subject areas. A thematic cycle activity, conversely, could involve students writing letters to the city government in support of an issue in which the students have a real stake. Science and social studies reading and research, interviews with public officials, report and letter writing converge on an authentic question or concern raised by students.

Sylvia Jackson's class study of recycling is an excellent example of a thematic unit of study. The topic itself touched directly on social studies and science issues. Moreover, functional reading and writing activities were integrated throughout the study. Students read books and articles on issues related to ecology. They met in small groups to discuss what they had read. They dictated stories on their field trip to a recycling center and about the importance of recycling. Students wrote reports and made signs about recycling. They interviewed other students about their home recycling efforts and opinions and displayed the results of various surveys in the form of bar graphs and pie charts. In short, students used their literacy and language skills to learn about an important and current topic for the world and their community.

Two important characteristics of more sophisticated implementations of whole language are literacy events that are group-based or that provide for social interaction among the members of the classroom community and literacy events that are grounded in students' experience. These characteristics are evident at any grade level in whole language classrooms, however, their specific manifestation may change as students mature. (See Figure 8.5.)

At the primary grade levels, shared or community-based literacy events include those activities in which children participate in reading an enlarged text that is visible to all students. The shared book experience (big book reading) and chart stories are, perhaps, the most common examples of group literacy events. Children read and reread, orally, in groups, pairs, and by themselves, the big books and chart stories that are an integral part of the classroom.

Beyond the primary grades, shared literacy events can be found in literature study groups. Here small groups of students read one book or other text. A copy of the book is provided for each student. The group meets

Figure 8.5
Community- and Experienced-Based Literacy Events

	Shared (Community) Published Reading	Experienced-Based, Literacy Activities
Primary level	Shared book experience (groups of students reading enlarged texts)	Language experience approach (experience, discussion, text creation)
Intermediate levels and above	Literature study groups (groups of students reading and discussing the same book)	"Foxfire" approach (students working on literacy projects for which the source of information is within the students, their families, or communities)

daily with the teacher to discuss what they had read over the previous day and share their personal reflections and responses.

Group activities in whole language classrooms are marked by heterogeneous and cooperative collections of students. Whole language teachers believe that social sensitivity, tolerance among individuals, and more comprehensive learning will occur when students work with all types of students in situations in which students need to help one another to be successful.

A second key characteristic of holistic literacy instruction is its emphasis on students' experience as the basis for growth in literacy. The prototypical example of this at the primary level is the language experience approach (LEA). In LEA activities, students follow up an experience (for example, field trip, nature walk) with a class discussion on the experience in which students share their observations, perceptions, insights, and feelings. This is followed by the students creating a text based on the experience. Students dictate the text to an adult who writes the text on a sheet of chart paper. The written text then becomes the reading material for later group activities.

A strong example of the connection of experience to literacy can be found in the Foxfire approach, named after the successful magazine and books written by teacher Elliot Wigginton's high school English classes in Rabun Gap, Georgia. In the Foxfire approach, students learn and write about the experiences of members of their family or community. Students may write personal family histories through interviews of their parents and relatives. They can develop essays on interesting places in their town or neighborhood by visiting such places, reading information about those places, and talking with people who are knowledgeable about the places. When finished, the individual essays can be collected, duplicated, and become the reading and subject area material for members of the class.

MAINTAINING GROWTH

Because altering an established and traditional curriculum is a risky undertaking, it is important for teachers to have a network of professional support. These support structures or groups can help to guide, assess, and validate the changes a teacher may be implementing. Moreover, these support groups help to facilitate further growth toward a whole language orientation. As with whole language itself, support structures can take a variety of forms. It could be one's classroom colleagues who themselves are attempting to innovate their curricula. Betsy meets regularly with first-grade teachers in her school to share ideas, insights, and plans. University faculty can also help support and work with teachers in their attempts to implement change. Many university faculty bring with them knowledge of a variety of manifestations of whole language. These people can assure whole language teachers that change can and should take a variety of forms. Some teachers maintain contact with the university through the student teachers and field experience students they accept into their classrooms.

Study and sharing groups not only offer support for teachers who wish to change, they are also opportunities to continue learning about whole language and to become reflective, theoretically oriented practitioners (Newman & Church, 1990). Professional groups dedicated to improvement in literacy, such as local councils of the International Reading Association, or that are specific advocates of whole language itself, such as the Whole Language Special Interest Group of the International Reading Association, the Whole Language Assembly of the National Council of Teachers of English, or Teachers Applying Whole Language (TAWL), offer the most formal kinds of support for teachers. More recently a confederation of whole language support groups has appeared. Known as the Whole Language Umbrella (WLU), the group acts as a clearinghouse and coordinator for whole language information and activities at the national and international level.

Groups such as TAWL meet regularly in an informal atmosphere to discuss issues related to whole language and to share ideas for implementing the principles of whole language in classrooms. Teachers are in charge of these groups and view themselves as experts in the classroom implementation of whole language (Watson & Stevenson, 1989). The groups, however, can and do include others such as school administrators and supervisors and university personnel. But the clear focus of the group is on teachers sharing and supporting other teachers' attempts to implement a whole language orientation in their own classrooms. The sharing for a particular meeting may be centered around a theme and teachers will be encouraged to bring in the ideas, material, books, and students' work that is related to the theme (Watson & Stevenson, 1989). Socializing is another important aspect of the meetings of these groups.

Growth rarely occurs in contextual vacuums. Taking the first step toward a whole language curriculum is usually a personal decision.

However, once that decision is made, a variety of opportunities are available for affirming the teacher's decision and nurturing further growth. It is highly unlikely that significant changes in curricula that occur when teachers decide to move toward a whole language orientation can be sustained and refined without the help of a loyal and like-minded group of supportive colleagues.

Whole Language and Teacher Empowerment

Joan, a whole language teacher, found that three second-grade students who moved to her school from schools with more traditional reading curricula have yet to develop fluency in their reading. Perhaps because of an overemphasis on phonics and practice in isolated word recognition in first grade these students read connected text in a rather slow, halting manner with a lack of expression that would suggest that they are not attending to the meaning of the passages they encounter.

Joan felt a bit unprepared to deal with the difficulties that these children encounter. Yet, she felt the need to help these students overcome their lack of fluency. She talked with some of her colleagues at school and called a faculty member in reading education at the local university. From these contacts, she was referred to several articles on fluency in professional journals. The professor mailed Joan copies of these articles.

As she read the articles, Joan began to develop a set of personal principles on fluency instruction. Modeling fluent reading, repetition of texts in functional ways, discussion of fluency, reading to and with others were some of the principles that Joan saw as important. From these, she designed an activity in which she asked the three students to read, with a fluent partner, a segment of the passages she presented to the class during read-aloud. She also contacted the parents and arranged with them to do paired reading with their children for five minutes every evening. She sent home information for parents on doing paired reading of real stories with their children.

Within two weeks of implementing this plan, Joan noticed definite improvements in the children's reading fluency, confidence, and desire to read.

In one of his graduate courses in reading, Tom had been reading about the decline in students' interest in reading and motivation to read as they move through the elementary grades. The articles that he read, as well as the discussions in class, seemed to suggest that by fifth grade many students develop a negative attitude toward reading and most had attitudes that had declined substantially since first grade.

This issue intrigued Tom since he had been moving his fifth-grade reading curriculum toward a more holistic orientation in recent years. He knew that one of the fundamental principles of whole language was that reading should be enjoyable and functional for students. Students should see value and have interest in reading at all levels. If this were true, he hypothesized, then his fifth-grade students' attitude should be above average and near the level exhibited by first graders.

With the support and assistance of a university faculty member, Tom decided to explore this hypothesis. A survey that assessed attitudes toward reading was found. It was administered near the end of the year to students in his class and another, more traditional, fifth-grade class in the same building. Scores were determined for both groups. Tom found the results gratifying. Students in his class maintained attitudes toward reading that were above what would be expected for fifth graders. This study validated Tom's approach to reading instruction. Moreover, he decided to use the same survey in future years to assess his students' feelings about reading at the beginning and end of the school year. Indeed, this experience led Tom to conduct periodic interviews of students in his class to assess their reading, to allow students to assess their own progress in reading, and to give encouragement and support to each student's efforts in reading.

Central to whole language is the concept of empowerment of teachers. Teachers need to be empowered to develop curricula, make decisions about instruction, and truly guide the course of reading instruction in the classroom.

In traditional systems, teachers take their cues from the reading textbook. Once a basal series is chosen, teachers are often required to follow the teacher's manual to the letter. Not only does such an action imply a fundamental distrust of teachers' ability to teach, it leads teachers to divorce themselves from responsibility for guiding children on the road to reading. It can be argued that since teachers are merely the implementors of instruction that was planned and designed by others, the responsibility for any of the difficulties in literacy learning that some children may experience is attributable to the instructional plan, materials, and philosophy they are required to follow.

In a whole language curriculum, teachers plan and take responsibility for their own curriculum using a set of principles of learning and teaching

as a guide. Implicit in this approach is the notion that teachers are knowledgeable of children, reading, and teaching. Whole language teachers
need to become scholars of reading education. Planning and taking responsibility for a reading curriculum require a much wider knowledge
base than what is necessary for implementing the instruction dictated
in a teacher's manual. Moreover, when problems or questions arise for
which there is no readily available answer, teachers must be able to address the problems or questions in a scholarly manner and arrive at satis-
factory solutions. This implies that teachers need to be researchers or
scholars of reading pedagogy. They need to be able to find informed answers through disciplined inquiry to questions for which answers do not
presently exist.

In sum, teacher empowerment in whole language requires teachers to
aspire to become scholars in their own classrooms. Teachers cannot rely
on "pat" answers or solutions to problems rooted in pedagogical folklore
or tradition. Teachers need to be able and willing to explore important
questions in their classrooms in order to improve their teaching and their
students' learning.

Becoming a Whole Language Scholar

For many teachers, the thought of doing research is antithetical to the
reasons why they went into teaching in the first place. They want to
teach children, not experiment with them. Nevertheless, since whole language assumes teachers have control over their curriculum, a whole
language orientation demands that teachers inquire into the nature of
problems and questions they encounter in the classroom. Newman and
Church (1990) say that whole language teachers are not expected to be
"big researchers, but careful observers" interested in finding out about
questions in their own classroom.

A first step in becoming a whole language scholar or action researcher
is realizing that uncertainties exist in teaching. (See Figure 8.6.) With
each new group of students comes a new set of challenges and questions.
Teachers need to become aware of those questions, prioritize them, and
begin to plan ways to explore them. Mohr and MacLean (1987) recommend that teachers keep a research log in which they record questions,
curiosities, observations, and insights about their students, classroom, or
their own teaching. These logs document the teachers' thinking and can
help to clarify those issues in the classroom that are in most need of being

Figure 8.6
Steps in the Action Research Process

- Recognize that there are many questions that need to be addressed and answered in any classroom.

- Focus on a question or set of related questions that, if answered, can have a positive impact on students.

- Develop a workable plan for answering the question. Decide on which methods are best suited to collect data that is related to the question.

- Implement the research plan. Collect relevant information (i.e., data).

- Analyze the data. Try to make sense out of the information collected. Ask, what does this information have to say about the original question.

- Arrive at a conclusion or answer to the question. Use the conclusion to make appropriate changes in the classroom.

- Disseminate the results to others, either informally (through discussion or school staff meetings) or formally (through presentations at professional meetings or publications in professional newsletters or journals).

addressed. These issues are often ones that can be addressed through scholarly inquiry.

At the beginning of the school year, teachers may ask how much reading and/or writing do these students do at home? What are their interests in reading? What books have they read? Do they know how to work in groups? Do any exhibit difficulties in reading? What motivates these students? The answers to these questions are well worth knowing and teachers can answer them through a variety of means.

Methods and Plans

The next step in action research is deciding upon a method or approach for answering the questions. Small and informal discussion-and-support teacher groups can be invaluable throughout the inquiry process (Mohr & MacLean, 1987) and especially at the point of determining procedures for conducting the inquiry. Members of such groups meet regularly to share each other's work, to react in a constructive and nonthreatening way to members' plans for research, and to support each other in the difficulties that are inevitably encountered in carrying out research. Mohr and MacLean note that membership can cut across grade levels as well as buildings. The key characteristic that must be shared by group members is a dedication to inquiry and improvement. Often, such inquiry groups form among teachers taking graduate level coursework. Several teachers described in these case studies meet in university-connected research groups to discuss and plan research initiatives. These post-baccalaureate teachers often find a great deal of shared interests and camaraderie among fellow students in their graduate courses. Brenda, for example, has an interest in how and why students write. She recently completed a project in which her students corresponded regularly with undergraduate students at Kent State. This project came about through Brenda's sharing with a colleague who taught education courses at the university level.

Inquiry methods can range from observation and note-taking in the classroom to more formal assessments of literate behavior. Questionnaires and surveys, personal interviews and informal reading and writing assessments are among the more popular methods used in classroom-based research.

Investigative methods need to focus on the problem at hand. They also need to be efficient. That is, methods should provide only enough information to answer the question and no more. Elaborate research schemes that involve multiple and complex methods and instruments often become unmanageable and turn the teacher's attention away from instruction. Methods need to be of sufficient power to answer satisfactorily the question with the least amount of effort.

To get a general sense of students' reading behavior and interests, a teacher may find that a quick three- to a five-question, group-administered, written survey will suffice. While individual interviews of parents may provide additional information, the time and effort required to conduct the interviews will take the teacher away from actually responding to students' behaviors and interests in the classroom.

The chosen approach to the scholarly inquiry should be contained in a plan developed by the teacher-scholar. Before beginning the research the teacher should be able to specify the question to be studied, the approach for answering the question, the instruments to be used and the way in which the data, whether quantitative or qualitative, will be analyzed to answer the questions.

Because teacher-based research is grounded in the culture of the classroom, it is important that the research itself be classroom oriented as much as possible. Teachers need to observe children within the context of their own classrooms and curriculum. Questions regarding students' reading performance in social studies might be better answered by observing students read in their textbook than by administering a standardized reading achievement test. Research methods and materials should be congruent with the research questions and the specific instructional context out of which the questions emerged.

Results

Action research is usually conducted to improve teachers' practice. In such cases, the teacher mentally gleans results and conclusions from the collected "data" or information and goes about changing the way she or he teaches. There is no formal written report or presentation of the results.

In some cases, however, a more formal analysis and presentation may be necessary. The results of the research may be interesting enough to share with other teachers in a staff development meeting or with school administrators. Teacher-researchers, then, need to consider effective ways for presenting their results. If the data collected were in the form of field notes, journal entries, or anecdotal records, the results are best presented in narrative form. The teacher-researcher simply tells the "story" of the project with strong reliance on the qualitative data to document the conclusions that are made. Should the data be in the form of test scores or other quantitative form then a statistical analysis would be more appropriate. Usually descriptive statistics such as means (group averages) and ranges are enough to allow the teacher to determine if differences exist between groups or treatments. Further statistical analyses to determine the significance of the results can be made through consultation with a colleague having some expertise in such analysis. Normally a university-based colleague or a colleague from the evaluation department of the school district should have access to such expertise.

What to Do with Results

A key question to doing action research is what to do with the results? Since the questions that guide the research come from the classroom practice, the results of the study should be used to inform or modify practice. Given the new knowledge, gained as a result of conducting the study, teachers should change their instructional practice to make instruction more interesting, meaningful, and effective for students. Informing the teacher's classroom practice is the primary use for which action research should be conducted.

If the questions that initiated the study have relevance for other teachers, the teacher-researcher may wish to consider disseminating the results of the study. Medical doctors, lawyers, and other professionals disseminate information and new knowledge through their professional journals and meetings. Teachers should do the same. This is normally done through publication in a professional journal or presentation at professional or school meetings. Teachers need to choose the type of journal or newsletter, practitioner-oriented or research, and level of dissemination, national, state, or local, appropriate for the study. Most journals, such as *Reading Teacher, Language Arts,* and *Reading Horizons* welcome articles written by and for teachers. Similar considerations need to be addressed in oral presentations. Colleagues at the school or university or in professional support groups may provide guidance in getting the study published or presented at the appropriate level. All of the teachers contributing to this book have engaged in research that has been published in professional journals or presented at professional meetings.

Action research is an integral part of any whole language approach to literacy instruction. It is based on the assumption that in any classroom questions or uncertainties about children, curriculum, and instruction exist, that answering those questions will improve instruction, and that teachers themselves are in the best position to find answers to those questions. As empowered professionals, teachers have the responsibility to explore issues which impact on the quality of instruction and learning in the classroom.

Given such a mandate, teachers need to become scholars within their own classrooms. This means being observant for questions or concern in the classroom, developing plans for exploring those areas, collecting and making sense out of information related to the question or concern, making conclusions from the research, and deciding how to act on the conclusions in the classroom and to what extent the results of the research should be shared withothers.

In a sense, the classroom research engaged in by teachers in classrooms mirrors the reflective and inquiring attitude that whole language teachers wish to foster in their students (Newman & Church, 1990). Indeed, one of the major goals of whole language is to develop in students the capacity to question the status quo, to consider new worlds and new ways of thinking, and to develop novel and reasonable approaches for answering questions and satisfying unmet needs. When teachers approach their work as inquiring scholars and reseachers and when they allow their classrooms to become the focal point of that scholarship, it is very likely that students themselves will begin to approach their own worlds as thoughtful and reflective scholars and researchers.

THE ROAD NOT TAKEN

Whole language is more an idea or philosophy rather than a specified and prescriptive curriculum. How whole language is manifested can be quite different depending upon the teacher, children, grade level, community, and school culture. There is no universal whole language curriculum.

Thus, to suggest that there is one road to achieve a whole language curriculum is fallacy. There are many possible paths. What cannot be compromised, however, are the principles upon which the whole language orientation rests and by which the various manifestations of whole language should be judged. Teachers who wish to belong to the whole language club need to subscribe to these principles. However, variation in the interpretation of these principles for classroom practice can be wide ranging and remain valid.

The fact that whole language relies on the professionalism and scholarly interpretation of informed teachers is both powerful and potentially self-destructive. By empowering teachers with the responsibility for interpreting and implementing whole language principles, teachers who become whole language advocates must be highly committed to the success of whole language. On the other hand, wide berth in interpretation provides the potential for implementation that is neither whole language nor good instruction. All teachers, teacher educators, and other school personnel dedicated to whole language must constantly analyze and assess their own implementation, seek evaluation from others, and be on watch for inappropriate interpretations of whole language principles. In its fullest sense, teacher empowerment means not only responsibility for one's own classroom but also for the ideals and principles that a person values. Thus, whole language, by its very nature, demands thoughtful, knowledgeable, caring, and empowered teachers.

REFERENCES

Edelsky, C., Altwerger, B., & Flores, B. (1991). *Whole language: What's the difference.* Portsmouth, NH: Heinemann.

Hiebert, E. H., & Fisher, C. W. (1990). Whole language: Three themes for the future. *Educational Leadership, 47,* 62–63.

Lukasevich, A. (1991). Organizing whole-language classrooms. In V. Froese (Ed.), *Whole-Language: Practice and Theory,* pp. 221–253. Needham Heights, MA: Allyn & Bacon.

Mohr, M. M., & Maclean, M. S. (1987). *Working Together: A Guide for Teacher-Researchers.* Urbana, IL: National Council of Teachers of English.

Newman, J. M., & Church, S. M. (1990) Myths of whole language. *The Reading Teacher, 44,* 20–26.

Ridley, L. (1990). Enacting change in elementary school programs: Implementing a whole language perspective. *The Reading Teacher, 43,* 640–646.

Robbins, P. A. (1990). Implementing whole language: Bridging children and books. *Educational Leadership, 47,* 50–54.

Shanklin, N. L. and Rhodes, L. K. (1989). Transforming literacy instruction. *Educational Leadership.*

Watson, D. J. & Stevenson, M. T. (1989). Teacher support groups: Why and how. In G. S. Pinnell & M. L. Matlin (Eds.), *Teachers and Research: Language Learning in the Classroom.* Newark, DE: International Reading Association.

Weaver, C. (1990). *Understanding Whole Language.* Portsmouth, NH: Heinemann.

INDEX